IMAGES
of America

WESTERN NEW YORK AMUSEMENT PARKS

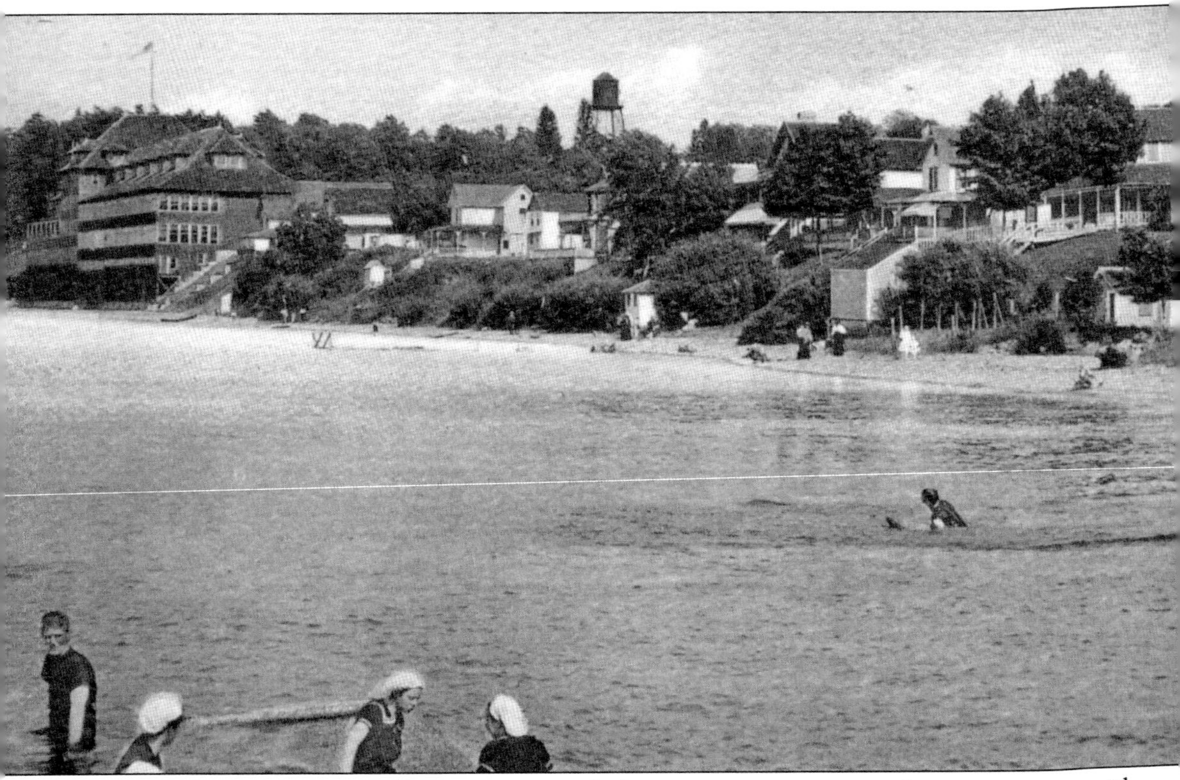

Many of Western New York's amusement parks began as picnic groves and summer resorts with magnificent hotels, top entertainment, and thrilling rides that attracted pleasure-seekers from all over the region and Canada. Olcott Beach was one of those resorts that eventually became only memories in a scrapbook. (Author's collection.)

ON THE COVER: Crystal Beach Park photographer Harry Woolever took this image in the late 1920s. The pony track in the foreground was one of the exciting attractions on the midway during this period. Directly across from it is Harry Burnett's Circus. The frightening, twisted track of the Cyclone roller coaster is visible in the background. (Courtesy of Rick Doan.)

IMAGES
of America

WESTERN NEW YORK AMUSEMENT PARKS

Rose Ann Hirsch

ARCADIA
PUBLISHING

ISBN 978-0-7385-7456-1

Published by Arcadia Publishing
Charleston, South Carolina

Printed in the United States of America

Library of Congress Control Number: 2010936916

For all general information, please contact Arcadia Publishing:
Telephone 843-853-2070
Fax 843-853-0044
E-mail sales@arcadiapublishing.com
For customer service and orders:
Toll-Free 1-888-313-2665

Visit us on the Internet at www.arcadiapublishing.com

To my husband, Tim, and all of my family and friends who rode with me at our favorite Western New York amusement parks.

Contents

ACKNOWLEDGMENTS

I wish to extend my deepest thanks to my friends and associates who generously contributed their photographs, postcards, and information so this book could be completed: Rick Doan, Cathy Herbert, Paul Kassay Jr., Dawn Lewis, the late Norm (Cyclone) Liemberger, Kathy Loveland, Richard Mintz, Joan Smyth, C. Thomas, Timothy Wagner, and Dan Wilke. I also wish to thank Mary Ann Pendrys for helping research the history of Martin's Fantasy Island and providing photographs. Special thanks goes to Martin DiPietro, Dotty Moore, and all the office staff at Martin's Fantasy Island; Melissa Emhardt of Midway Park; Darien Lake's public relations supervisor Cassandra Okon, director of marketing Linda Taylor, and director of finance Roy Neeland; PARC Management; Peggy Hatfield and Daniel DiLandro of Buffalo State College Archives and Special Collections; and Doug Bathke of the Herschell Carrousel Factory Museum for their help in finding photographs and information, scanning images, and supporting this project.

And thank you to my husband who gave up our precious time together so I could work on this book. And last, but not least, I wish to thank my editor at Arcadia Publishing, Rebekah Mower, for her guidance and patience.

Some of the images in this volume appear courtesy of the Herschell Carrousel Factory Museum (HCFM), Buffalo State College Archives, Courier-Express Collection (BSCACEC), Darien Lake Theme Park (DLR), Martin's Fantasy Island (MFI), and the Norm "Cyclone" Liemberger Collection (NLC).

Introduction

The freshwater lakes, creeks, and rivers of Western New York have provided not only natural resources for the area, but also became prime locations for the area's amusement parks. There is a continuing debate over where the eastern border of the region ends— whether or not it encompasses Rochester and Wayne County. This book defines Western New York as designated by New York State Tourism, which states that it is comprised of eight counties: Allegany, Cattaraugus, Chautauqua, Erie, Genesee, Niagara, Orleans, and Wyoming.

Western New York is dotted with many cities. The largest is Buffalo, followed by Niagara Falls and Jamestown. Although these cities are situated on waterways, city residents were still drawn to nearby shoreline resorts in search of an escape from the urban heat, the day-to-day grind, and to enjoy some social interaction with neighbors, friends, and family.

Amusement parks positioned on the lakes and rivers offered swimming from sandy beaches, shady picnic groves, athletic fields, boating, dancing, roller skating, bowling, concerts, entertainment, and mechanical rides. Hotels sprang up around the resorts, boasting airy lake-view rooms with wonderful amenities such as private baths with hot and cold running water. Some hotels were noted for their restaurants, whose menus offered delicious dinners of locally caught yellow perch, bass, and trout.

Cottages ranged from tiny, one-room dwellings to large abodes two or three stories high, with spacious sleeping porches and fully equipped kitchens. The conveniences of the Industrial Revolution allowed for more leisure time for middle-class families. It was not uncommon for a family, along with a myriad of aunts, uncles, cousins, and grandparents, to rent a cottage at one of the resorts for the duration of the summer.

Resorts that sported beaches and direct access to bodies of water drew the most patrons. Owners capitalized on their natural resource, building contemporary bathhouses equipped with showers and automatic hair dryers. Lockers, beach chairs, umbrellas, towels, and sanitized bathing suits could be rented at the bathhouse. Resort owners also created water playgrounds at their parks by installing water toboggan slides, water swings, water seesaws, and diving platforms.

Mechanical rides were in demand. Resort owners often turned to independent business owners to pack their midways with rides, games, and food. This was a typical practice throughout the amusement industry. A concessionaire owning a ride or game would rent a place inside an amusement park for the season by paying rent to the midway's owner. The concessionaire and his family worked hard to attract patrons to their ride in order to make the rent and a profit during the short season.

In Buffalo, there were parks inside the city limits with plenty of amusing distractions inspired by the 1901 Pan-American Exposition. While the Pan-Am was not the success its backers had hoped it to be, its thrilling midway full of illusions and amazing rides motivated local entrepreneurs to recreate that excitement in smaller, easy-to-reach neighborhood venues.

Several of the region's amusement parks were built on the outskirts of the cities by trolley companies as a means to increase ridership on the weekends. As times changed and the automobile became the family's main mode of transportation, the trolleys became obsolete. The freedom automobiles gave their owners sent them out of the area in search of far-away vacation destinations earlier generations had only dreamed of. In-town amusement parks soon suffered from a lack of patrons, resulting in financial losses and closure.

Fire was a park's greatest enemy. It could easily wipe out an entire midway before the fire department arrived. Other factors and the Great Depression of the 1930s played a major role in the closures of many Western New York resorts, including Fort Niagara Beach and the fledgling Neptune Park in Niagara Falls.

Western New Yorkers loved their amusement parks. The parks were central to summer activities. Relationships flourished at the parks. Lifelong romances were sparked on a park's ballroom floor; friendships were forged between patrons, workers, and owners. Several famous area residents got their start at the local amusement parks, including composer Harold Arlen whose band played aboard Crystal Beach's steamship *Canadiana* during the 1920s. Arlen went on to create such memorable songs as "That Old Black Magic," and "Somewhere over the Rainbow."

Many of the region's amusement parks were family owned and operated. Employees included family members and local teenagers who swept the midway, manned concession stands, operated rides, cleaned restrooms, danced and sang in park shows, and portrayed characters and mascots.

Despite Western New Yorkers' love for their amusement parks, the financial difficulties and high insurance costs that plagued the parks in the later decades of the 20th century could not be averted. Even the amusement parks that had survived the Great Depression suddenly had patronage and monetary losses. Old rides broke down beyond repair; others simply lost their appeal. The days of the independent concessionaire were over, and new rides were too costly to be purchased by owners already feeling the burden of maintaining their existing rides. Modern technology finally caught up with Western New York amusement parks. Rides had become bigger, faster, and higher; the thrills had become more intense. Family-owned parks buckled under the pressure. Since it was no longer feasible for the younger generation to make a living operating an amusement park, they closed the park after their parents retired. For many waterfront amusement parks, the profit from the sale of the land far outweighed the profit the park generated, resulting in closures.

Of all the amusement parks that once were scattered around Western New York, three have struggled through adversities and continue to operate today. One amusement park has been reborn. All offer unique experiences to Western New Yorkers as they continue a local summertime tradition.

One

The First Summer Resorts

The earliest record of an amusement park in Western New York is a small advertisement in the *Buffalo Courier Times*, dated July 1853, for a picnic grove and man-powered carousel in Olcott. The addition of summer cottages and the palatial Olcott Beach Hotel helped Olcott thrive as a summer resort. The opening of Olcott's Luna Park in 1898, with its Dreamland Ballroom and other amusements, drew day-trippers as well as overnight visitors. A terrible fire destroyed Luna Park in 1927.

Grand Island's position in the middle of the Niagara River lent well to the development of 12 summer resorts on its shores between 1878 and 1896. Competition, financial losses, fires, and other tragedies led to the closing of nearly all the Grand Island parks before the turn of the 20th century.

Fairyland Park opened on East Ferry Street and Jefferson Avenue in the city of Buffalo in 1905. Thirty rides and attractions filled its midway. The park never made a profit. Additionally, it faced competition from Carnival Court located only a few blocks away. By 1909, Fairyland had disappeared.

Woodlawn Beach, near Lackawanna, opened in 1891 with several rides and attractions. A modern roller coaster was added during the 1920s. The park survived the Great Depression of the 1930s, but it never fully recovered. It managed to remain open until 1962, but by then, several of its rides, including the roller coaster, had been idle for years. The amusements were finally torn down, and the property became a New York state park.

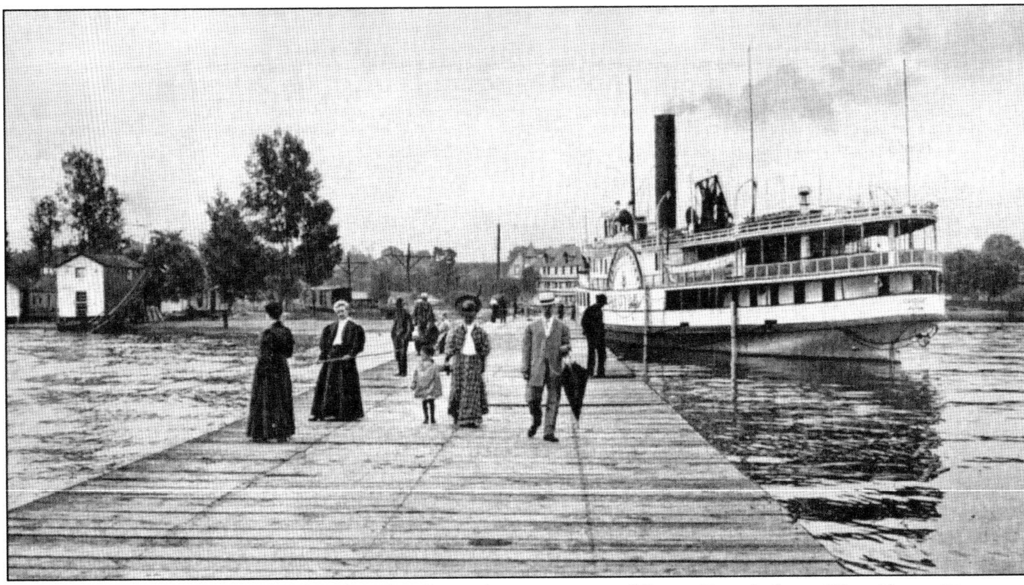

Numerous steamships and side-wheelers brought patrons to Olcott Beach from Hamilton, Toronto, Rochester, and as far away as the Thousand Islands. In the early days of the resort, people came for the concerts, vaudeville acts, and other entertainment. By 1904, Olcott Beach was so popular that a buggy could not be driven down the crowded Main Street during the summer. (Author's collection.)

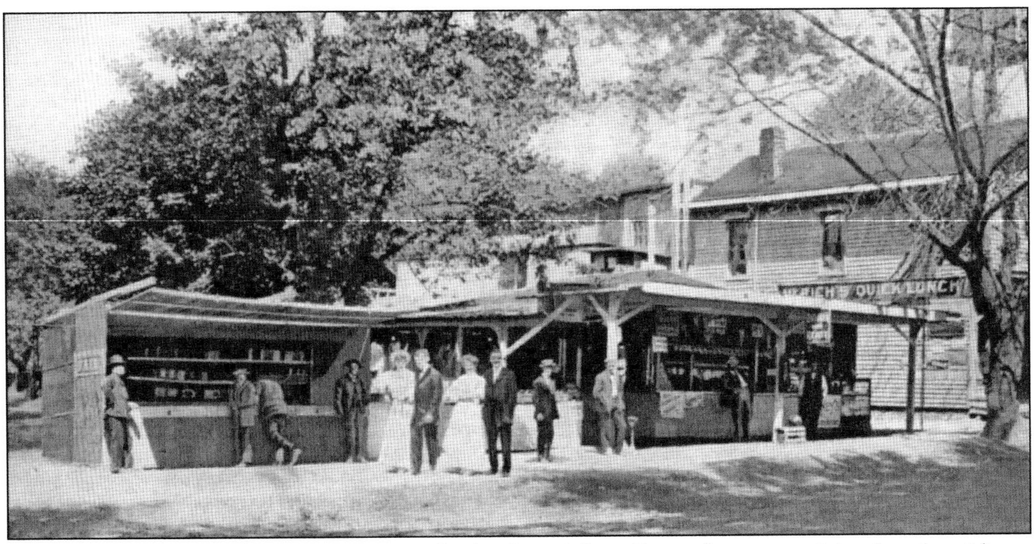

Independent rides and attractions were built along Main Street by enterprising local residents right on their front lawns. The stands offered games of chance, novelties, ice cream, refreshing drinks, or souvenirs. Some residents turned their homes into businesses like Ulrich's Quick Lunch to the far right of the photograph. (Author's collection.)

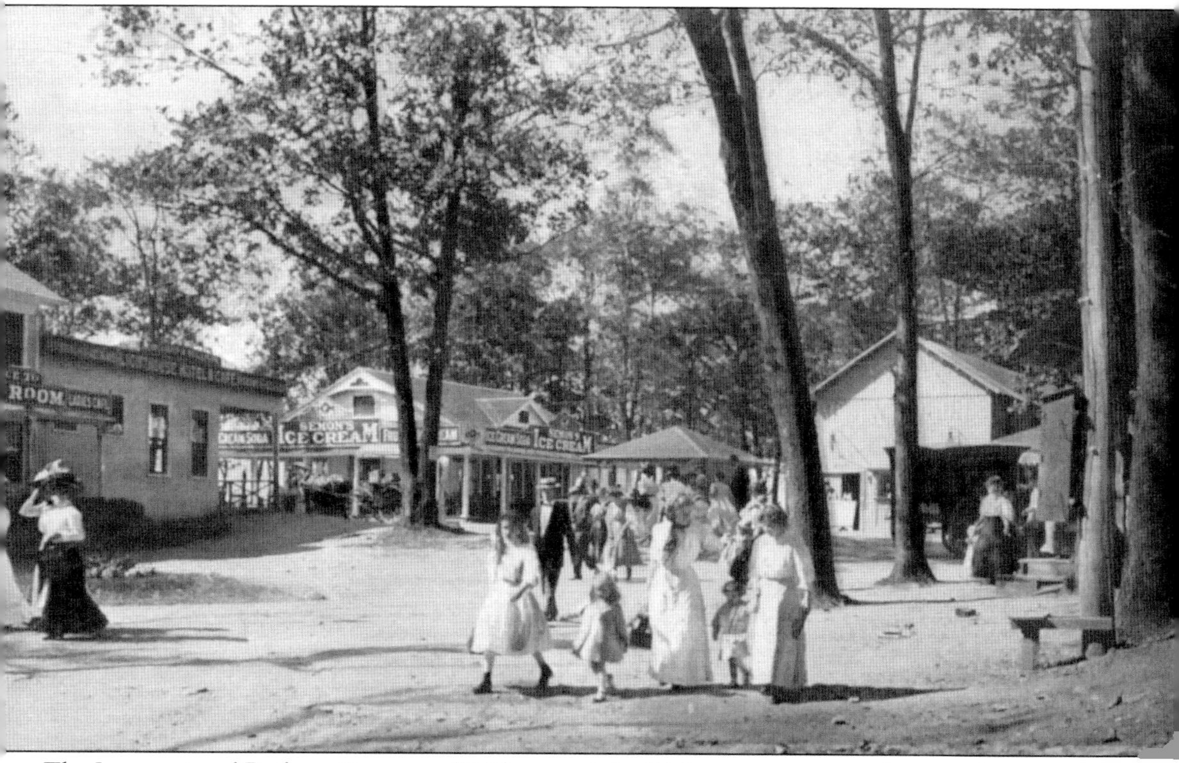

The International Railway Company (IRC) opened the Rialto amusement park across the street from the pine grove (now Krull Park) around 1902. The park included a carousel, bowling alleys, roller-skating rink, Whip, refreshment and game stands, and a fortune-teller. The IRC's trolleys brought people from Buffalo, North Tonawanda, Tonawanda, and Niagara Falls. Thousands jammed the midway throughout the summer. The Figure-Eight roller coaster was built in 1902 and was one of the few rides owned by the IRC itself, rather than run as a concession. Public interests began to change after World War I. Patrons wanted fast, thrilling rides, which the Rialto did not offer. Additionally, people who once rode the trolley were now arriving in automobiles. The IRC was losing money operating the Rialto, so it closed the park in 1925. (Courtesy of Dawn Lewis.)

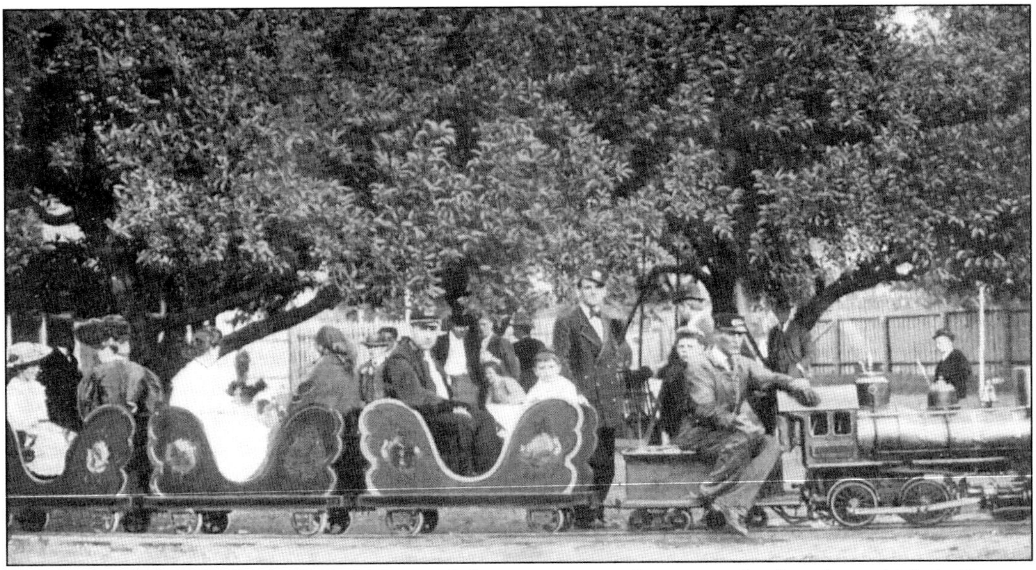

The pine grove stretched along the top of the escarpment between the beach and Main Street. Visitors enjoyed outdoor concerts at the Rustic Theater. A carousel and a miniature railroad operated in the pine grove. Patrons of the Olcott Beach Hotel often used the little steam train for transportation from the hotel to the railroad station. (Courtesy of Dawn Lewis.)

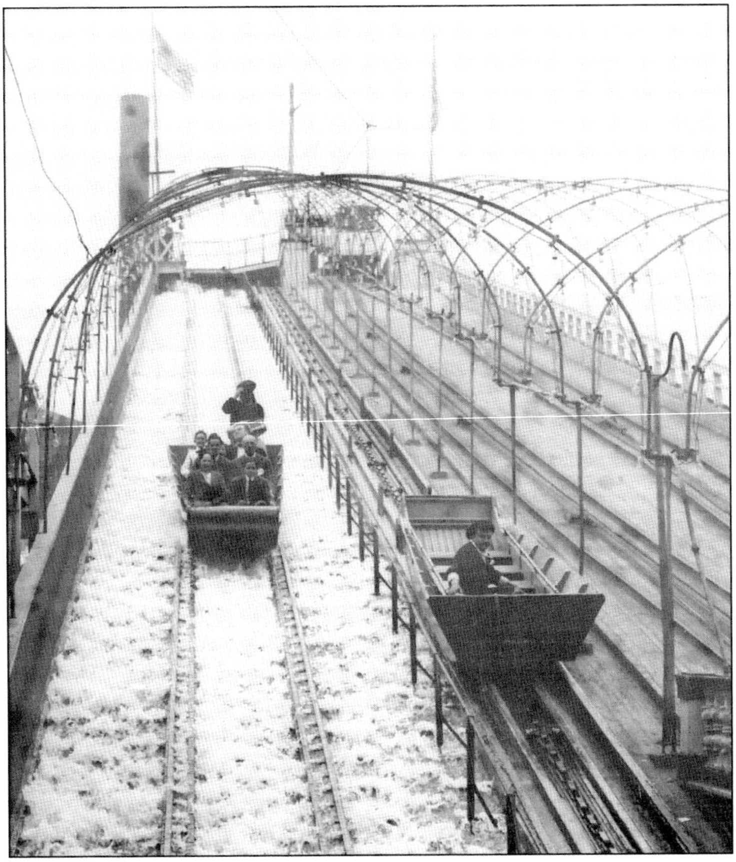

Athletic Park opened on Main and Ferry Streets in Buffalo in 1904. Attractions included the Scenic Railway and Temple of Mirth from the 1901 Pan-American Exposition, Old Mill, Mystic Swing, Circle Swing, a carousel, and the Shoot-the-Chutes. The "best vaudeville in the city" was featured in the Theatorium. Athletic Park suffered financial troubles from the beginning, however, and it was sold in 1906. (Courtesy of Dawn Lewis.)

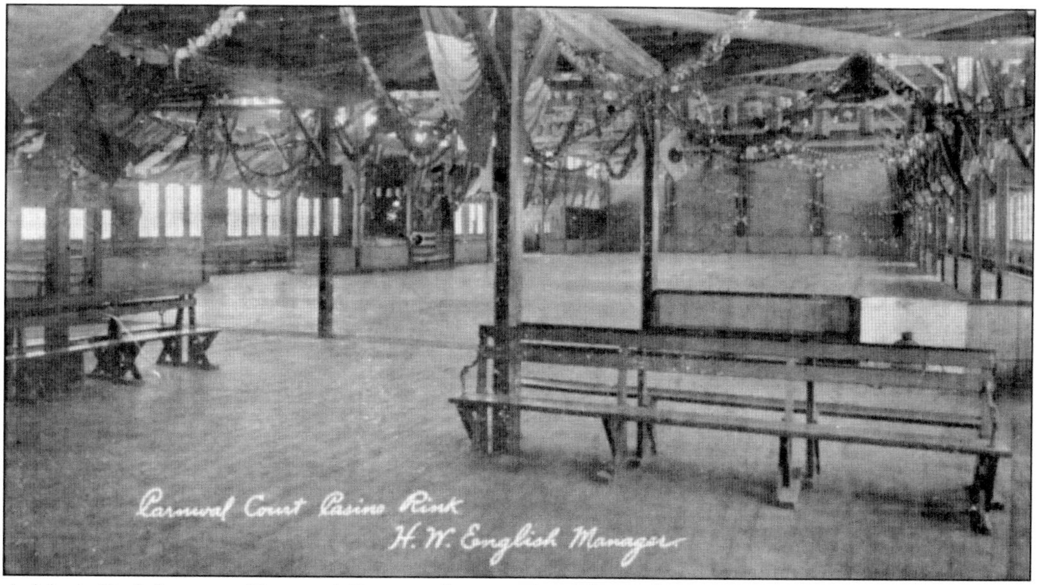

Athletic Park became Carnival Court, advertised as "the only court in Buffalo which sentences you to unlimited enjoyment." New rides and attractions were added, including a spacious casino that doubled as a roller-skating rink and dance hall. The older rides were revamped and renamed. Despite the improvements, Carnival Court could not keep up with the lakeside resorts. It operated sporadically for several years, and the lights went out permanently in 1920. (Author's collection.)

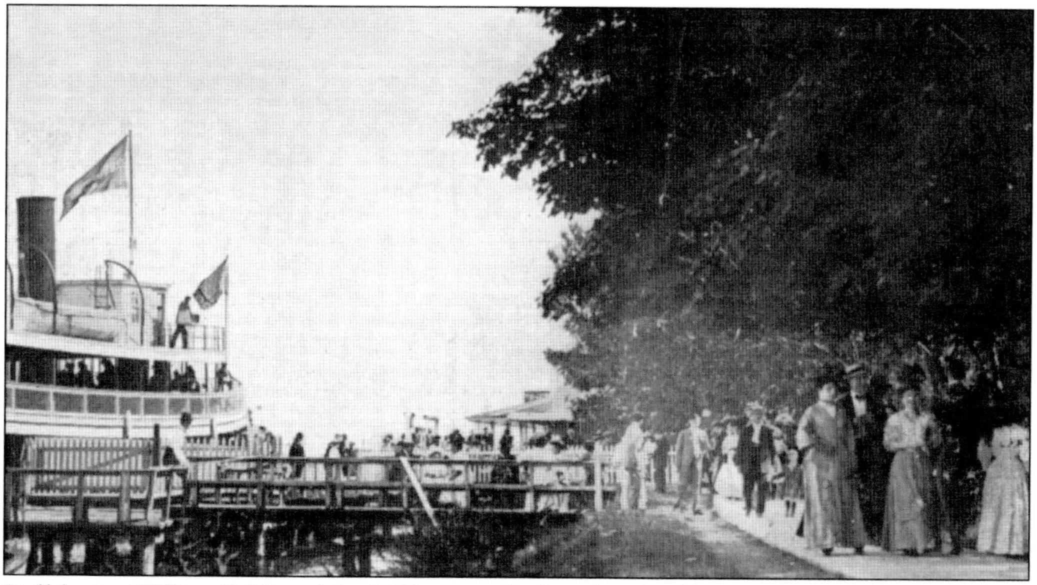

Buffalonian William E. Voetsch built Edgewater Park on farmland he purchased on East River Road on Grand Island in 1886. Crowds arriving via steamship enjoyed dancing, boating, bathing, and mechanical rides. The Depression and the opening of the Grand Island Bridges in 1935 took their toll, and the park was sold to a New York City concern around 1937. (Author's collection.)

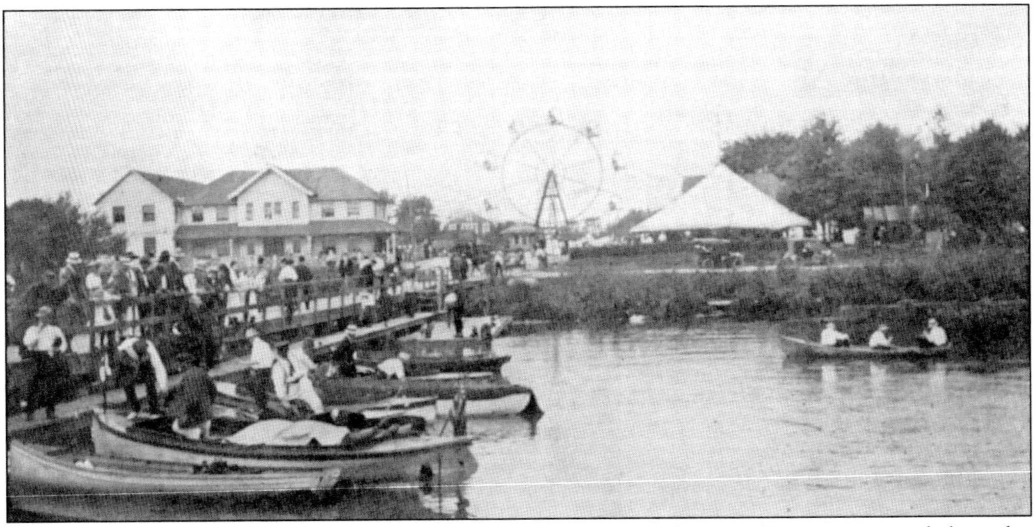

Edgewater Park's financial problems did not improve. The park ceased operation, and the rides were sold off sometime during the 1940s. A series of owners operated the Edgewater Hotel and restaurant until 1973, when the aging building was shuttered. A large section of the hotel collapsed during a storm in April 1974. It was finally demolished in 1978, and the last bit of Edgewater Park vanished into history. (Courtesy of Dan Wilke.)

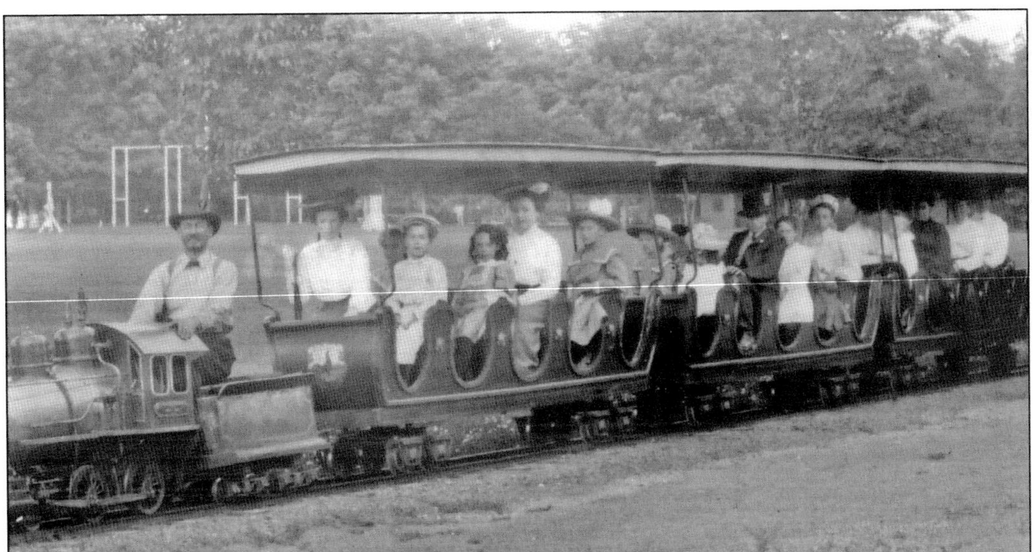

Sheenwater Park debuted in 1878 on what are now West River and Love Roads on Grand Island. It was the first amusement park in Western New York to have decorative electric light. Sheenwater featured a carousel, concessions, miniature train, and Figure-Eight roller coaster. The Howard family, who owned and operated the park from its inception, sold it when business soured during the Depression. (Courtesy of Dawn Lewis.)

Two

Chautauqua and the Southern Tier

Chautauqua Lake's rolling shoreline became a center for recreation and amusement during the 1860s, when passenger railroad service connected the Chautauqua County communities with Pittsburgh, Cleveland, and Buffalo. The beauty and charm of the lake was the perfect setting for the development of grand hotels, summer cottages, and two amusement parks—as well as the famous Chautauqua Institute.

In the heart of the Enchanted Mountains lies picturesque Cattaraugus County. In 1964, Montgomery Shoemaker opened Cloud 9 Resort just off Route 16 on the side of Mount Hermann. The resort included picnic groves, camping, hiking trails, an oil-boomtown replica, and an amusement park that was mostly comprised of kiddie rides, including a tiny miniature train and a Ferris wheel. Unfortunately, the low admission price was not enough to cover all the resort's expenses. Profits turned into losses at a rapid rate. A very wet and rainy 1970 season sealed Cloud 9's fate. The resort went bankrupt, and Cloud 9 went dark forever.

In Allegany County, the remote Cuba Lake sits in the shadow of the Allegany Mountains. The man-made lake was actually constructed as a reservoir to feed the Genesee Valley. Stocked well with fish, it soon attracted locals and developed into a natural summer resort with a focus on fishing, boating, and swimming. The birthplace of Charles Ingalls, the father of author Laura Ingalls Wilder, Cuba Lake became home to a small amusement park, Olivecrest Park.

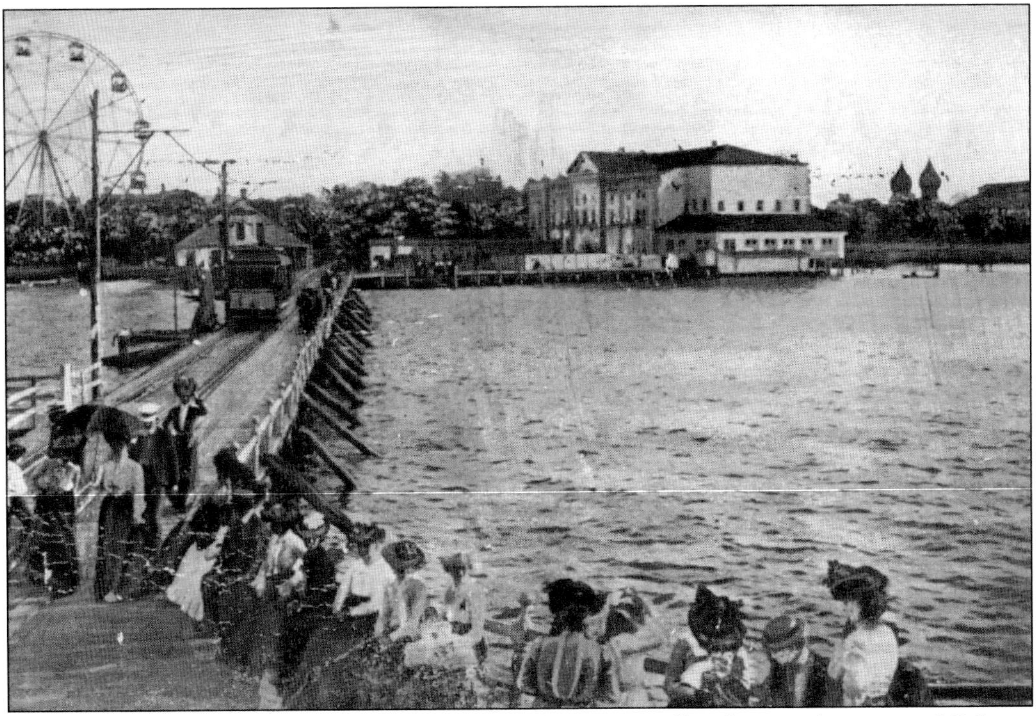

In 1894, the Celoron Amusement Company, with Almet N. Broadhead as president, opened Celoron Park on the banks of Chautauqua Lake in the village of Celoron just a short distance from Jamestown. Most patrons arrived by steamship. Because the dock was so far out from the shore, a trolley shuttled patrons back and forth from the end of the dock to the park. (Author's collection.)

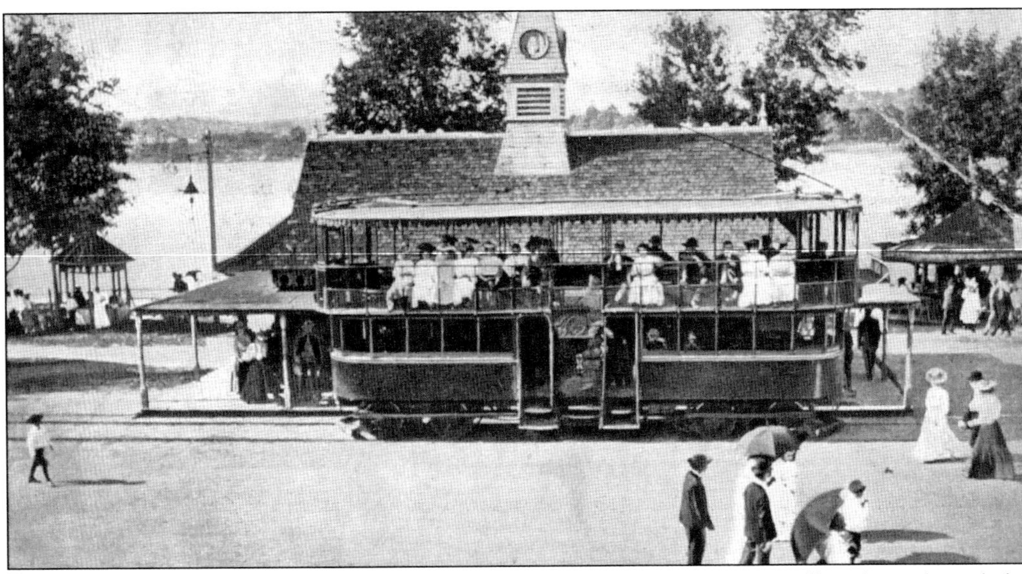

After the closing of the Columbia Exposition in Chicago in 1893, Broadhead purchased the *Columbia,* a double-decker streetcar built by the Pullman Company. Its only duty was to make the run between Jamestown and Celoron Park, and it did so every summer until it was retired in 1913. (Author's collection.)

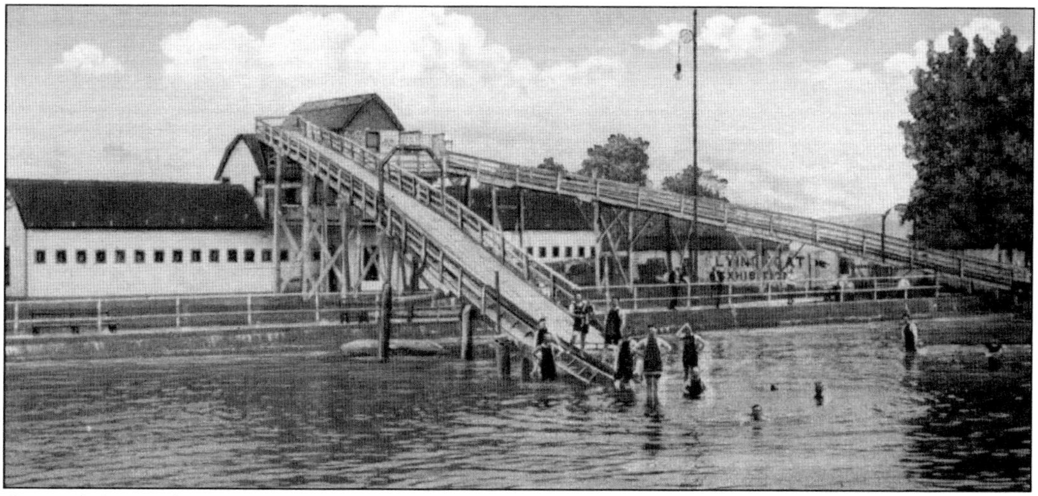

One of the early structures in Celoron Park was the bathhouse with three toboggan slides, including a camelback slide, which was removed in 1908. Each slide originated at the bathhouse's top floor. Riders sat on wooden toboggans with rollers underneath. The toboggan zipped down a track on the man-made hill and skimmed across the lake surface before sinking into the water. (Author's collection.)

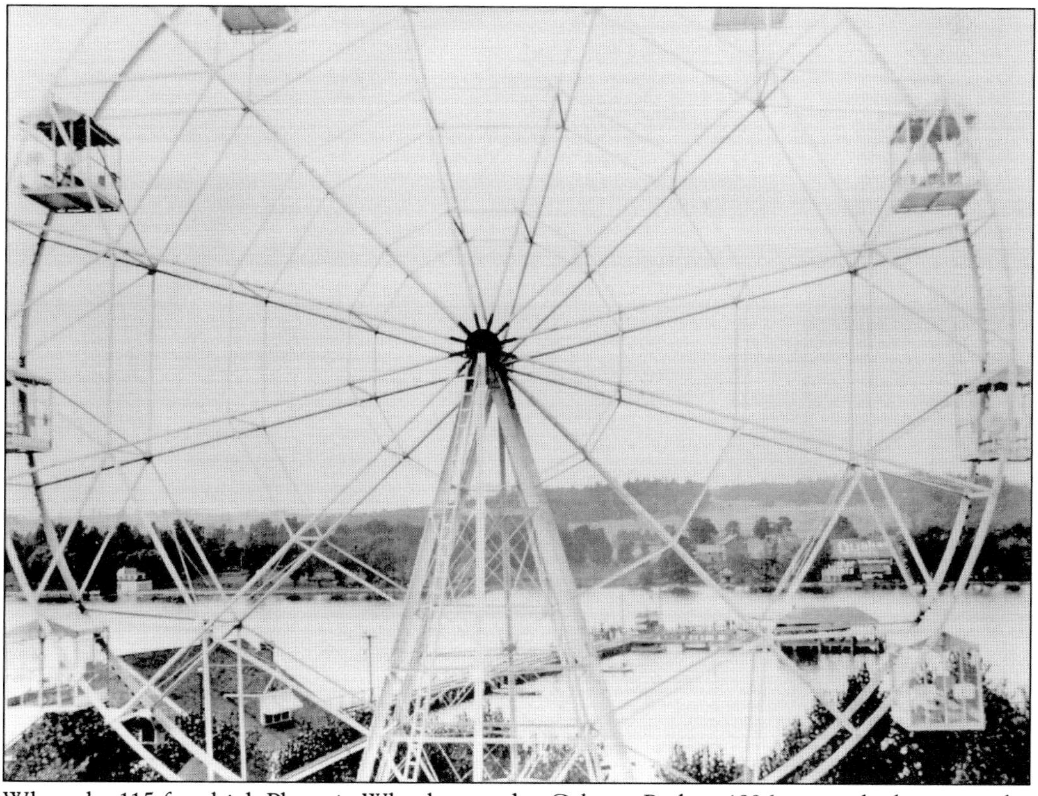

When the 115-foot-high Phoenix Wheel opened at Celoron Park in 1896, it was the largest in the world. Broadhead bought the Phoenix Wheel from the Cotton States and International Exposition in Atlanta. Its 12 cars were large enough to carry 15 riders or more either standing or sitting on benches. Some 350 colored lights turned it into a beacon at night. (Author's collection.)

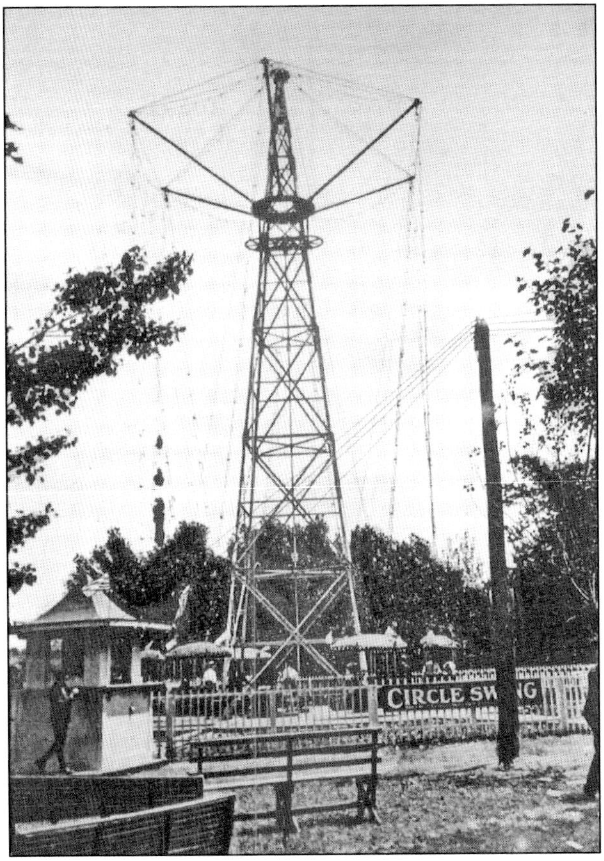

The Circle Swing debuted near the water in 1905. Riders climbed aboard wicker canopied gondolas attached to cables hung from sweeps at the top of the tower. The gondolas flew outward as the sweeps turned. Each of the cables was strung with incandescent lights that created a giant firefly effect in the nighttime sky. (Author's collection.)

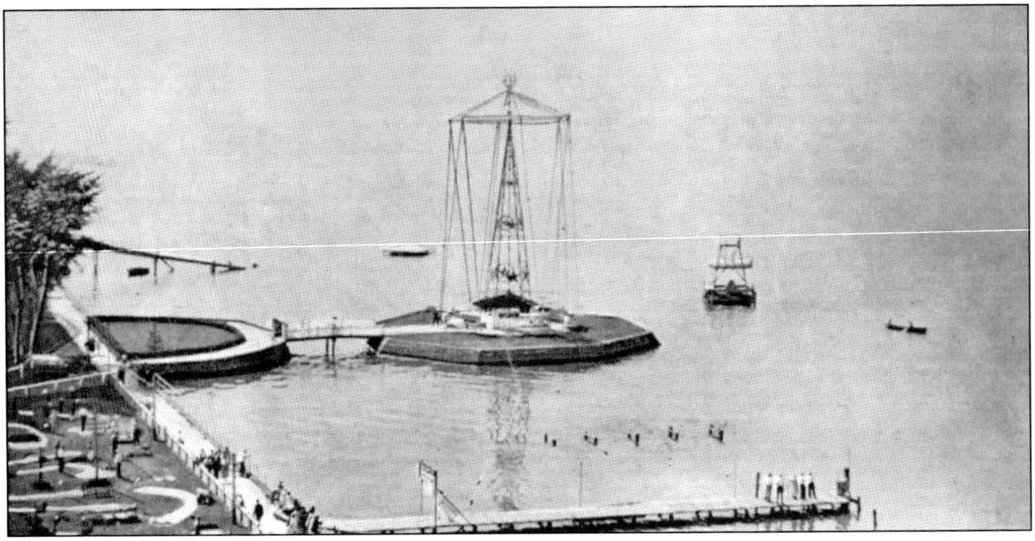

In 1925, the Circle Swing was moved to a small island just offshore. The wicker gondolas were replaced with wooden airplane-styled cars. The island was connected by a bridge to the former site of the band shell. A toboggan slide, the promenade, and a miniature golf course can be seen on the left. The island still sits in Chautauqua Lake, now overgrown with trees. (Courtesy of Dan Wilke.)

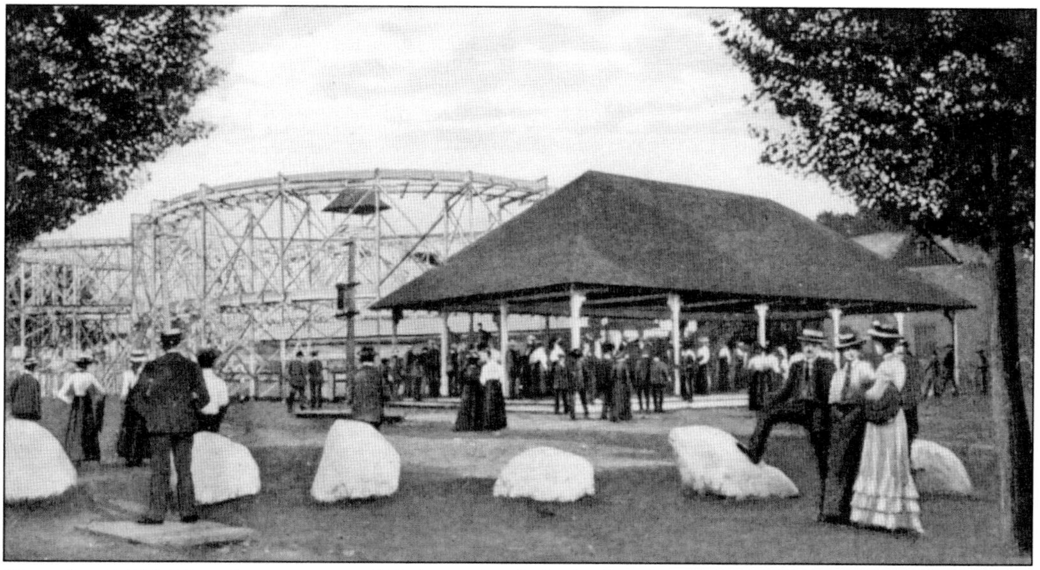

Crowds of 15,000 and more visited Celoron Park daily during its first two decades of operation. The park had a full lineup of rides, including the Figure-Eight roller coaster, which opened in 1903. It was the only figure eight roller coaster existing in Western New York when it ceased operation in 1933. (Courtesy of Dan Wilke.)

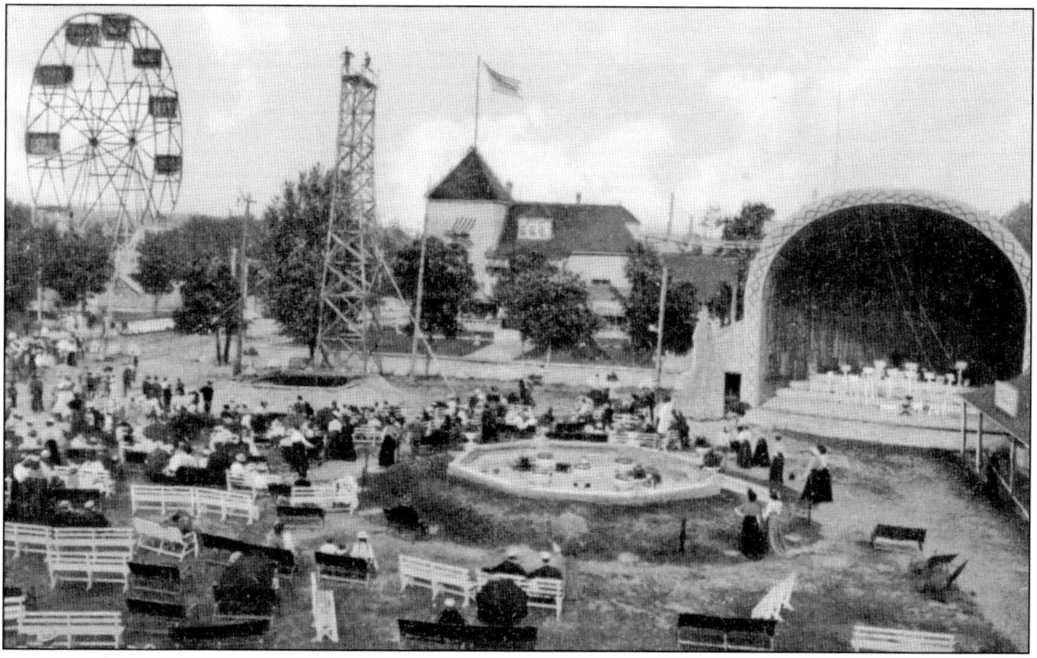

The band shell was moved to this location from the lake in 1896. Plenty of benches for comfortable seating during performances and concerts were clustered on the grass in front of the streetcar turnaround. Across from the band shell is the electric fountain. During the evening, the bursting spray was illuminated with multicolored lights and accompanied by music. (Author's collection.)

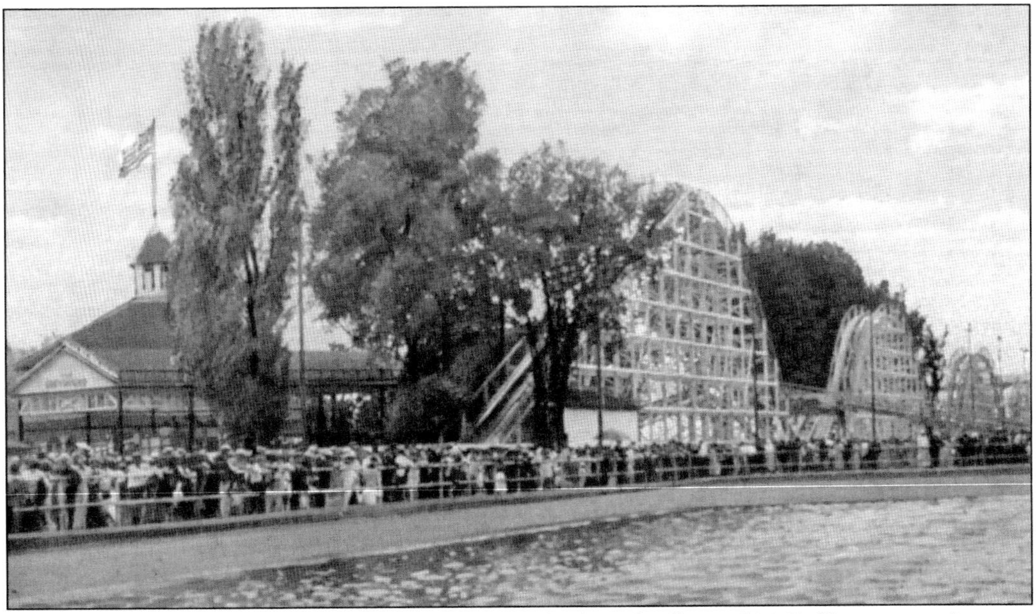

The Greyhound roller coaster was built alongside the boardwalk in 1924. Roller coaster designer T. M. Harton built, owned, and operated the Greyhound. Its out-and-back configuration included three major hills and a tight turnaround. It was covered with 6,000 incandescent lights. A tornado destroyed it in 1959. (Courtesy of Dan Wilke.)

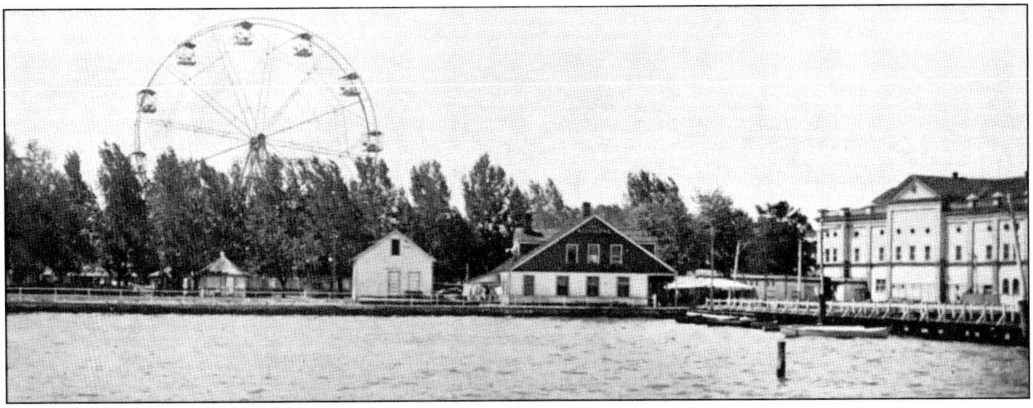

The Richmond Hotel, center, was home to traveling entertainers and sheltered park employees during the winter. To the far right is the magnificent Celoron Theater. Built in 1896, its lavish interior offered seating in the orchestra, mezzanine, and 16 box seats. In 1924, it was reconfigured into a very popular ballroom, consumed by fire in 1930. (Courtesy of Dan Wilke.)

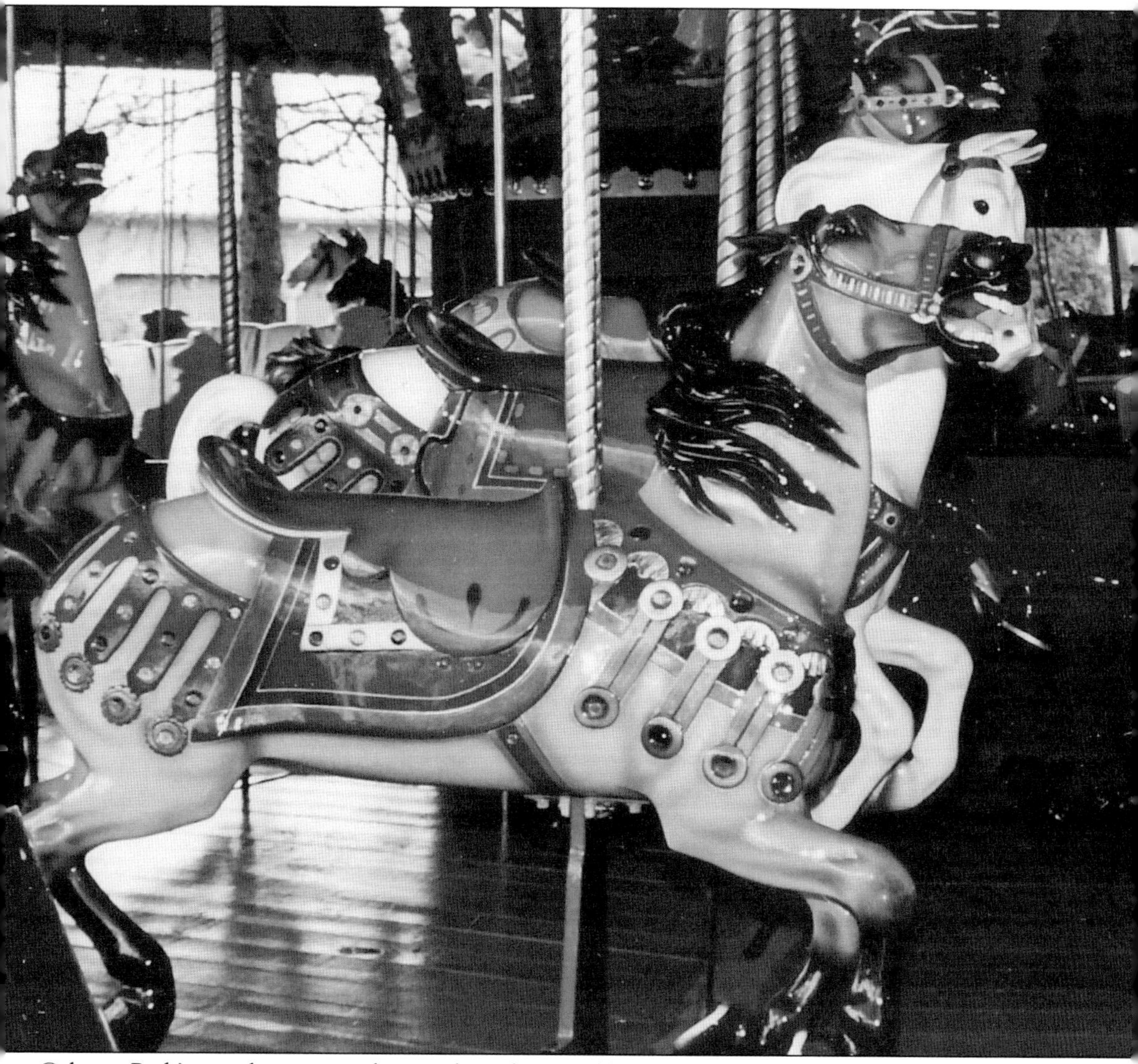

Celoron Park's popularity waned somewhat after World War I, despite the continual addition of new rides and attractions. The Coney Island Realty and Amusement Company took a five-year lease of the park from the Celoron Amusement Company in 1918. As droves of patrons arrived by automobile during the 1920s, more and more of the midway was requisitioned for parking lots. Celoron Park was sold to the Jamestown Street Railway Company and then changed hands again in 1930 when it was sold to park managers George and Thomas Carr. The Jamestown Street Railway Company ceased operation in 1938, ending streetcar service to the park. The Carr brothers sold Celoron Park to J. G. Campbell, president of Jamestown Motor Bus Transit Company. In 1943, Harry A. Illions purchased the park from Campbell. Illions brought a new carousel to the park, replacing the E. Joy Morris carousel that had been at Celoron since its opening. (Author's collection.)

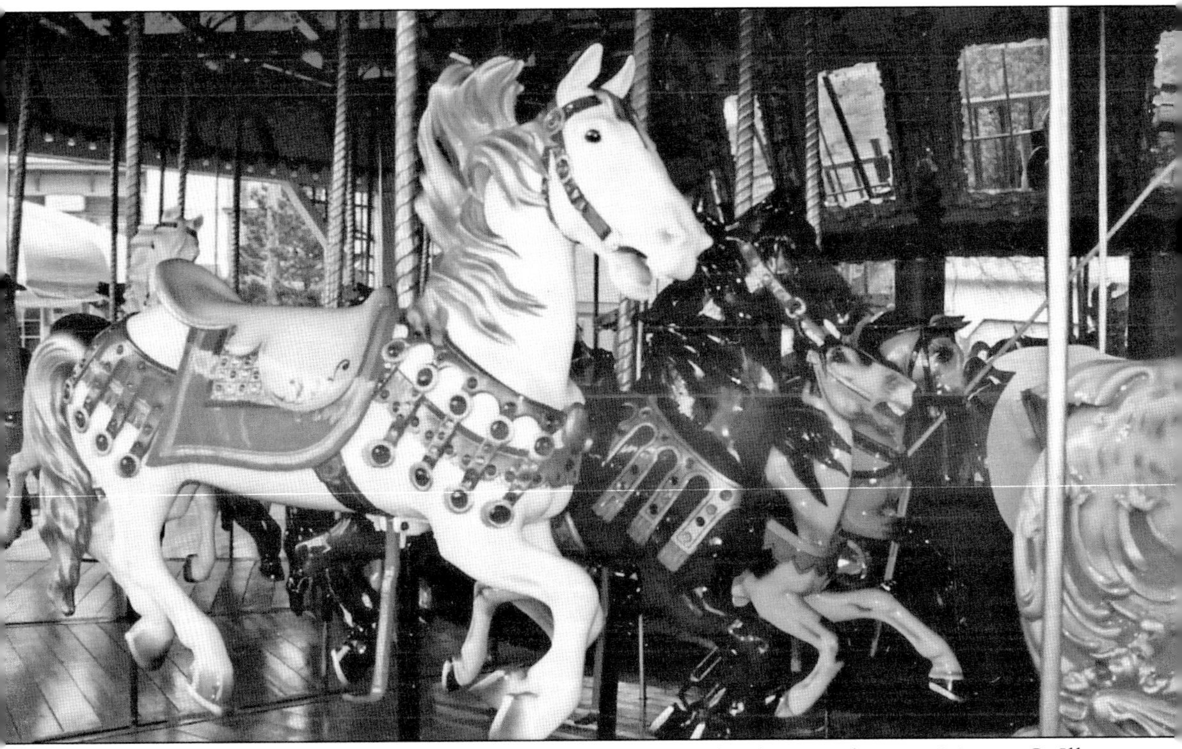

Harry A. Illions, one of five children of famous Coney Island carousel carver Marcus C. Illions, brought several new rides to Celoron Park in 1943: three Eli Bridge Company Ferris wheels from the 1940 New York World's Fair, Skooters, and a 1927 Illions Supreme Carousel from Coney Island. The Phoenix Wheel was struck by lightning in 1949 and dismantled. Illions hinted that Liberty Park in Cheektowaga, which he had purchased in 1948, might become the new home for the Phoenix Wheel—however, it was put back up at Celoron Park following repairs. The Los Angeles County Fair hired Illions to build a $1 million midway in 1952. He took the Circle Swing, the Supreme Carousel, and the Phoenix Wheel with him. The Phoenix Wheel remained in Los Angeles until 1981, when it was condemned and permanently dismantled. Celoron Park continued to decline. Illions put the park up for sale in 1960, but there were no buyers. After he died unexpectedly two weeks before the start of the 1962 season, his heirs sold Celoron Park, and it faded into history. (Author's collection.)

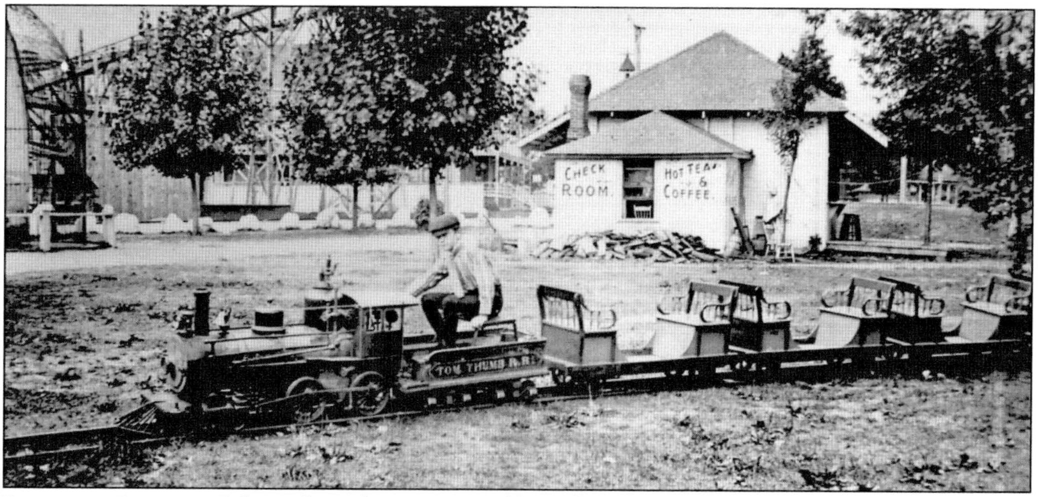

Jamestown's most celebrated resident was Lucille Ball. After her father died, Lucy, her brother, and their mother lived with her maternal grandparents, whose house was within easy walking distance of Celoron Park. As a child, Lucy saw performances at the Celoron Theater. She even worked at the park as a teenager, selling tickets for the Tom Thumb Miniature Railroad. (Author's collection.)

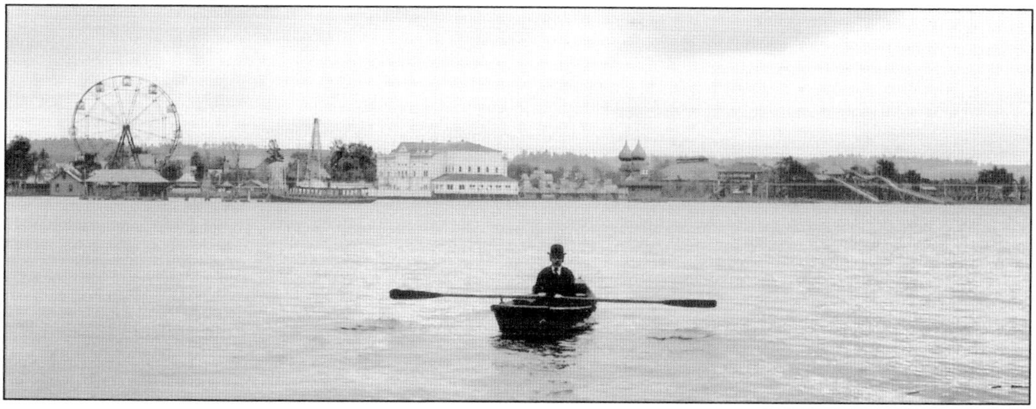

In 1965, the board of the Village of Celoron authorized the $30,000 purchase of the 7-acre Celoron grove, to the left of where the Phoenix Wheel is seen in this photograph. Originally named Pier Point Park, the grove was renovated and renamed Lucille Ball Park in 1991. A bandstand was built and named in honor of Lucy's first husband and television costar, Desi Arnaz. (Courtesy of C. Thomas.)

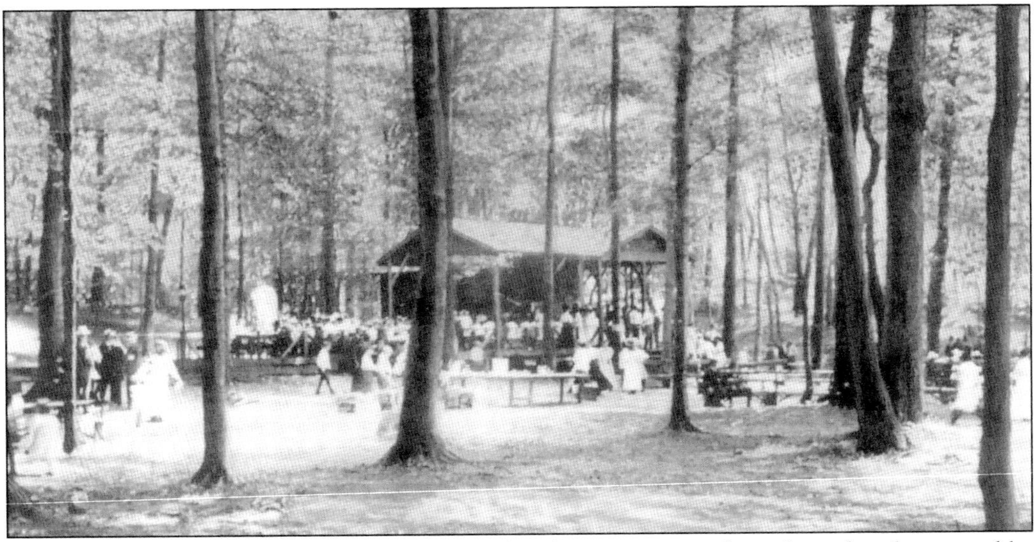

July 12, 1898, was opening day for Midway Park. The 17-acre parcel was leased and operated by the Jamestown and Lake Erie Railway as a way to attract passengers to ride the trolleys to the northern side of Chautauqua Lake. The park's name derived from a steamship dock built on the site in 1894 that was midway between the Maple Springs Inn and Hotel Whiteside. (Courtesy of Midway Park.)

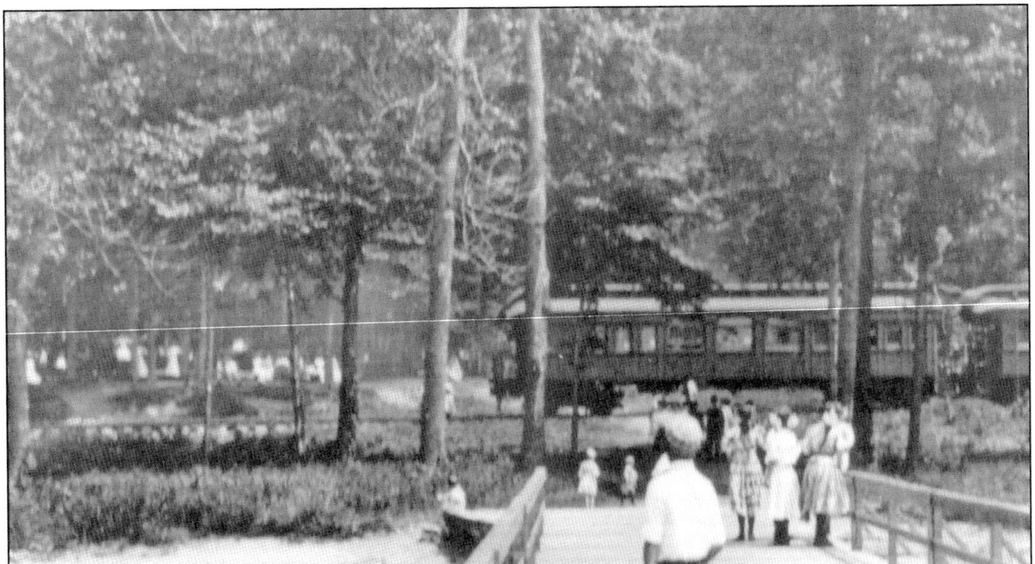

The park's amenities included a beach, dance pavilion, dining room, tennis courts, ball fields, rowboat rentals, and croquet. The trolleys arrived at the park with carloads of passengers. Round-trip fare from Jamestown was 25¢. A 450-foot dock was built in 1907 to accommodate the steamships. (Courtesy of Midway Park.)

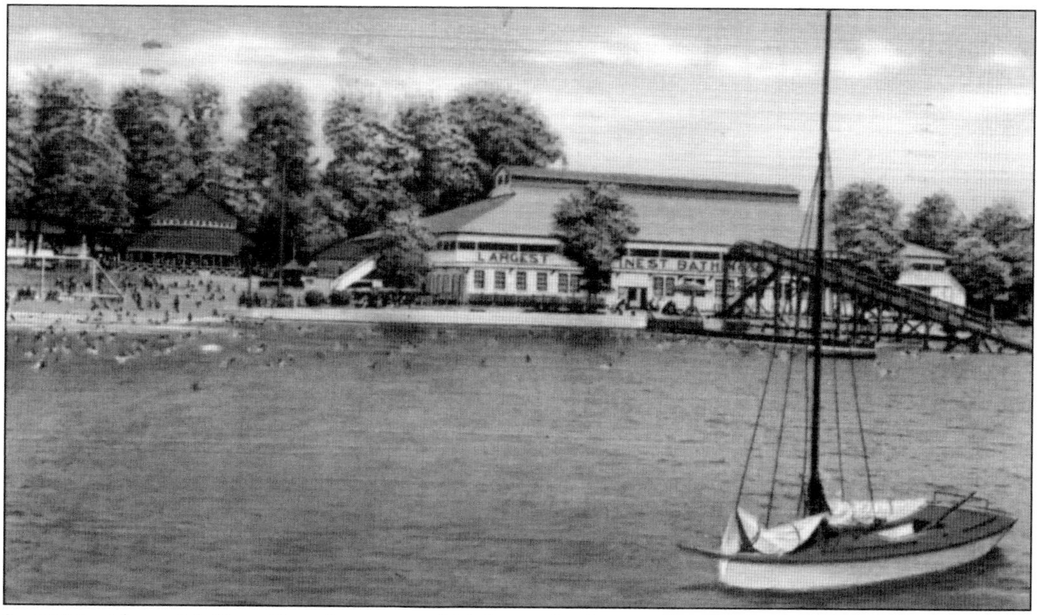

In 1913, Almet N. Broadhead, owner of Celoron Park, purchased the steamship and railroad companies and electrified the railroad tracks for trolley runs. The Chautauqua Lake Navigation Company bought the park in 1915. A 40,000-square-foot lakeside pavilion was built along with a toboggan slide supplied by Sellner Manufacturing, creators of the Tilt-A-Whirl. The new owners added picnic shelters and a carousel. (Author's collection.)

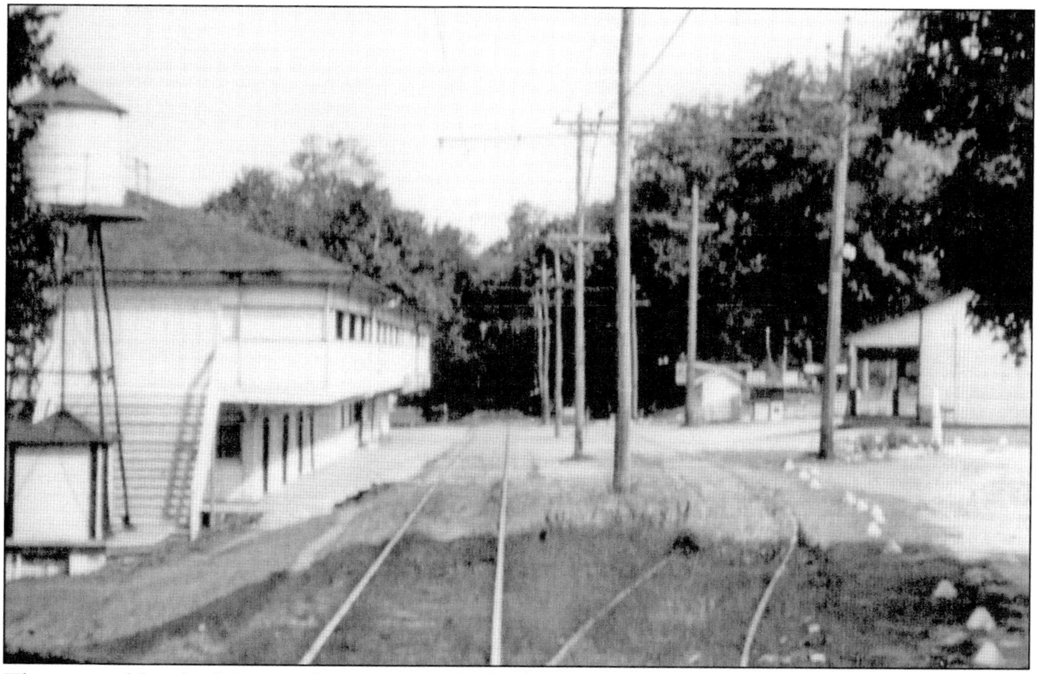

The ground level of the pavilion consisted of a dining room, concessions, shooting gallery, and bathhouse. An open-air roller-skating rink occupied the entire upper level. The rink also served as a dance floor. Lucille Ball and her friends often skated at the rink. The trolley stopped beside the pavilion. (Courtesy of Midway Park.)

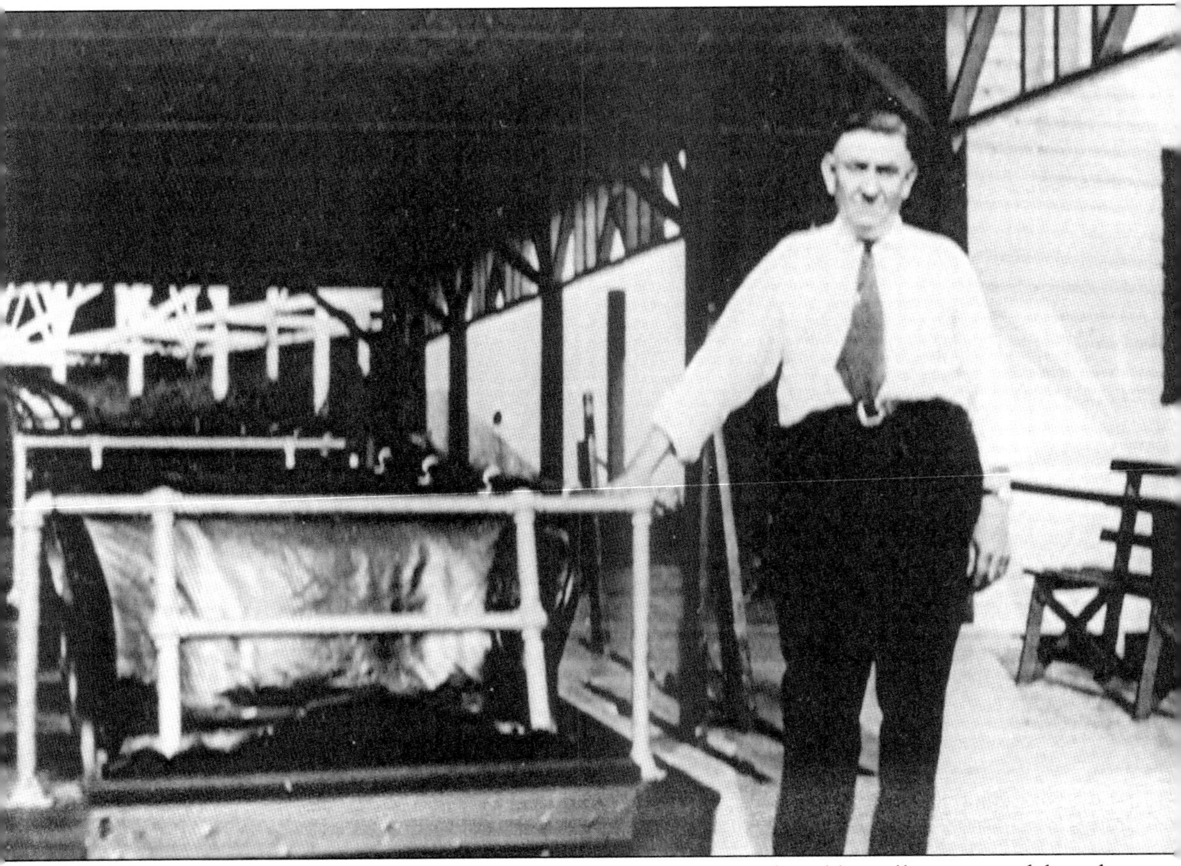

Built by roller coaster designers Miller and Baker, Inc., the Jack Rabbit roller coaster debuted in mid-summer 1934. Massive in size, it was meant to compete with nearby Celoron Park's Greyhound roller coaster. The Jack Rabbit's loading station was situated on the lower level of the park with the major portion of the ride built on top of the hillock alongside the baseball diamond. The lift hill took the open-front train to the upper level and the first drop. Its out-and-back configuration gave a thrilling ride with deep dips, rolling hills, and flat turns. The finish took riders down a steep dip back to the lower level of the park. Few photographs remain of the Jack Rabbit. Bill Johnson, operator of the roller coaster until it was torn down in 1939, stands beside the train in this image. (Courtesy of Midway Park.)

Thomas Carr, who had bought Celoron Park in 1930, leased Midway Park from the Jamestown, Westfield, and Northwestern Railroad in 1934. He purchased the park outright in 1939. Martin "Red" Walsh had been with the park's management staff since 1927. He remained on with Carr as administrative assistant, procuring the park from Carr's estate in 1951. (Courtesy of Kathy Loveland.)

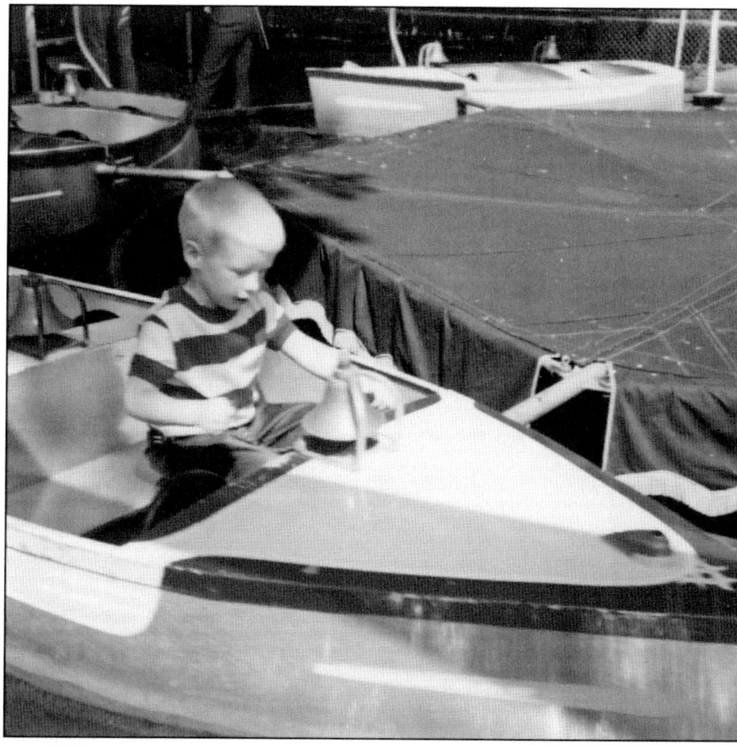

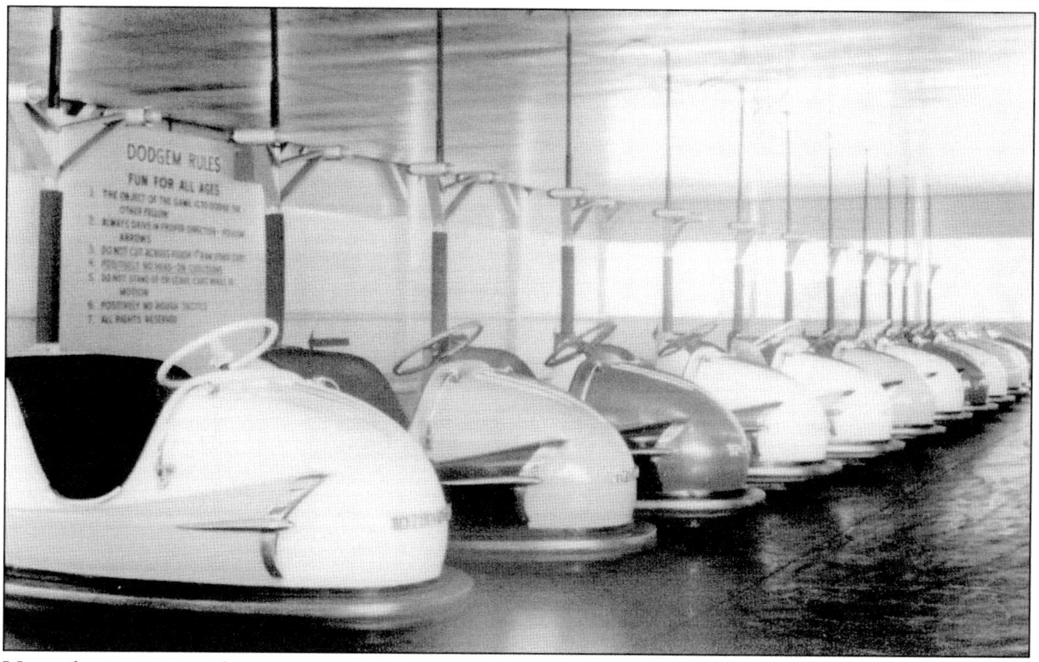

Upon becoming park owner, Walsh immediately brought his younger brother, Frank, on board and added four kiddie rides from the Allan Herschell Company of North Tonawanda. Large group picnic pavilions were erected and additional land was acquired, bringing the park's total parcel to 27 acres. The Dodgem ride opened in 1958. The classy art deco Dodgem cars were replaced with fiberglass ones in 1994. (Courtesy of Midway Park.)

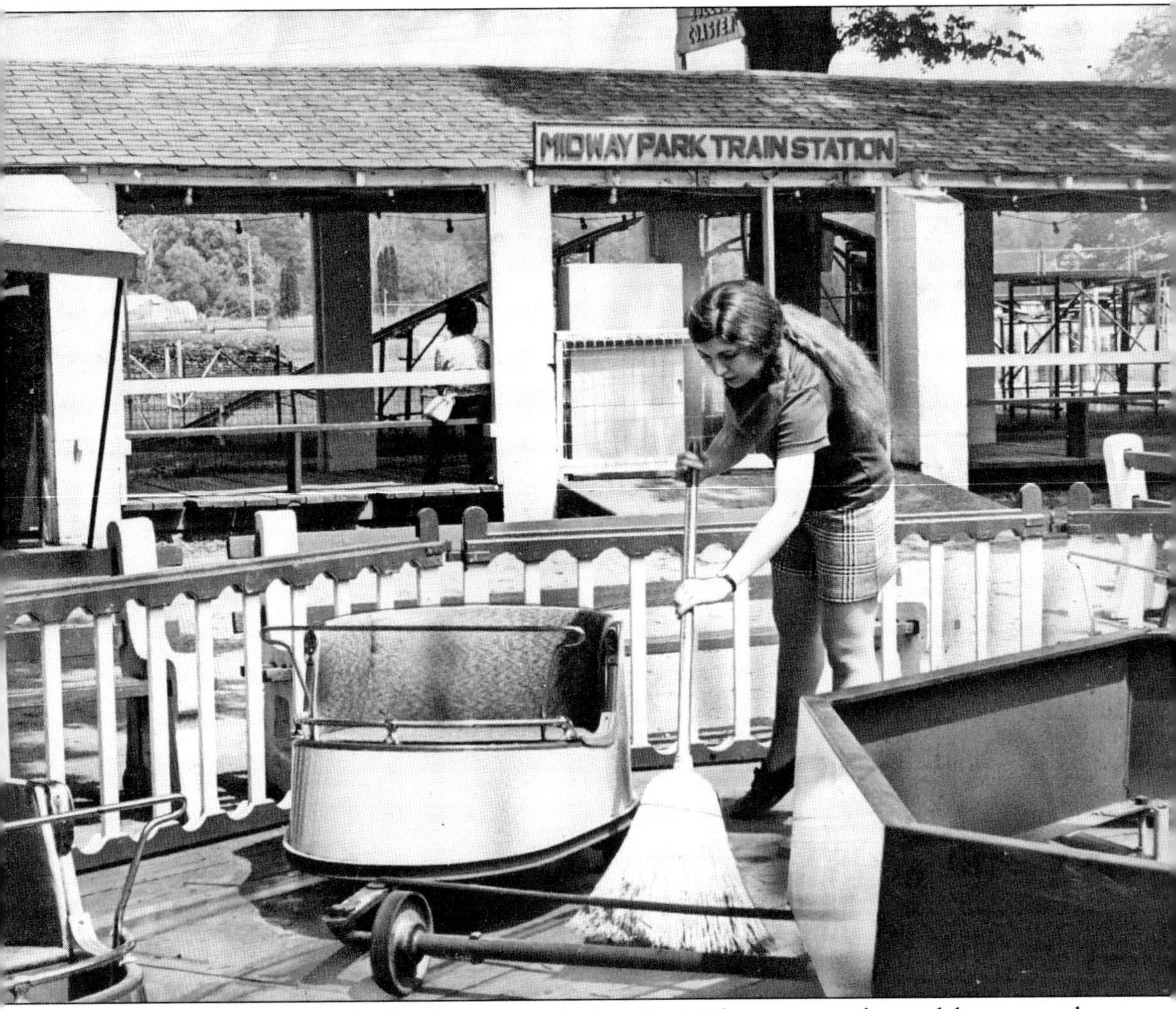

The Walsh brothers worked hard to promote Midway Park. They concocted special discount packages to attract company outings, made Wednesdays "5¢ Kiddie Days," created a school picnic program, and gave large families discounts. The attitude and treatment of staff was equally important to park operations. The Walsh brothers designed a curriculum that trained their personnel to be kind and courteous to all guests. A focus on appearance meant that staff had to be uniformly dressed and well groomed. Employees were expected to take pride in their jobs and in the park. This young lady kept the kiddie Roto Whip neat and clean, sweeping up the platform between ride sessions. Behind her are the train station and the Roller Coaster. Although considered a kiddie ride, the Roller Coaster, from the Allan Herschell Company, had cars large enough to fit the average adult so that parents could ride with their kids. (Courtesy BSCACEC.)

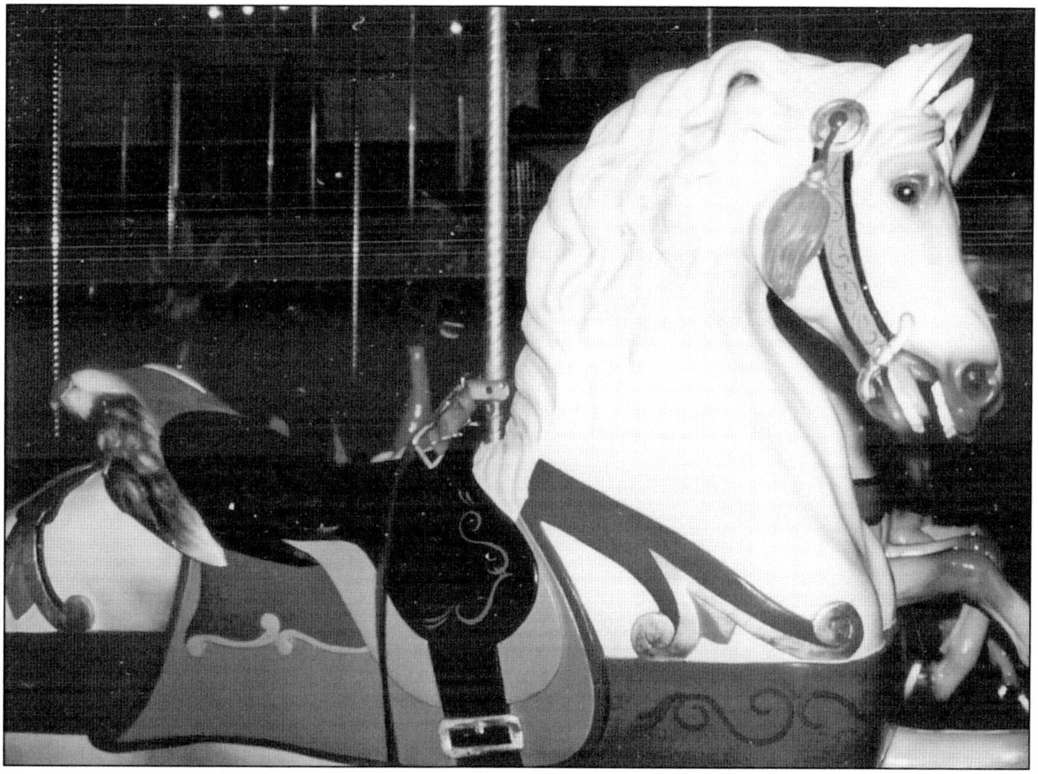

Several rides were added during the 1960s. These included the Chair Plane ride from the Smith and Smith Company of nearby Springville and a Sellner Manufacturing Tilt-A-Whirl. When the carousel roundhouse had been built in 1928, a used Gustav Dentzel menagerie carousel was installed. In 1968, the animals were sold separately from the frame, which went to George Long at Seabreeze Park in Rochester, New York. (Author's collection.)

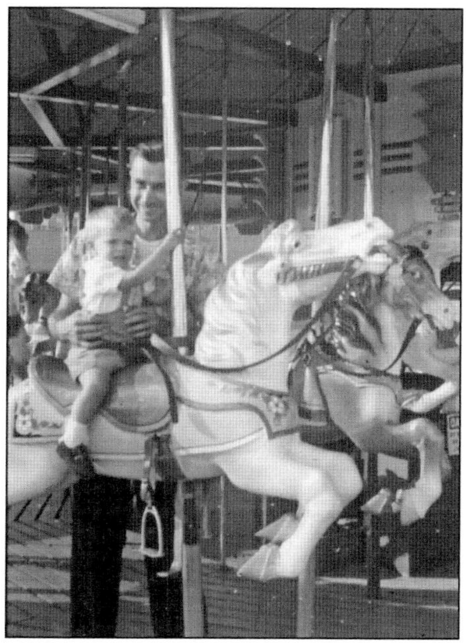

A 1946 Allan Herschell Company aluminum, three-row, art deco carousel was purchased in 1968 from Owasco Lake Park in Auburn, New York. It remains an important ride at Midway Park as adults and children alike enjoy riding on the jumping horses. Here a young boy takes what may have been his first carousel ride. (Author's collection.)

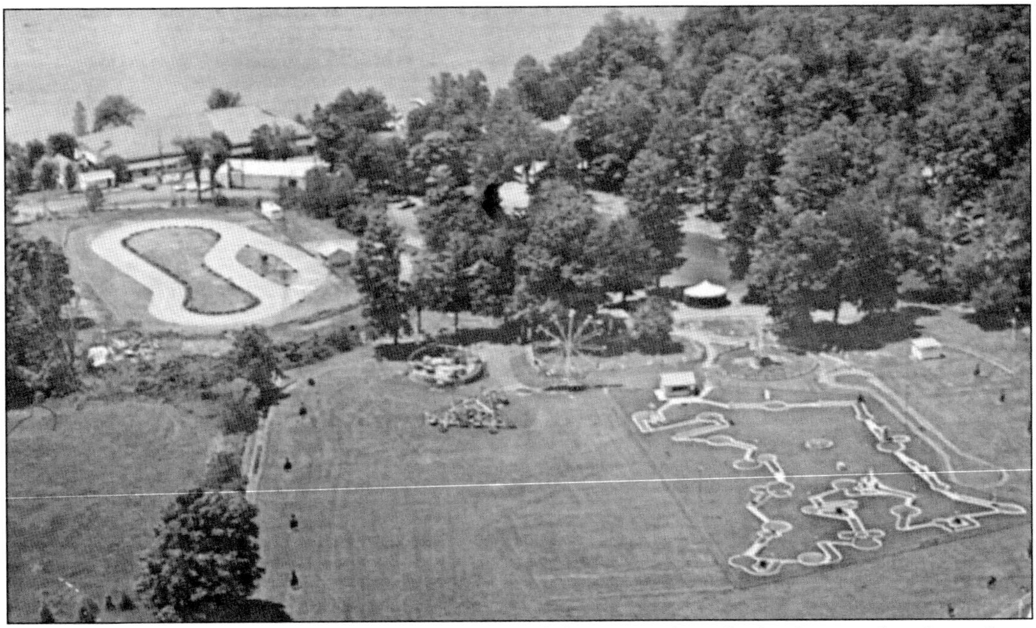

This view of the park from 1966 shows the lake and skating rink in the background and a go-kart track on the left where the Jack Rabbit roller coaster once ran. A Tilt-A-Whirl, Scrambler, and Ferris wheel are in the center, and miniature golf on the right. The park looks very much the same today except for the addition of several family thrill rides. (Courtesy of Dan Wilke.)

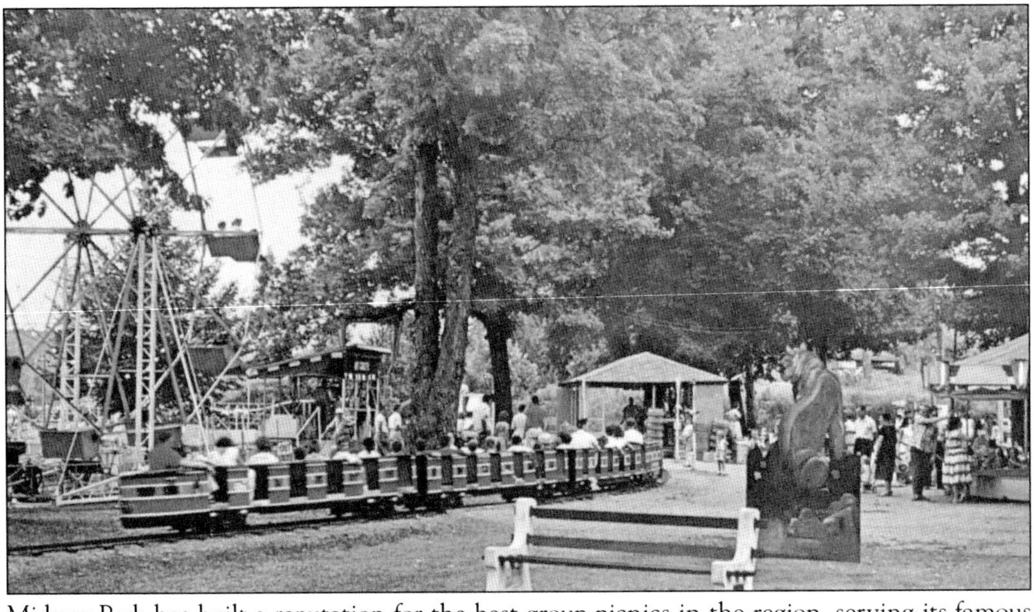

Midway Park has built a reputation for the best group picnics in the region, serving its famous chicken barbeque for company and school picnics. An annual Shrine Kiddie Day is held at the park with proceeds benefiting the Shrine Children's Hospital. In 1984, Red Walsh's son Michael and daughter-in-law Janis took over operations of Midway Park. Red Walsh remained active in the park until 1991. (Courtesy of Midway Park.)

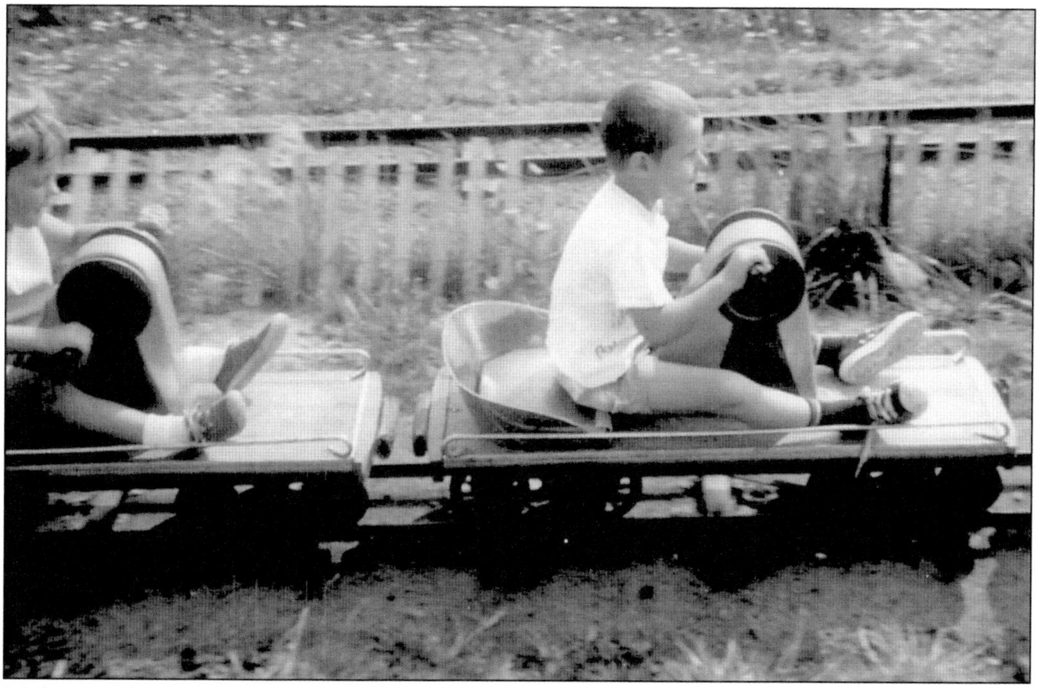

Midway Park continued to prosper under the direction of Michael and Janis Walsh. The park's offerings of modern family thrill rides and traditional kiddie rides appealed to families with preadolescent children. Free admission and free parking encouraged grandparents to join their families for a day of fun at the park. (Author's collection.)

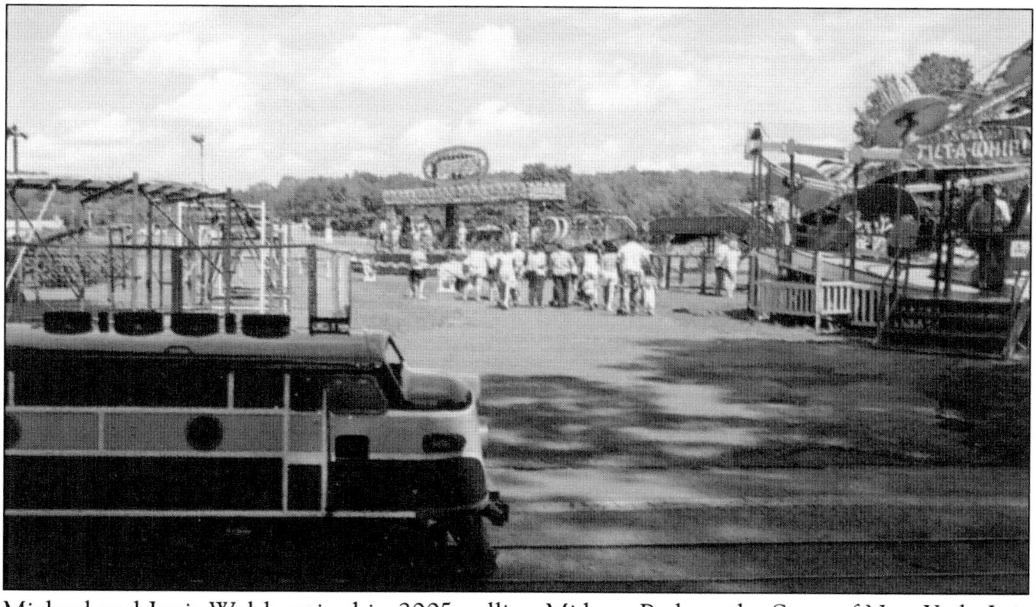

Michael and Janis Walsh retired in 2005, selling Midway Park to the State of New York. It is one of only two amusement parks owned by the state and one of the last surviving trolley parks in the nation, having celebrated its 100th birthday in 1998. Midway Park resonates with the charm of a bygone era when people came to enjoy a relaxing summer afternoon—and still do. (Author's collection.)

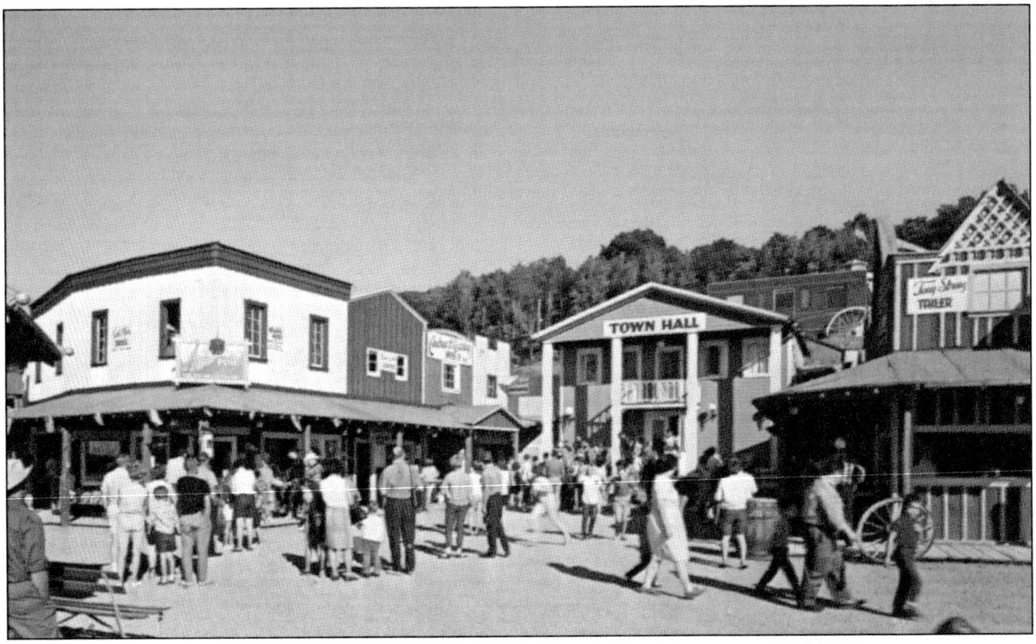

Ned Fenton Jr.'s idea of a fun-filled family vacation was visiting every Wild West attraction in the United States and Canada. His dream of owning his own Wild West park came true in 1966 when he opened Fentier Village, "where the Old West comes east," in Salamanca astride the tiered South Mountain. (Author's collection.)

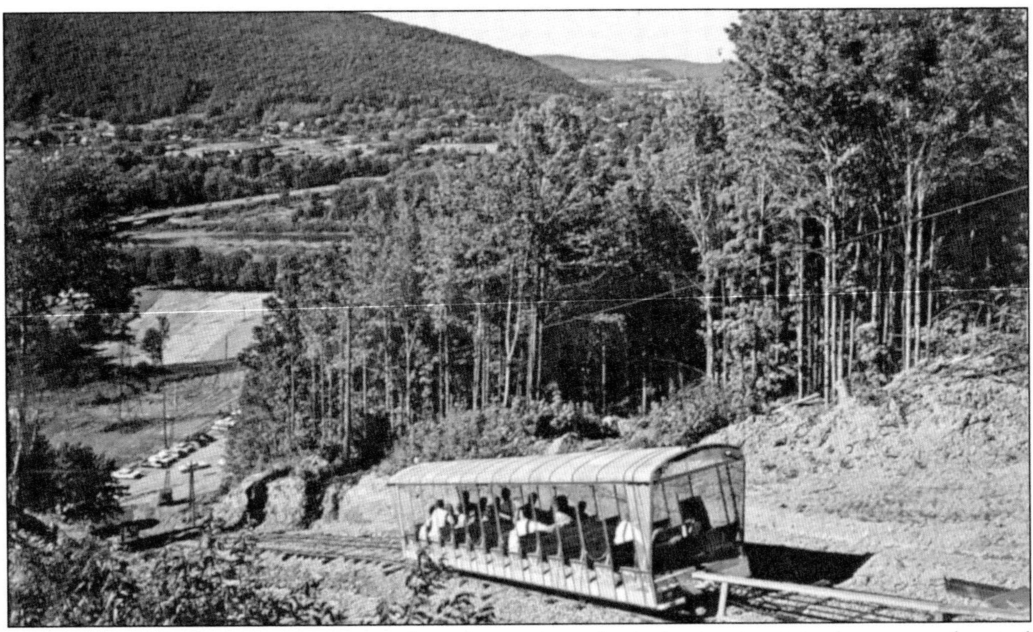

Fentier Village had New York State's only incline railway. In the beginning, it had many mechanical problems. Local resident Jim Crosby was asked to take over and revamp the entire system. Resembling a giant covered wagon, the car carried visitors up and down the mountain between the village and parking lot. (Author's collection.)

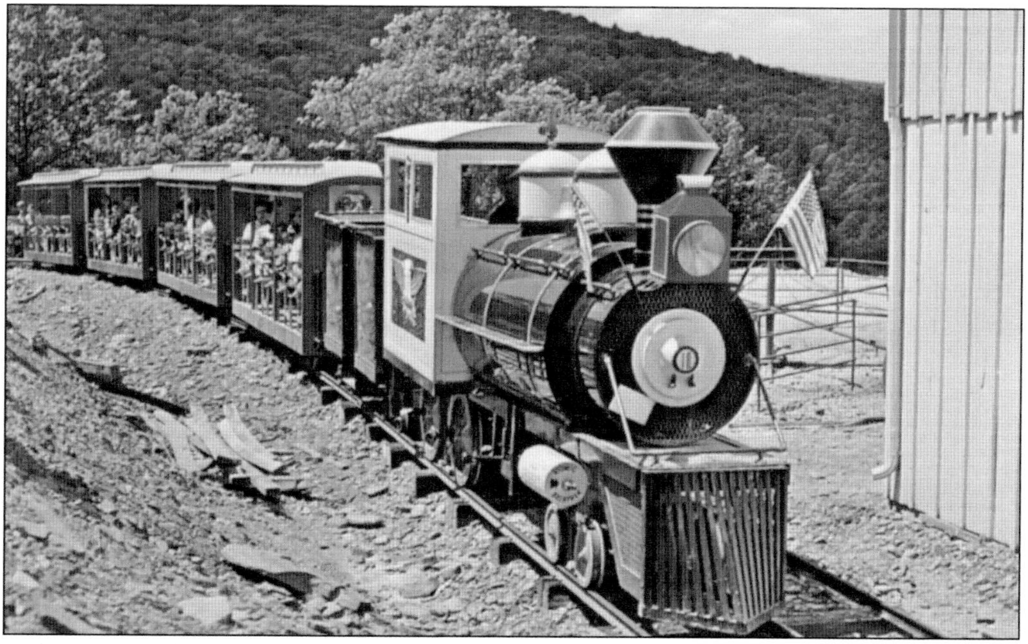

Park guests could enjoy a mile-long scenic ride through the woods on an old-fashioned train. Young cowpokes had the chance to experience a live pony ride, a trip down the "longest slide in the world" or a walk through the phenomenal Mystery Shack with a tilted-room illusion billed as "gravity on the rampage." (Author's collection.)

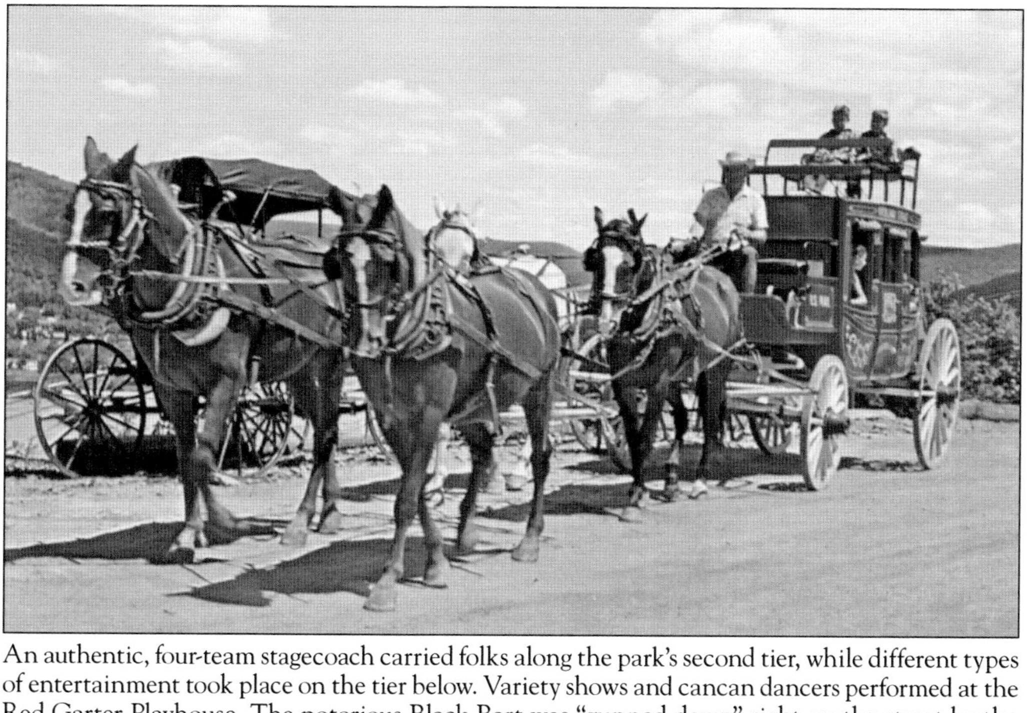

An authentic, four-team stagecoach carried folks along the park's second tier, while different types of entertainment took place on the tier below. Variety shows and cancan dancers performed at the Red Garter Playhouse. The notorious Black Bart was "gunned-down" right on the street by the local sheriff several times a day. Celebrities like Hank Williams Jr. and Lassie made appearances at the park. (Author's collection.)

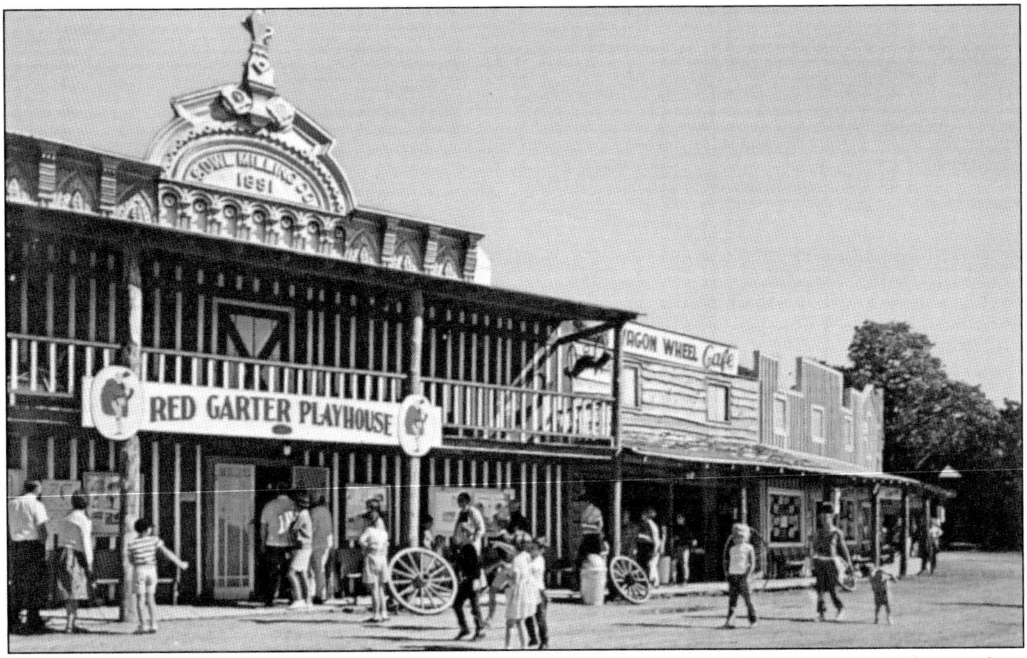

Fentier Village was such a unique amusement park that it drew around 1,000 visitors a day—often more than that on the weekends—yet the park only lasted for four seasons. At the end of the summer of 1969, New York State forced the park to close due to the planned construction of I-86, the Southern Tier Expressway. Fentier Village became a memory existing only in photographs. (Author's collection.)

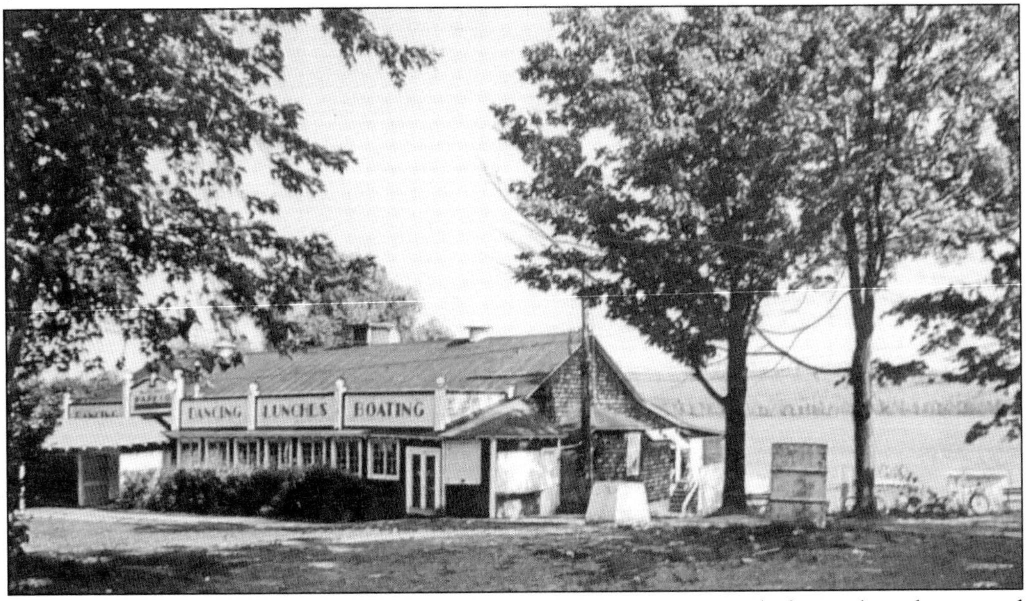

Fenton Olive opened Olivecrest Park on Cuba Lake in 1915. It consisted of a pavilion that served as dance hall and restaurant, game stands, and a few kiddie rides. He purchased a used 1915 Herschell Spillman carousel around 1933. Wesley Wakefield was the park's last owner. When he sold off the rides in 1970, the carousel went to the New York State Museum in Albany, where it operates today. (Author's collection.)

Three

Western New York's Coney Island

Buffalonian John Evangelist Rebstock purchased a combination of three farmlands totaling 100 acres on the Canadian shore of Lake Erie in Ontario. His intention was to sell the sand to Buffalo construction companies, but he found the beach and clear water so appealing that he decided to open a religious campground instead. The campground debuted the summer of 1888. As a way to relieve the intensity of religious lectures and sermons, Rebstock allowed sideshows of "high quality" to be set up on the fringes of the camp. These sideshows became so popular that Rebstock decided to convert his religious campground into a summer pleasure resort, eventually called Crystal Beach.

Crystal Beach was an immediate success, and by 1906, the midway was bustling with exciting rides and attractions. Western New Yorkers and folks from Southern Ontario, Ohio, and Pennsylvania flocked to the resort to socialize and to enjoy new experiences, such as an exhilarating ride aboard the Figure-Eight roller coaster. The park became so popular that it was dubbed "Western New York's Coney Island."

Crystal Beach continued to entertain thousands every summer for the next several decades. It survived the Great Depression and afterwards experienced a resurgence in popularity that lasted from the late 1940s until well into the 1960s. Changing times, increased competition, changes in ownership, receivership, and other factors contributed to the demise of the park. In 1989, after 101 years of entertaining the masses, Crystal Beach Park closed forever.

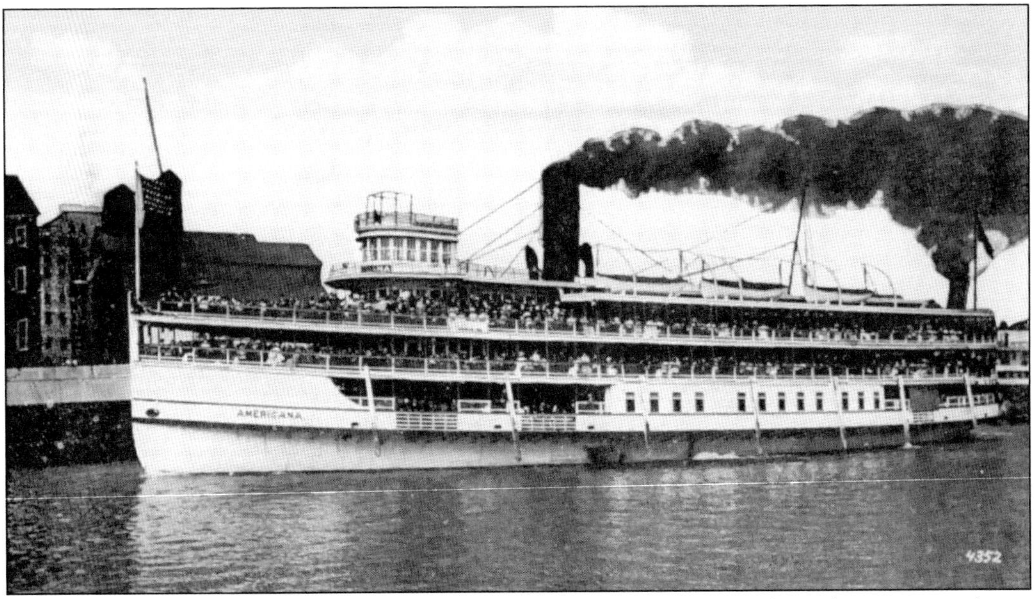

In 1890, the *Dove* side-wheeler began ferry service from Buffalo to Crystal Beach. Numerous boats were added to the fleet until 1908, when the *Americana* took its maiden voyage across Lake Erie. Built by the American Shipbuilding Company in Buffalo, it was the first steamer on the Great Lakes built specifically for pleasure cruises. (Author's collection.)

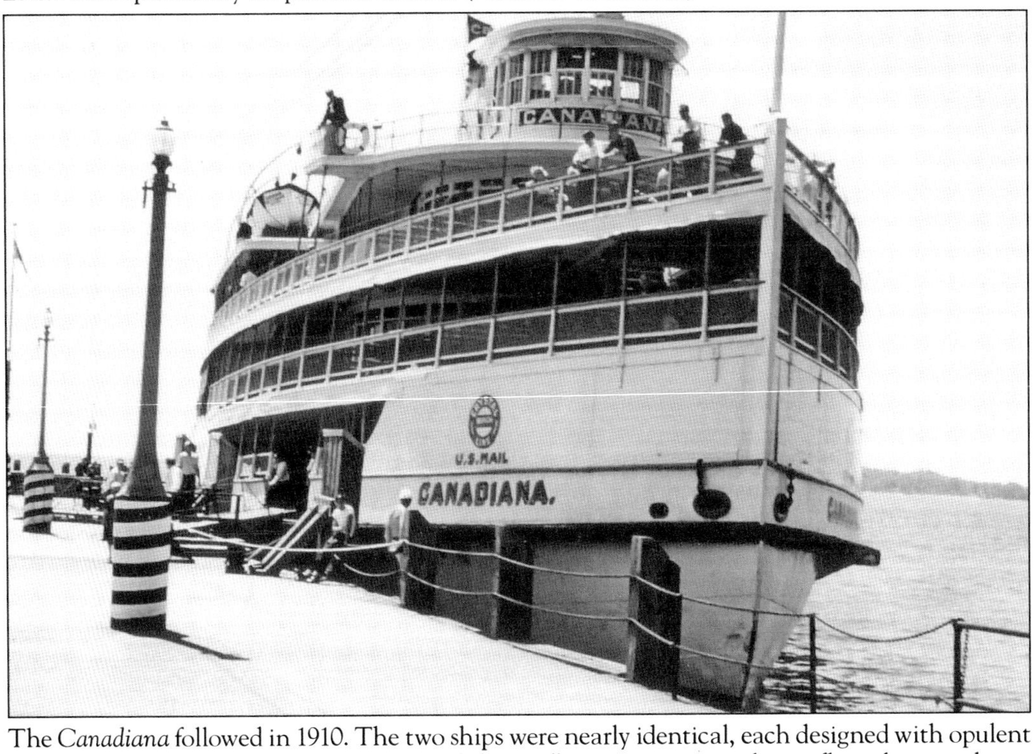

The *Canadiana* followed in 1910. The two ships were nearly identical, each designed with opulent salons, stained-glass windows, an enclosed dance floor, an open-air dance floor, brass railings, beveled mirrors, and crystal chandeliers. The steamships were licensed to carry 3,500 passengers at a time, but often carried more. (Courtesy NLC.)

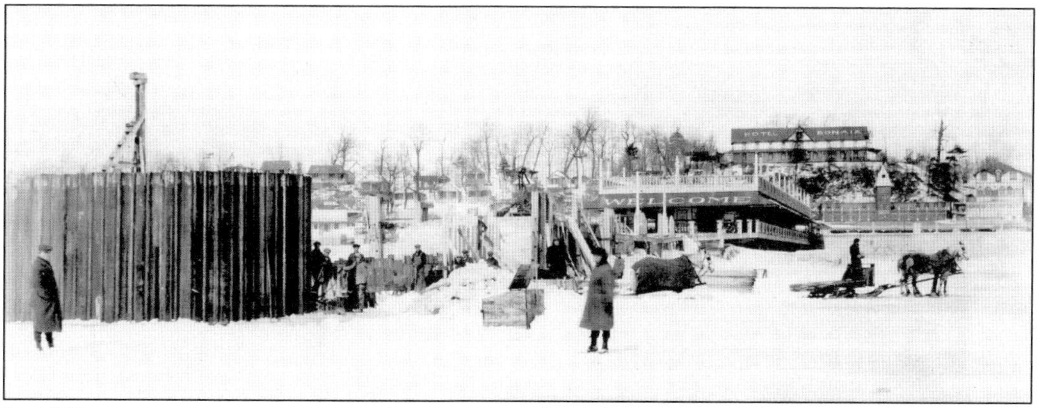

In 1912, a new pier was constructed to accommodate the new steamships. However, it was not large enough to handle the crowds, so the Lake Erie Excursion Company, the owners of the park, made the decision to build a larger pier, which was constructed over the winter of 1920–1921. Cottages and the Bon Air Hotel are visible in the background. (Courtesy of Rick Doan.)

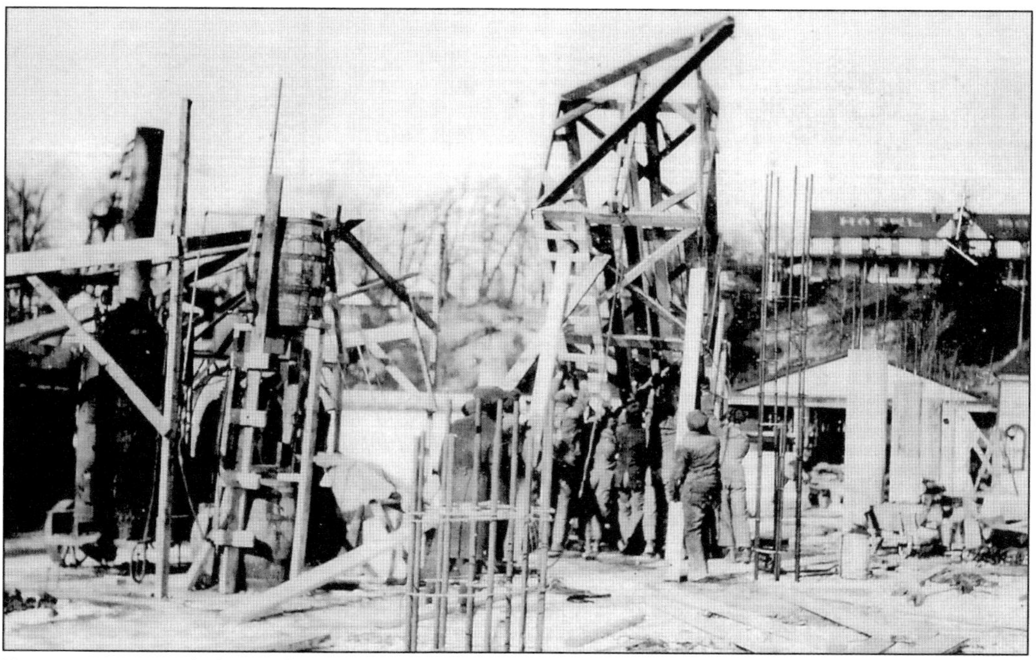

Forms were pounded into the ice, rebar was set, and concrete was poured to create the pylons that would support the concrete pier. Blizzards often deterred the progress of the pier's construction. Lake Erie, in her fury, kicked waterspouts up through the ice onto the men and their equipment, yet the brutal conditions did not deter them from completing the job. (Courtesy of Rick Doan.)

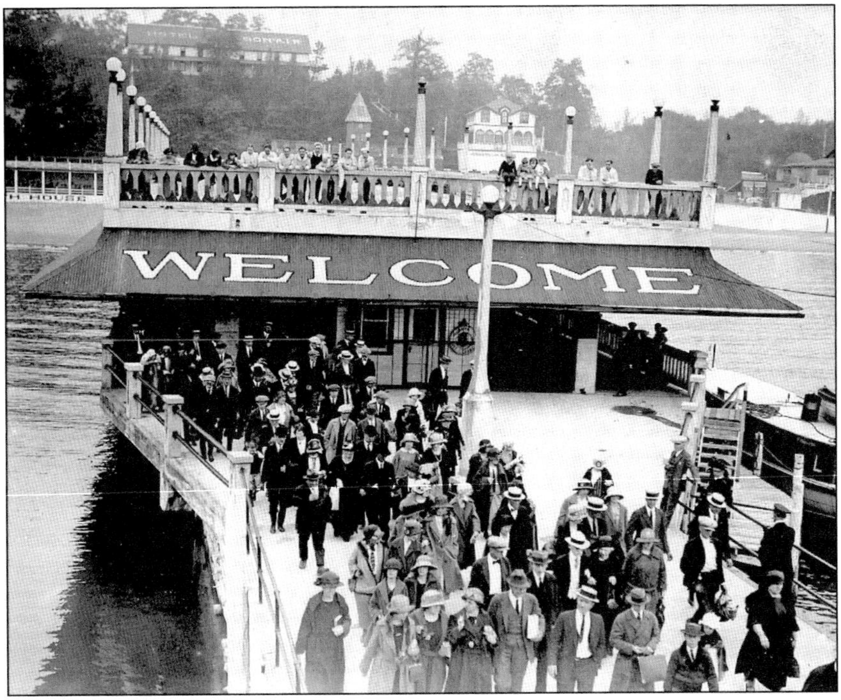

The pier was finished in time for opening day of the 1921 season. It extended more than 200 feet into the lake. The waiting area had an observation deck, which also doubled as a launching pad for fireworks. This view was taken from one of the steamships on opening day. (Courtesy of Rick Doan.)

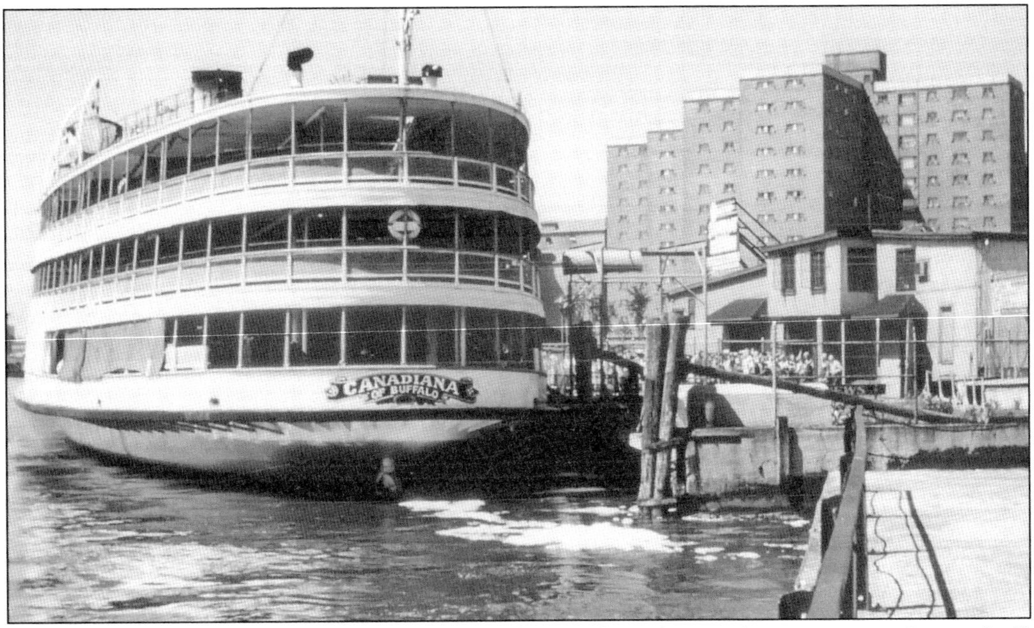

With the opening of the Peace Bridge in 1927, the number of steamship passengers dropped off, as patrons favored a quick ride to the park instead of a leisurely cruise. The *Americana* was sold to Rye Playland amusement park on Long Island, New York. The Canadiana worked alone and was soon dubbed "the Crystal Beach boat." This photograph shows the *Canadiana* at Buffalo's Commercial Street Pier. (Courtesy NLC.)

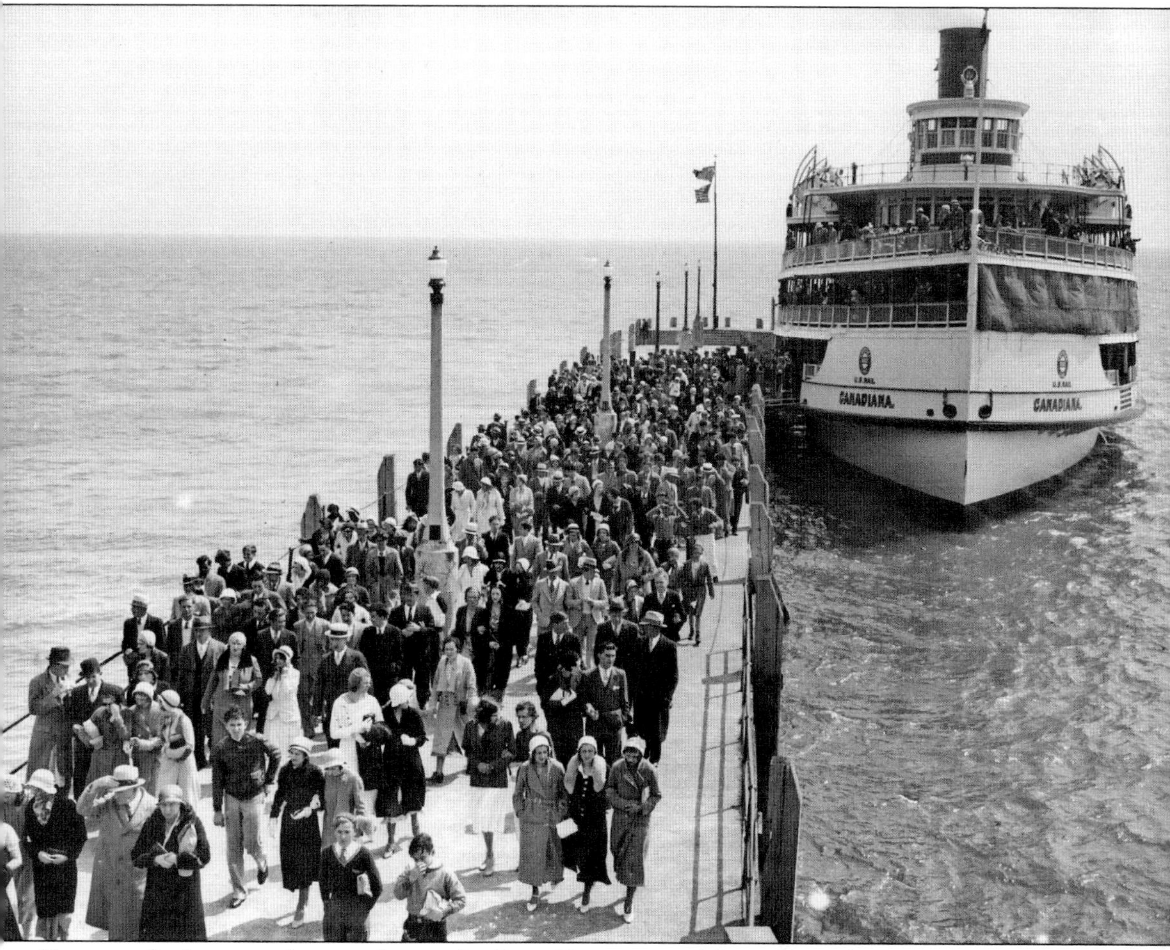

Because of a shortage of money during the Great Depression of the 1930s and gas rationing during World War II, many patrons took advantage of the *Canadiana*'s services. After the war ended, Buffalonians returned to taking their cars to the park, and once again, steamship patronage dropped off. Soon there were other troubles: union problems, a lack of funds, a boat that needed maintenance and was not up to Coast Guard standards, and gang-related problems. Following an on-board riot in 1956, park owners decided to cease steamship service to Crystal Beach. The boat was sold several times and suffered a myriad of mishaps. The Friends of the Canadiana, a preservationist group, rescued it after it sank into the Cuyahoga River in Cleveland, Ohio, and brought it back to Buffalo with intentions of restoring it. Those plans also fell through, and the *Canadiana* was cut up for scrap in 2004. (Courtesy of Rick Doan.)

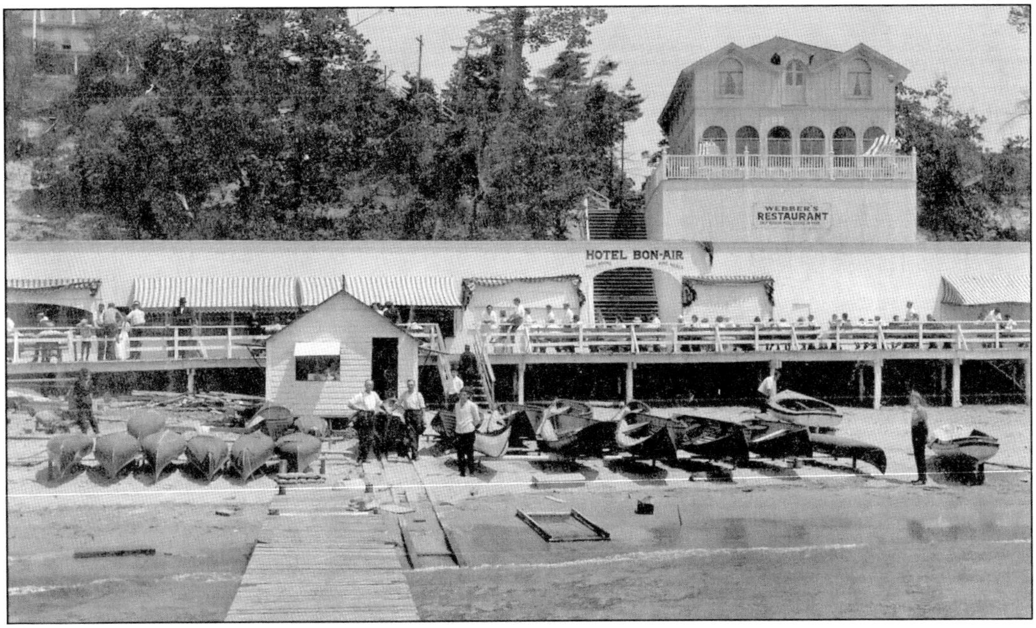

The boardwalk along the beach stretched from the bathhouse to the park entrance. A staircase led from the boardwalk up the sand dune to the Bon-Air Hotel and Webber's Restaurant, which would later become the Administration Building. Stands housing games of chance and refreshments vied with the canoe-and-boat-rental concessionaire for customers. (Courtesy of Rick Doan.)

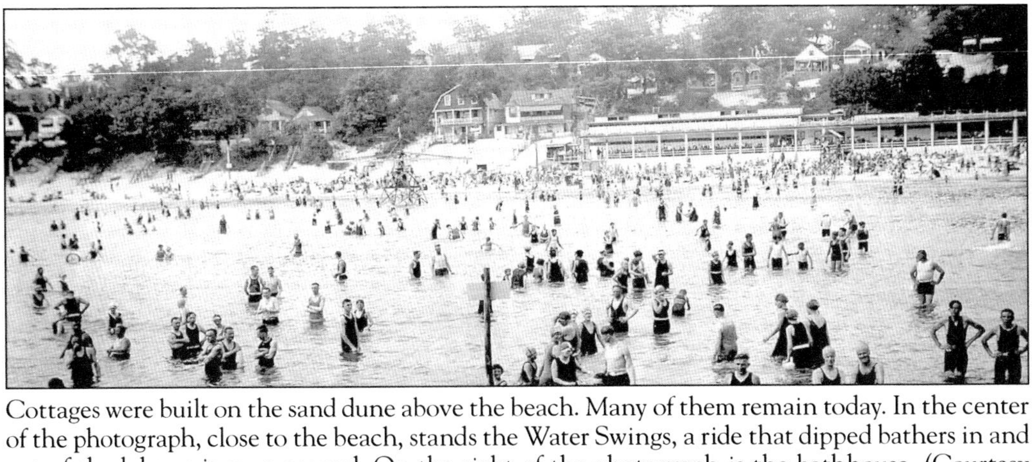

Cottages were built on the sand dune above the beach. Many of them remain today. In the center of the photograph, close to the beach, stands the Water Swings, a ride that dipped bathers in and out of the lake as it spun around. On the right of the photograph is the bathhouse. (Courtesy of Rick Doan.)

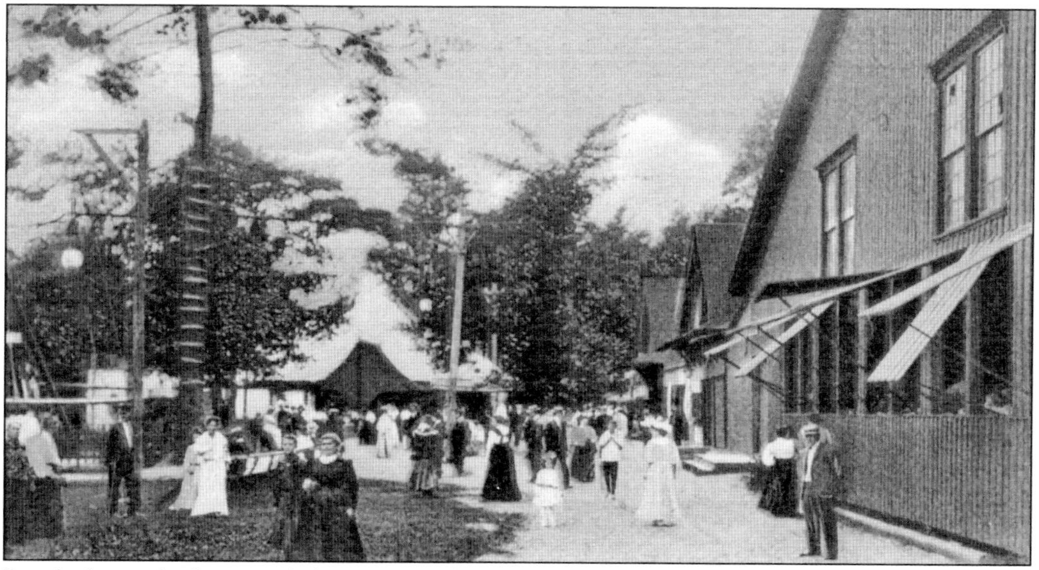

Besides large, shady trees, shelters provided relief from the sun for picnickers. A few man-operated rides, like the Razzle Dazzle, on the left, and children's playground equipment were tucked in between the trees. The picnic grove was lit at night by large incandescent lights. On the right of the photograph is the Midway Restaurant. The wooden window flaps opened so that diners could stay cool. (Author's collection.)

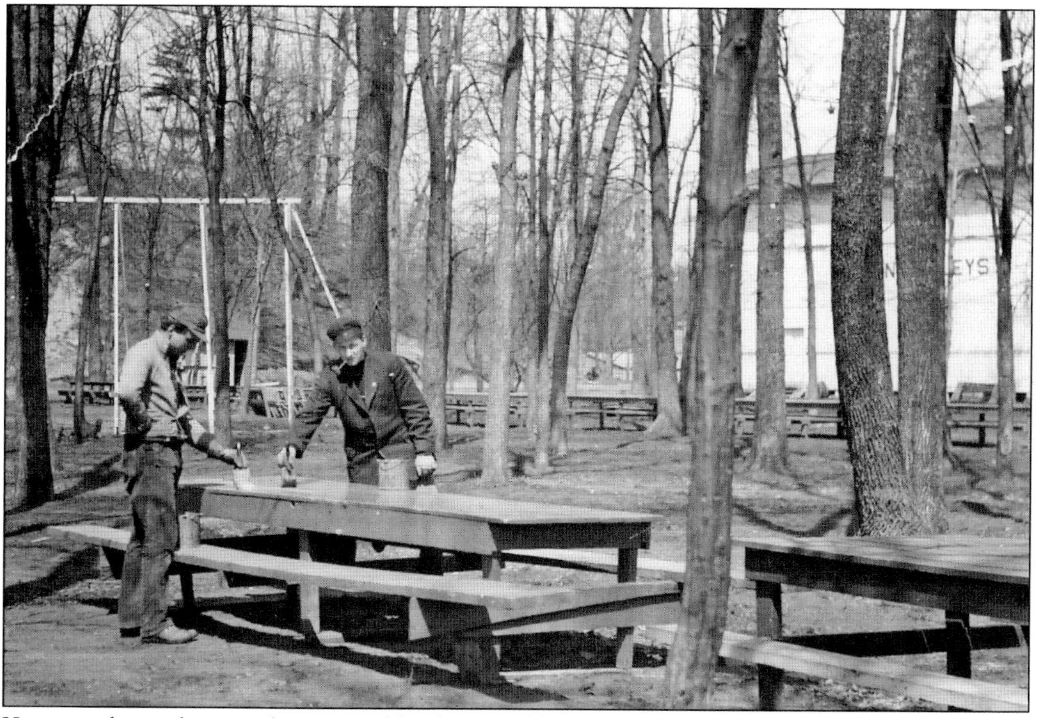

Keeping the park grounds impeccably clean and bright was important to getting customers to return year after year. These men are busy painting picnic tables. The tables were so sturdy that they served picnickers for many decades. Rows of them were placed under the new shelters built during the 1920s. (Courtesy of Rick Doan.)

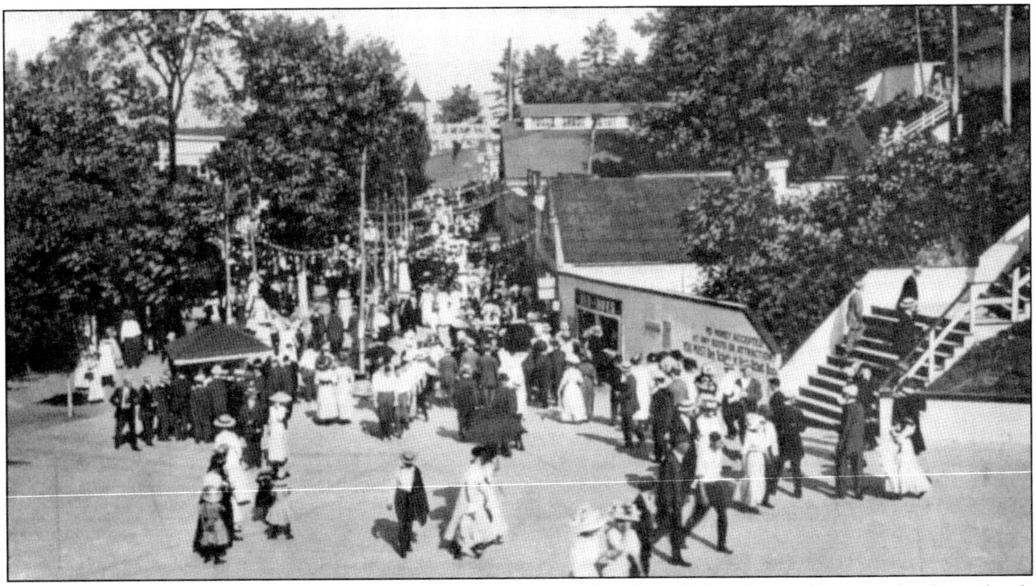

Attractions were built on the 60-foot-high sand dune that lined the shore. Patrons had to climb stairs to reach them. Cash was not accepted at any of the rides, shows, attractions or concessions stands. Visitors had to purchase tickets, which were used by the owners to collect rent from concessionaires. By 1900, strings of incandescent light bulbs were draped across the midway, turning it into a nighttime fairyland. (Author's collection.)

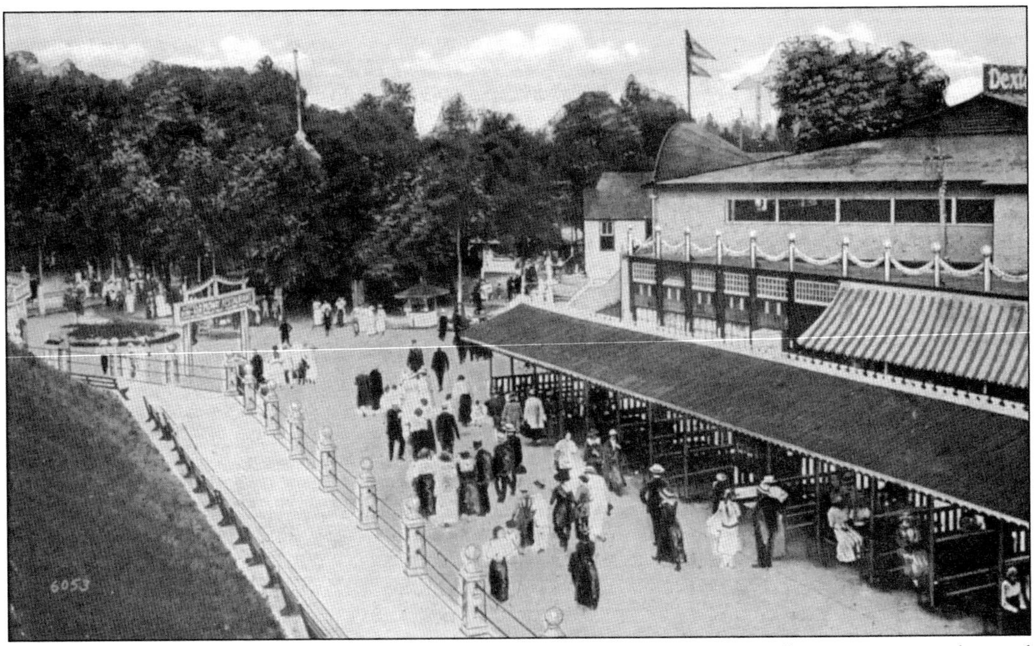

Although the picnic grove had many trees, the midway did not. To alleviate sun stroke and heat exhaustion, park owners erected a covering over part of the walkway. Beneath the slanted roof were benches where patrons could sit and rest their tired feet. Over time, the covered walkway stretched down the midway. Dexter's Roller Rink is directly behind the covered section. (Author's collection.)

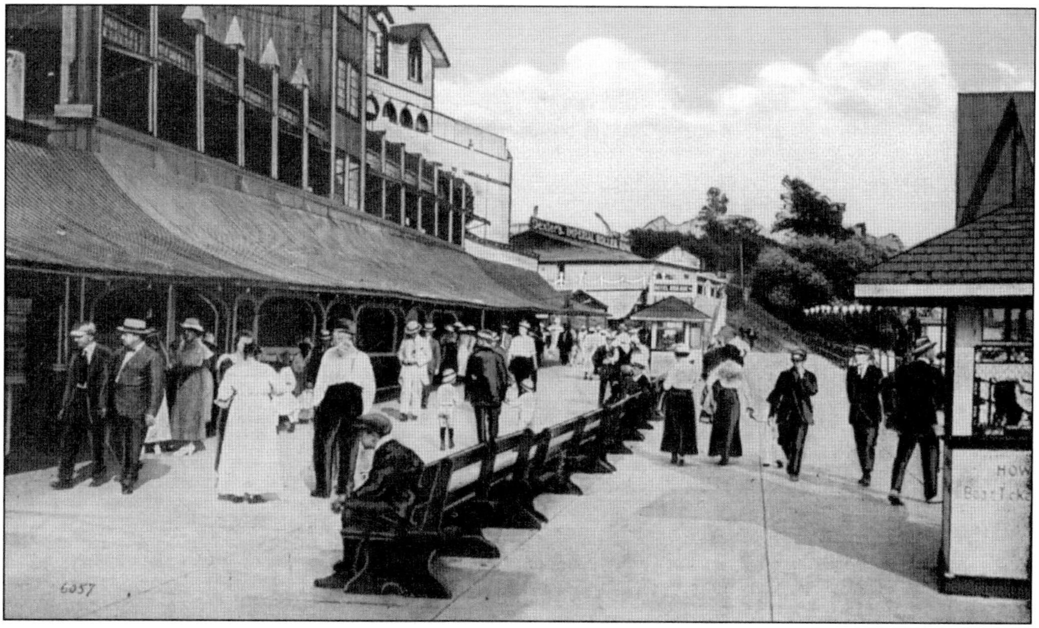

The original promenade ended at the sand dune where Dexter's Roller Rink was situated. When the sand dune was removed to build the ballroom, the promenade was extended to the front of the park. The building on the left housed numerous souvenirs, food and game stands, and the park offices on the second floor. (Author's collection.)

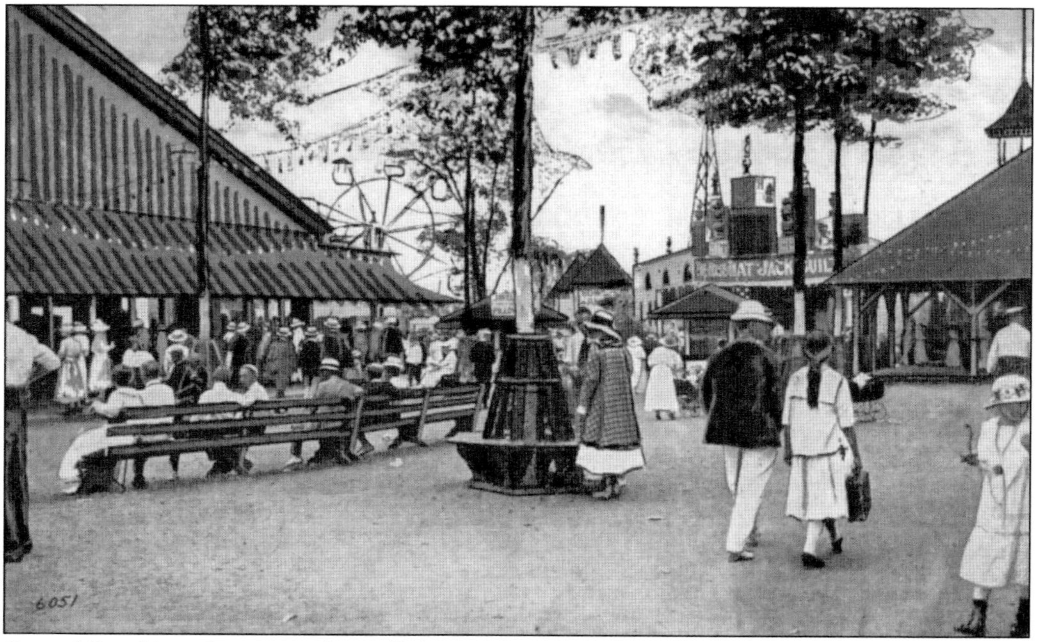

Crystal Beach's midway was where all the excitement happened. Behind the building on the left is a Ferris wheel. The twin towers next to it belong to the Bowling Alley, which would eventually become the Laff in the Dark ride. To the far right is the loading station for the Figure-Eight roller coaster. Built in 1901, it had a top speed of 5 miles an hour. (Author's collection.)

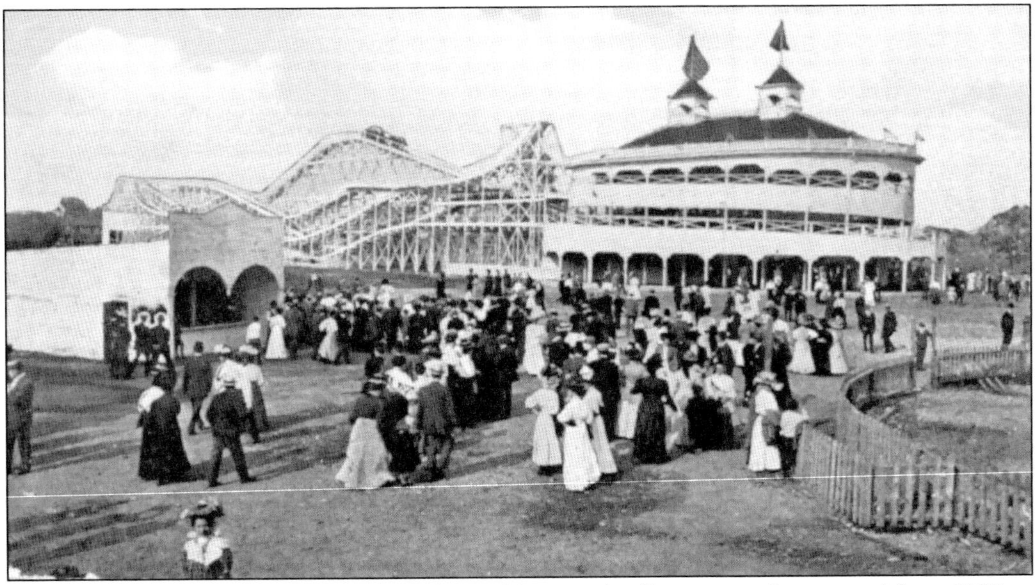

The Backety-Back Scenic Railway was the park's second roller coaster. It operated from 1909 to 1926. Built for $50,000 by John H. Brown of Pennsylvania, it included two lift hills and a dark, curved tunnel. The trains rode up the dead-end section of track sticking up in the air, then rolled down backwards after the switchman moved the track below onto the second course. (Author's collection.)

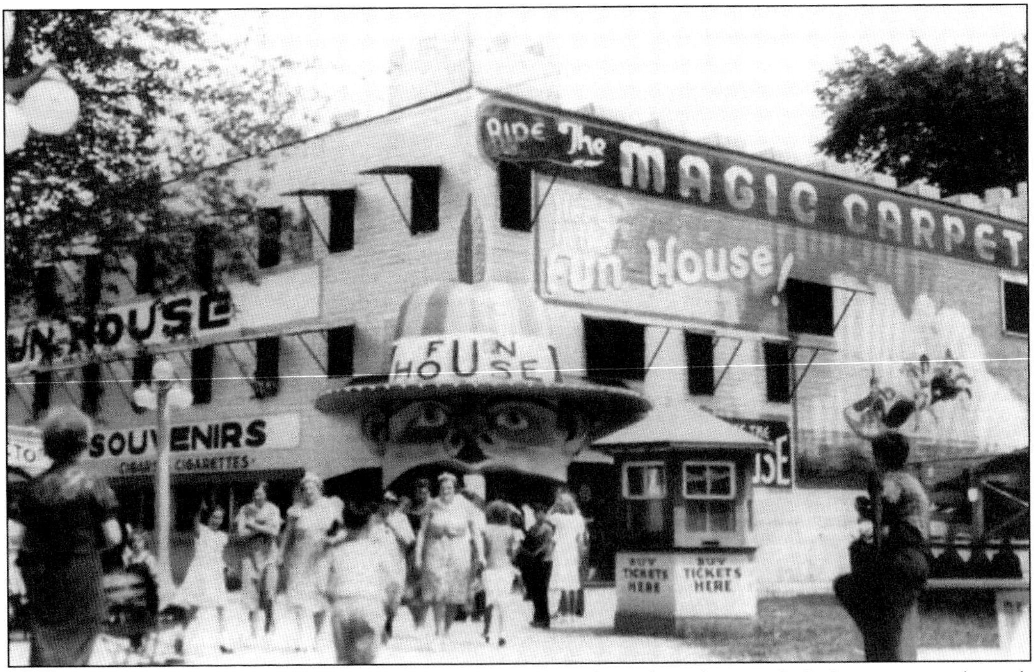

Burnett's Fun House was two stories of delightful madcap fun that included a rotating barrel, distorting mirrors, and moving floors. The advertised Magic Carpet ride was a slide that ended in a large, highly polished wooden bowl patrons had to climb out of. On the ground floor, E. M. Sherrif operated the souvenir stand, which sold periodicals, postcards, candy, and gum. (Courtesy of Rick Doan.)

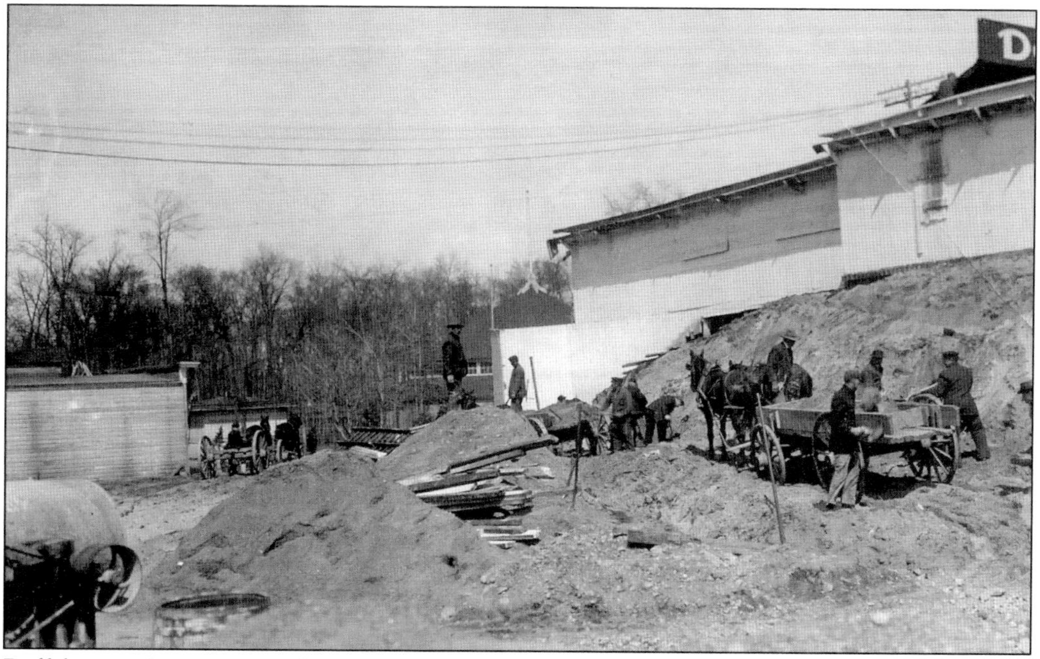

Buffalonian George C. Hall had been selling popcorn and candy at Crystal Beach Park since 1901. In 1924, he purchased the park. The first thing he decided to do was build a ballroom. This required removing all the buildings on the sand dune. Local fire companies loaned out their steam pump trucks to blast the sand into Lake Erie. (Courtesy of Rick Doan.)

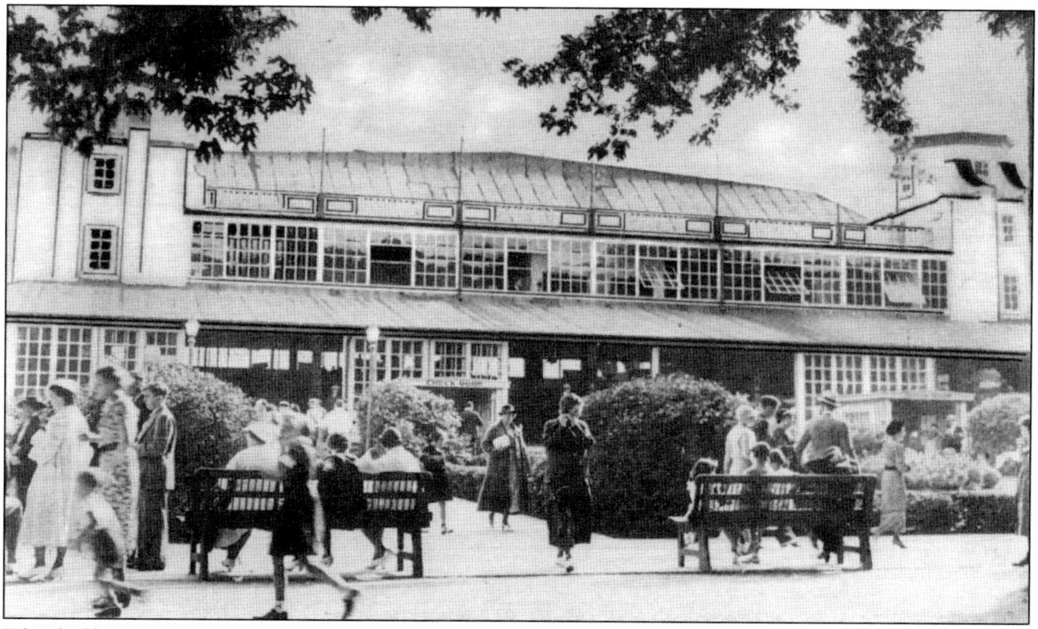

The ballroom opened in 1925. Its cantilevered design was unique with 20,000 square feet of unobstructed maple dance floor. Large, sliding glass doors allowed lake breezes to circulate throughout. Coat checks and restrooms were located in the basement along with an archery range and bowling alley. Les Brown, Kay Kaiser, the Dorsey Brothers, and other famous big bands played at the ballroom. (Author's collection.)

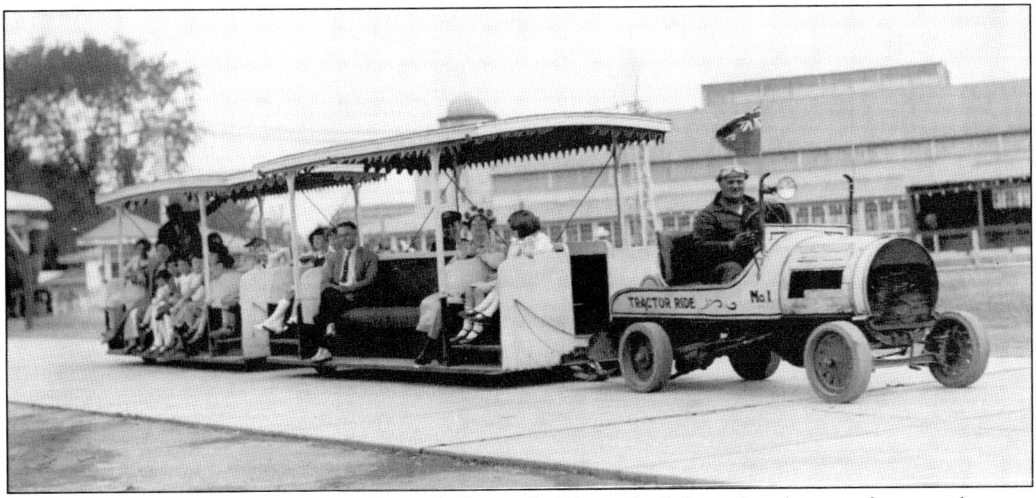

The Tractor Ride moved patrons through the park. The ride did not last long as few people were willing to pay the fee to ride it. Roller skating replaced dancing in the ballroom when the big band era ended. An antique car ride was placed on the ballroom's patio in 1964. (Courtesy of Rick Doan.)

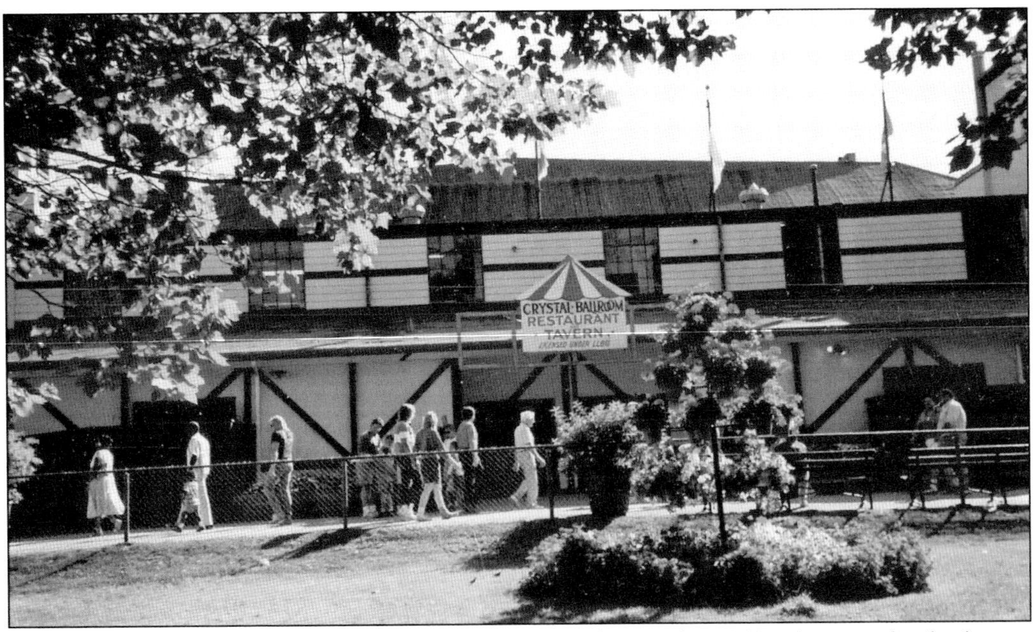

Two wax museums opened in the ballroom basement during the 1960s. A tragic fire broke out in one of the attractions in August 1974. No one was injured; however, the ballroom was forever changed. It was reconfigured with restrooms and a restaurant in the front half and a pirate dark ride in the back. The ride was removed in 1984, and dancing returned to the ballroom. (Courtesy of MaryAnn Pendrys.)

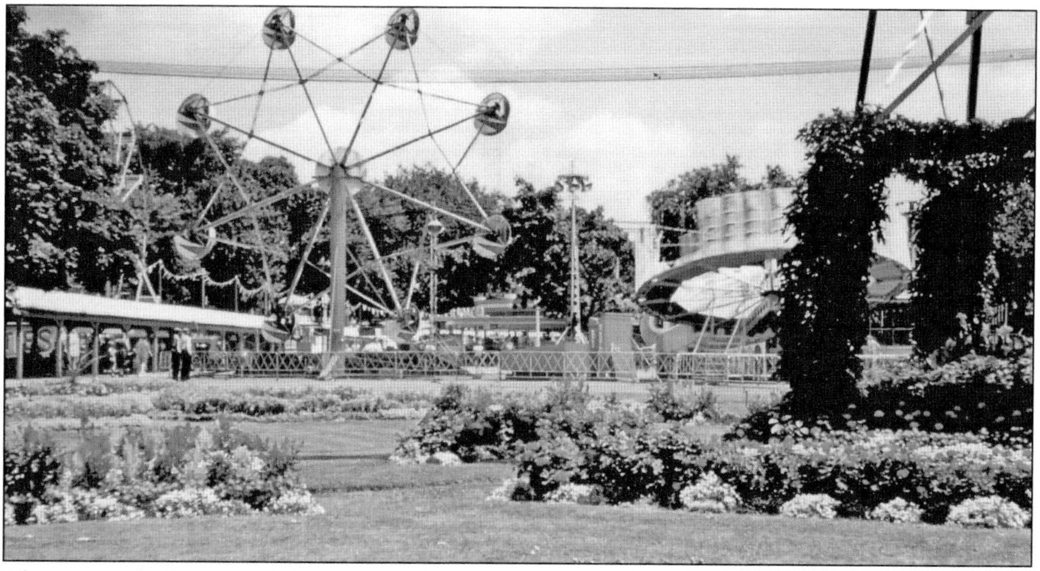

The removal of the sand dune not only made room for the construction of the ballroom, but also opened up the midway for additional rides, attractions, and a garden. The promenade was extended as was the covered walkway. From left to right is the covered walkway, the Rock-O-Plane, and Round-Up. (Courtesy NLC.)

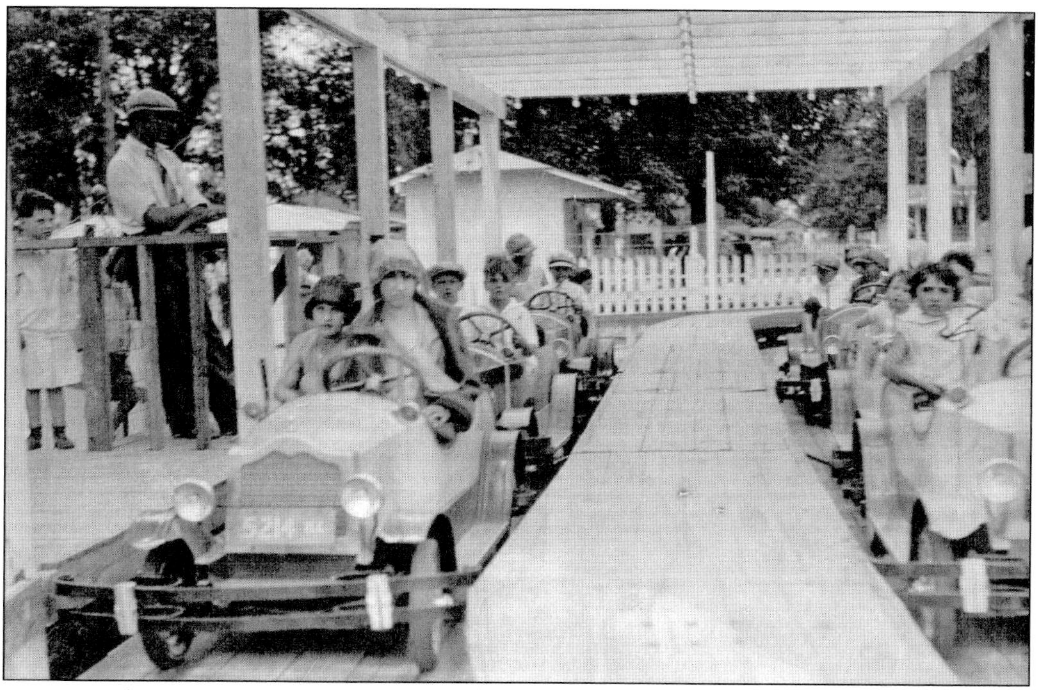

Youngsters learned to drive on Harry Traver's Auto Speedway, which debuted in 1929. The small electric cars ran on an undulating wooden track that went out to Erie Road and back. The LaJuene family purchased the ride in 1932 and added an art deco station complete with neon lights. The ride was removed in 1980 to make room for the flume. (Courtesy of Rick Doan.)

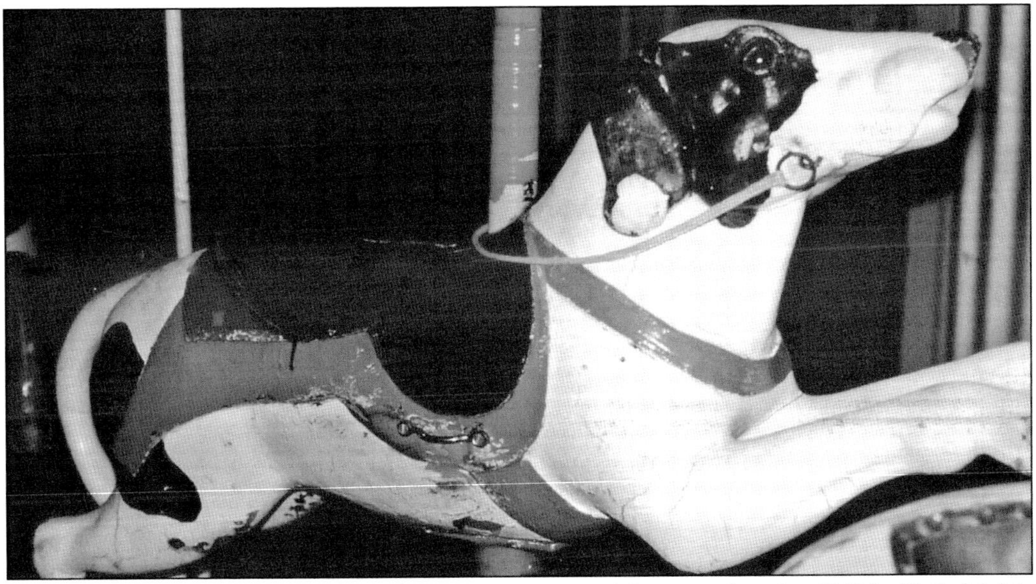

The very first carousel at Crystal Beach was steam operated. It was replaced in 1910 by Philadelphia Toboggan Company carousel number 12. Built in 1906, it originally operated at Chestnut Hill Park in Philadelphia. It consisted of two rows of jumping animals, two elaborately carved chariots, and an outside row of standing animals. (Courtesy of Dan Wilke.)

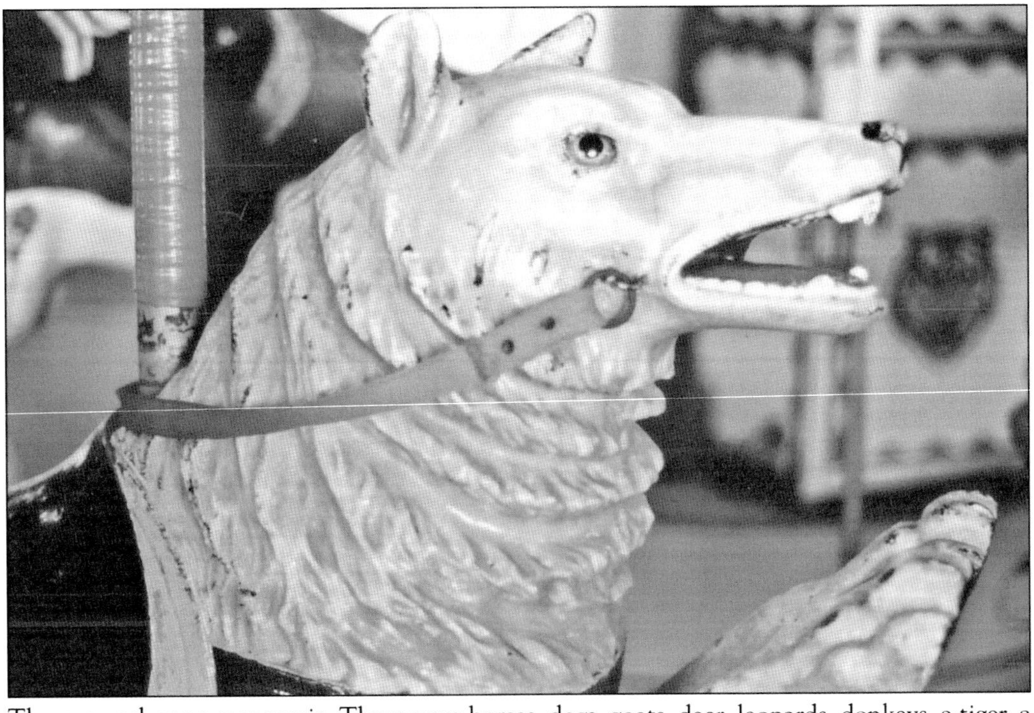

The carousel was a menagerie. There were horses, dogs, goats, deer, leopards, donkeys, a tiger, a lion, a camel, a giraffe, zebras, and a very rare wolf. By 1984, the wooden animals were showing their age. The expense of restoration was not an option for park owners. The carousel was taken to Fort Wayne, Indiana, and sold at auction, piecemeal, for a total of $500,000. (Courtesy of Dan Wilke.)

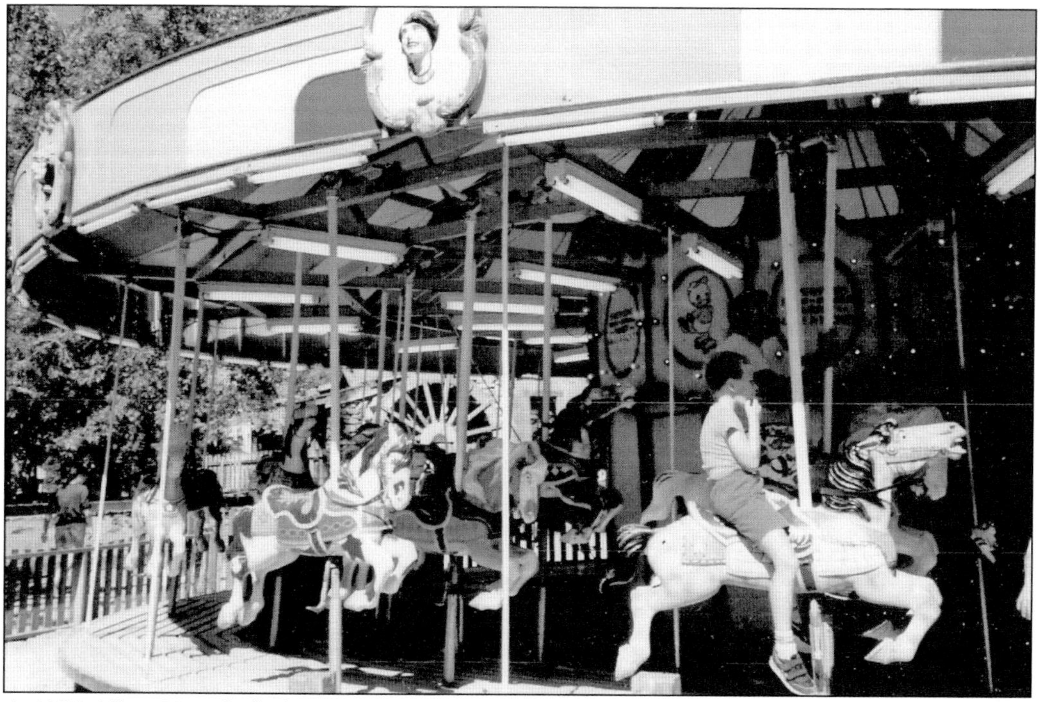

A 1956 Allan Herschell three-row aluminum carousel was purchased to replace the menagerie carousel. A second Allan Herschell carousel was purchased to use for parts but was sold instead to the Buffalo Zoo. After one season in the roundhouse, the carousel was moved outside, and the roundhouse was converted into a game stand. (Courtesy of MaryAnn Pendrys.)

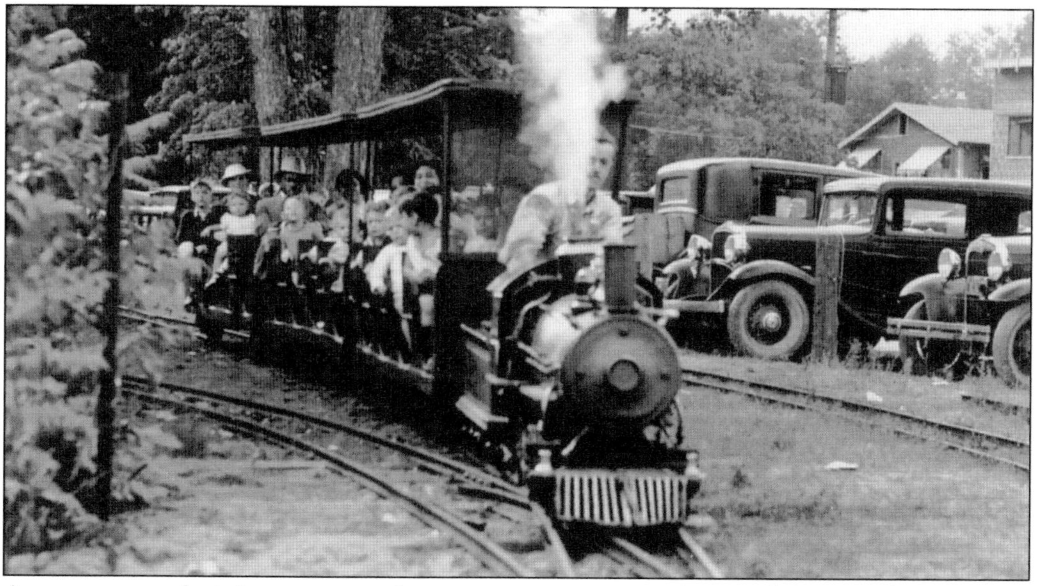

A steam-powered miniature train took passengers on a scenic ride towards Erie Road and into the wooded area along the back parking lot. The LaJuene family purchased the concession in 1932. They replaced the steam engine with a diesel engine a few years later and replaced that train in 1962 with a propane-powered C. P. Huntington train by Chance Manufacturing. (Courtesy of Rick Doan.)

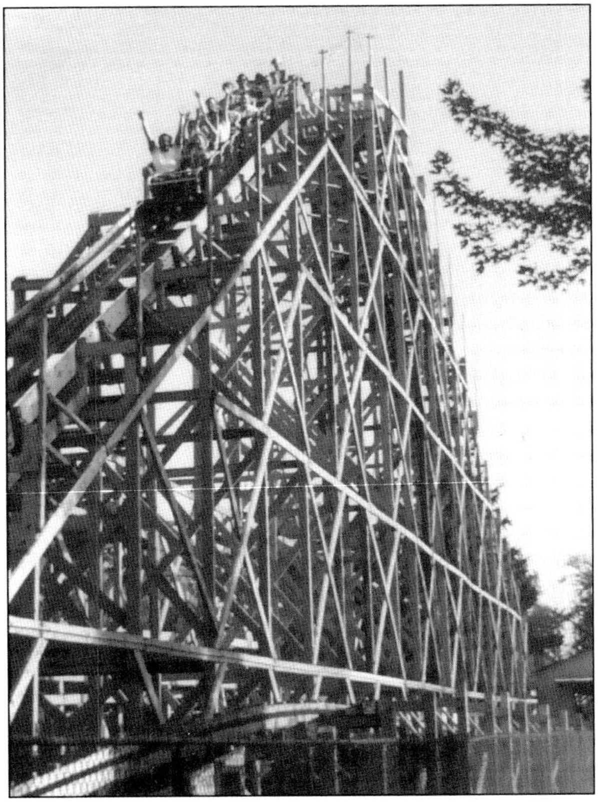

Known to many as the "yellow coaster" because of its color, the Giant Coaster became the park's third roller coaster in 1916. Built as a side-friction design, its sofa-like cars traveled on track set in a trench rather than on top of the track. Reaching heights of 57 feet, the 2,627-foot-long ride reached speeds of 35 miles per hour. (Courtesy of MaryAnn Pendrys.)

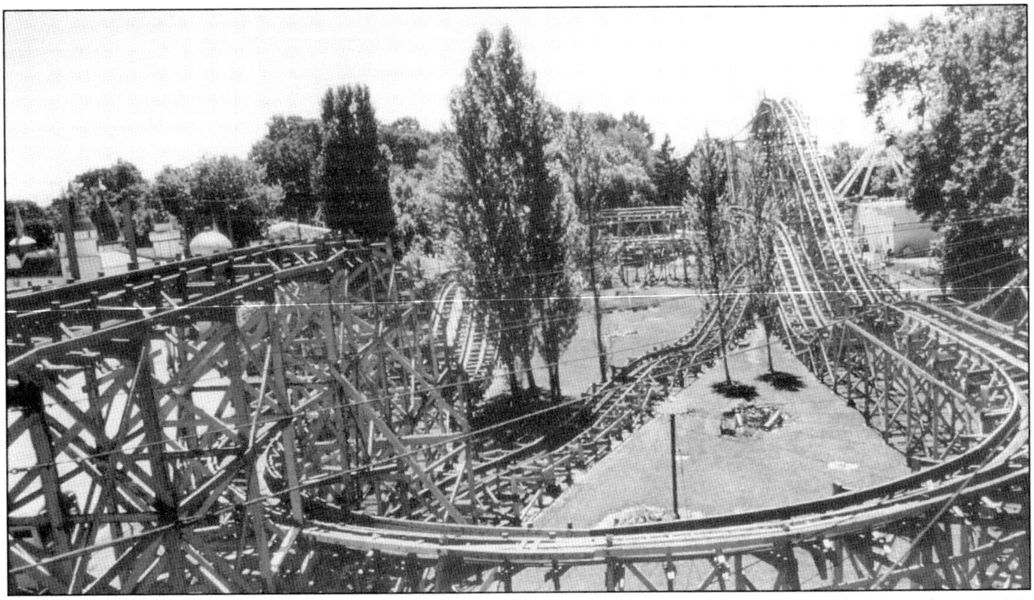

The Giant Coaster was Crystal Beach's oldest operating ride when the park closed in 1989. During the auction, several roller-coaster enthusiasts purchased the ride but were unable to find a home for it. The Giant Coaster was demolished in 1991. Its cars and sections of track were salvaged by those same enthusiasts, many of whom still have them in their homes. (Courtesy of Timothy Wagner.)

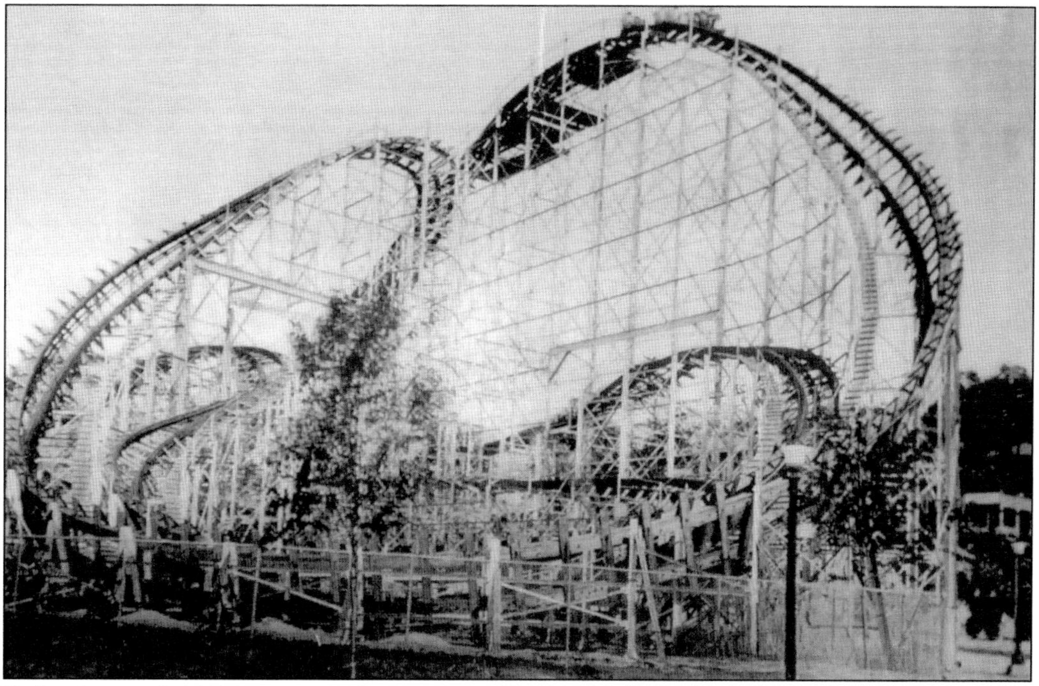

Rides during the 1920s were at the cutting edge in speed and danger. George C. Hall wanted the "roughest and meanest" roller coaster in the world, so he hired roller coaster builder Harry Traver, known for his horrific roller coaster designs, to build the Cyclone. Traver was ahead of his time, using prefabricated steel supports. He created the spiral dip first drop known as "the drop into hell." (Author's collection.)

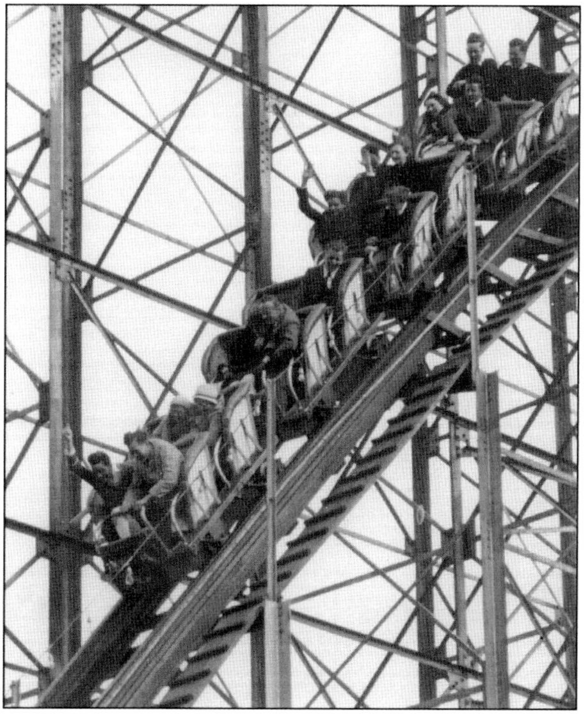

Unveiled in 1926, the Cyclone dominated the park as no other ride had before it. Its twisting, convoluted track slammed riders from one side of the car to the other. Neck injuries and fainting were so common that a nurse was stationed on the loading platform. Only one rider in this photograph, fifth seat back, was brave enough to raise both hands on the severe second drop. (Courtesy of Rick Doan.)

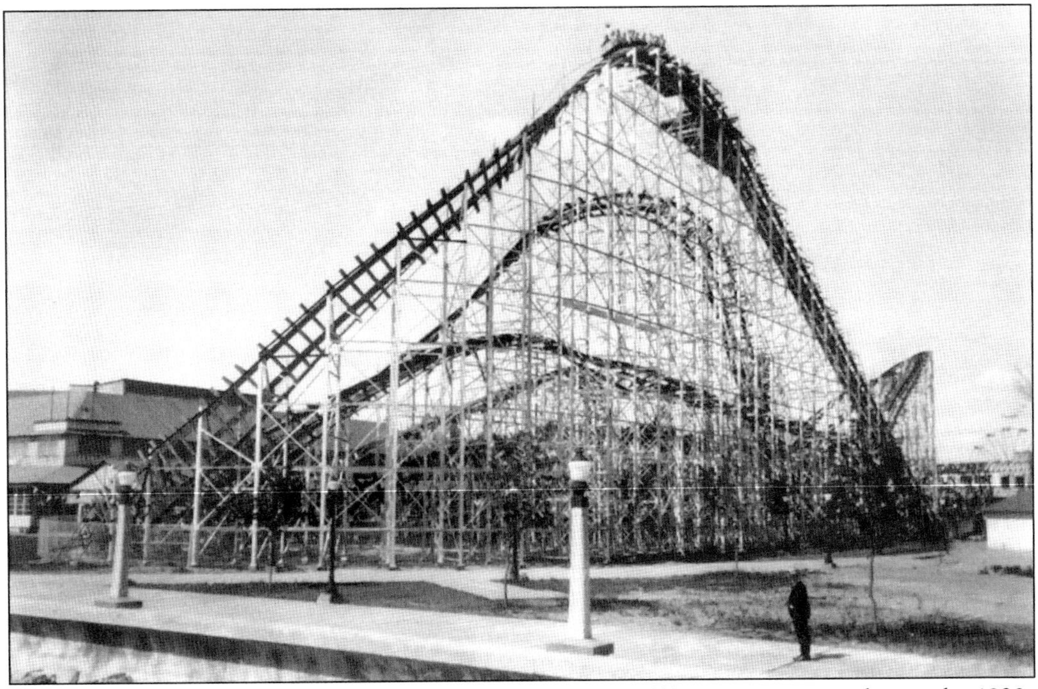

The Cyclone proved to be a maintenance nightmare, yet Hall kept it operating during the 1930s because he could not afford to take it down. He hired Philadelphia Toboggan Company engineer Herb Schmeck to overhaul it, extending its life by nearly 10 years. The Cyclone was finally disassembled in 1946, but it is still considered the most terrifying roller coaster in the world. (Courtesy of Rick Doan.)

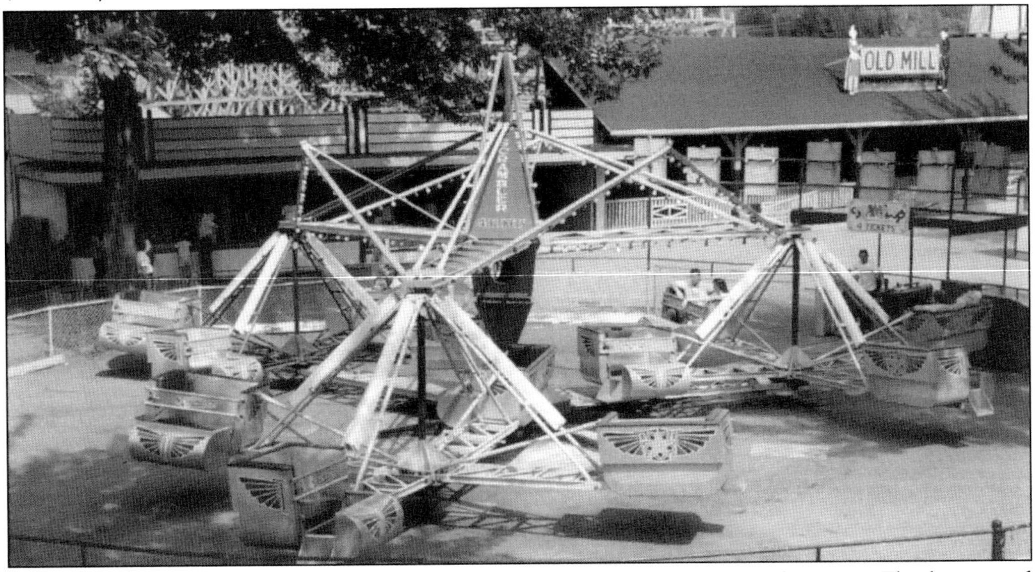

The Old Mill, to the right rear of the photograph, dated back to the early 1900s. Flat-bottomed boats were propelled along a serpentine waterway inside a darkened tunnel where scenes lit up along intervals of the ride. The ride was revamped in 1964 into Jungle Land, with cannibals, animated crocodiles, and water-squirting elephants. The Scrambler is in the foreground. (Photograph by Paul Kassay Jr.; courtesy of Rick Doan.)

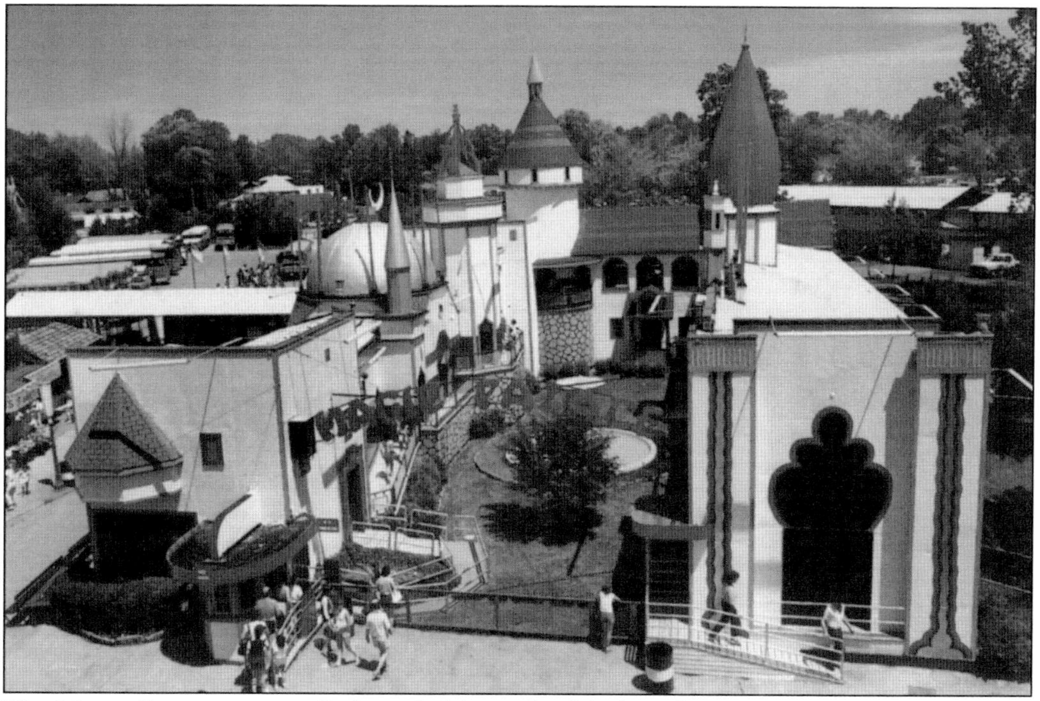

The Magic Carpet was a walk-through labyrinth of darkened rooms and hallways with tilted floors, tipping barrels, crazy mirrors, wooden slides, and optical illusions. Air jets fixed into the outside walkway lifted women's skirts with blasts of air. The big finale was a ride down an actual carpet. The worn-out carpet was removed in 1974, and the attraction was renamed the Magic Palace. (Courtesy of Cathy Herbert.)

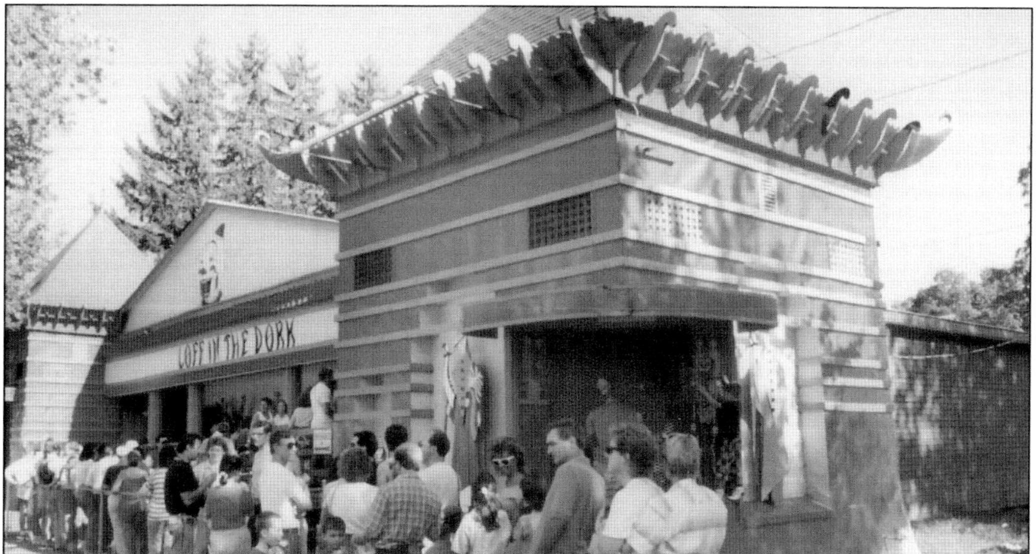

An Oriental-themed facade deceived riders expecting much of the same inside the Laff in the Dark. Two-person cars wove through the building in a disorienting route past stunts that lit up and moved as the cars passed. Dancing skeletons, snakes, and other two-dimensional figures startled riders almost as much as the near-miss collision into a brick wall. (Courtesy of Timothy Wagner.)

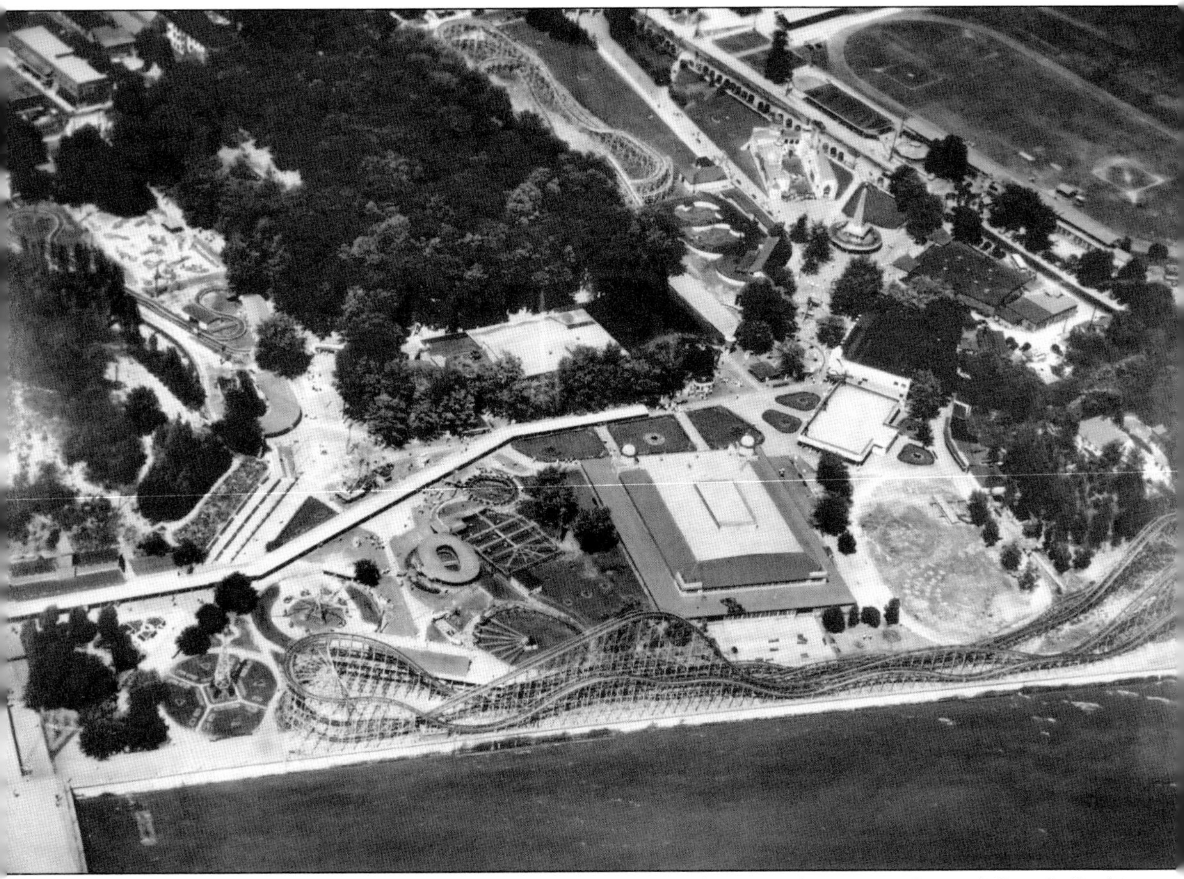

Folks arriving on the *Canadiana* in May 1948 saw a distinct change to Crystal Beach Park's waterfront. Stretching nearly the length of the old promenade was a new roller coaster, the Comet. More than 300 tons of the steel superstructure came from the Cyclone, and it was durable enough to withstand the ferocity of Lake Erie. In the bottom half of this photograph, behind the Comet, from left to right are the Coronation Tower and gardens, Flying Skooter, Tumble Bug, (closest to the Comet), Hey Dey, Water Skooter, Caterpillar, Ballroom, Auto Skooter, and game booths. The large empty space clearly shows the footers left from the Cyclone. In the upper half of this photograph, above the covered walkway, from left to right are the concession stand, rock garden, Ferris wheel, miniature train, Auto Speedway, miniature golf, carousel, Lunch Counter, roller rink, Giant Coaster, Old Mill, Octopus, Loop-O-Plane, Fun House, Laff in the Dark, Rocket Ship ride, Magic Carpet, and—across the road—the athletic field. Kiddieland was tucked away in the tree-shaded picnic grove across from the train. (Courtesy BSCACEC.)

Rising 96 feet from the ground, the Comet's first drop seemed higher when riders looked down and saw the bottom of Lake Erie. The Comet's double out-and-back configuration totaled a length 4,197 feet. The wood track was constructed of seven laminated layers of British Columbia Douglas fir. Carrying 24 passengers in three trains, the Comet was known for its unbridled speed of 55 miles per hour. (Courtesy of Timothy Wagner.)

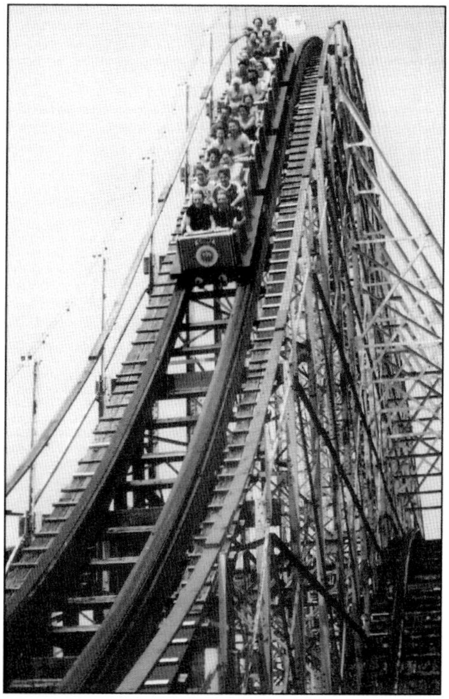

The double-down hill and low-to-the-ground profile were elements that made the Comet an exhilarating ride. It was considered one of the top 10 roller coasters in North America. Charley Wood, original owner of Great Escape in the Adirondacks, bought it for $210,000 at the auction in 1989. It debuted at Great Escape in 1994, making it the only roller coaster in the world built three times. (Courtesy of Timothy Wagner.)

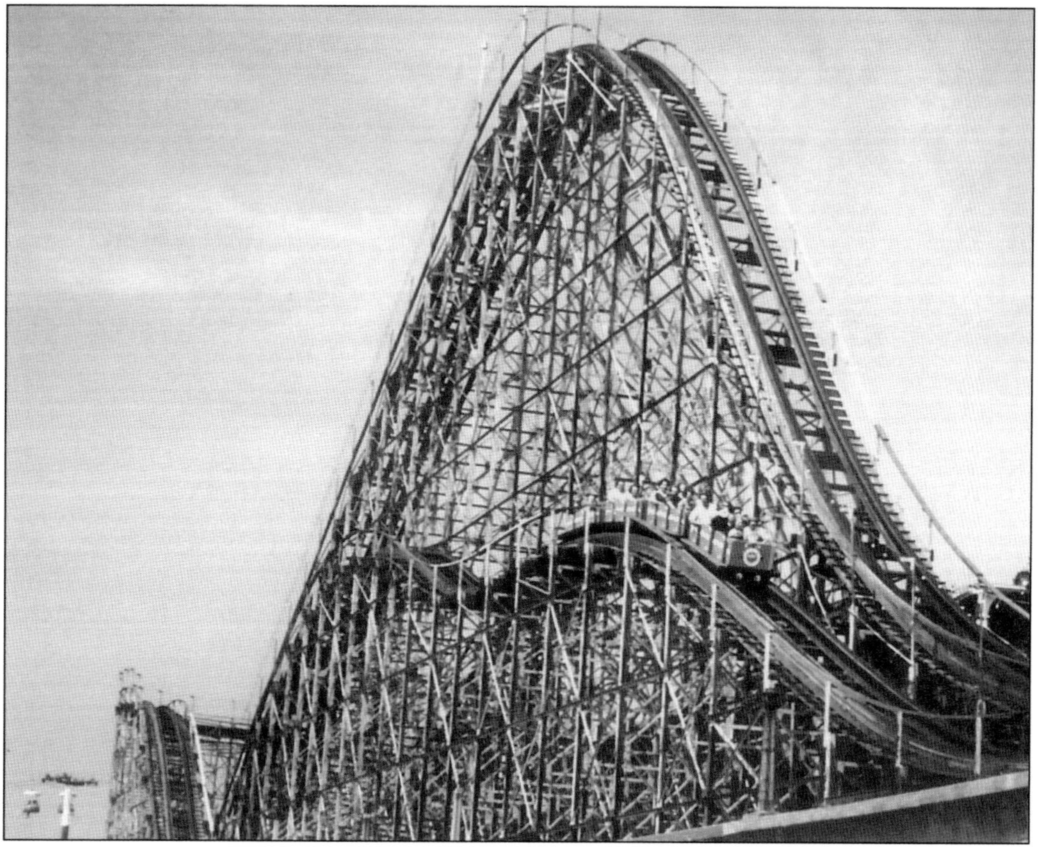

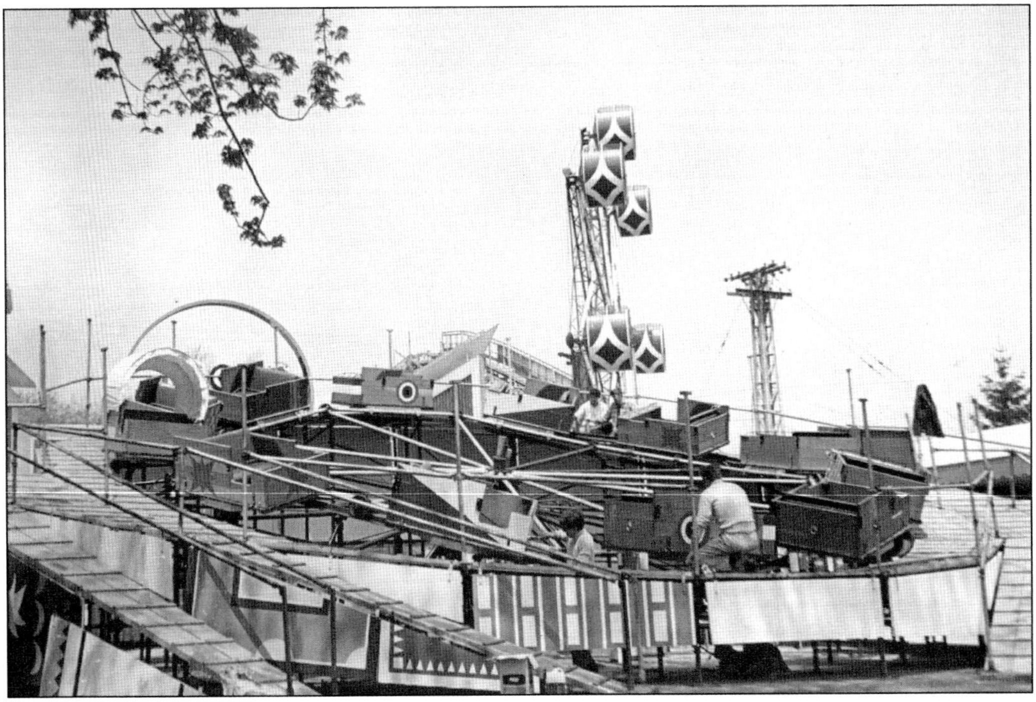

The 1950s and 1960s were the most profitable years for the park. Exciting rides like the Wild Mouse were added. Thrilling portable rides, like the Conestoga Wagon, front, and the Roll-O-Plane, back, filled the midway. Company and school picnics brought in decent revenue. Teenagers from Kenmore, Cheektowaga, Williamsville, West Seneca, and other areas thronged the midway on community days. Crystal Beach was the place to be. (Courtesy BSCACEC.)

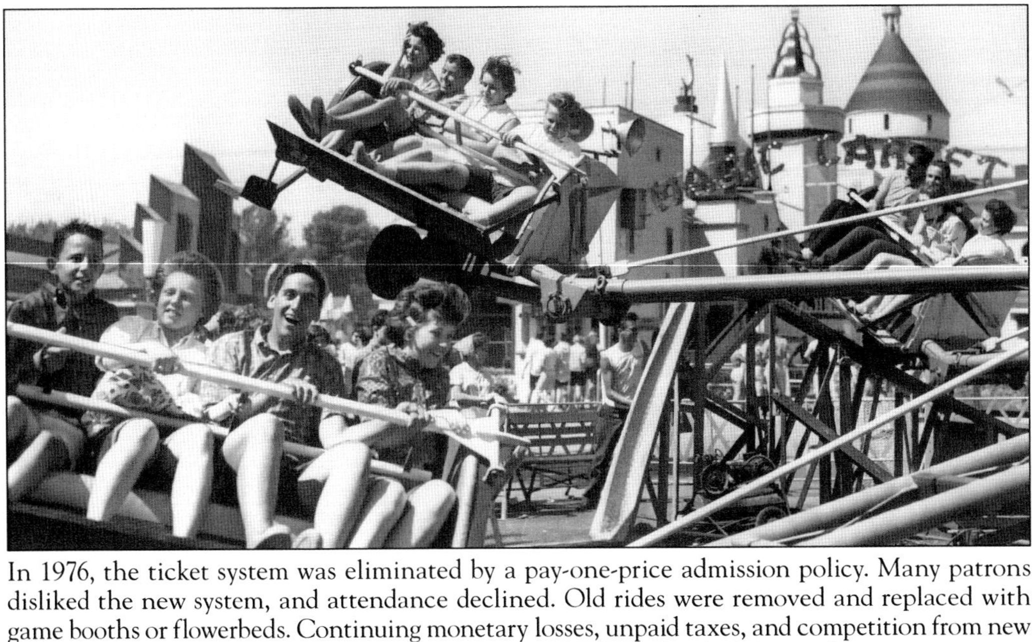

In 1976, the ticket system was eliminated by a pay-one-price admission policy. Many patrons disliked the new system, and attendance declined. Old rides were removed and replaced with game booths or flowerbeds. Continuing monetary losses, unpaid taxes, and competition from new theme parks on both sides of the border added to Crystal Beach's decline, resulting in permanent closure in 1989. A gated community now occupies the property. (Courtesy BSCACEC.)

Four

The Lost Neighborhood Parks

The advent of the baby boomer generation brought about a boom in small neighborhood kiddie parks. They could be found throughout Western New York in town parks, shopping plazas, street corners, backyards, drive-ins, and hot dog stands. Privately or family owned, most of them opened during the 1950s, usually offering rides that came right from the Allan Herschell Company in North Tonawanda.

The neighborhood parks were the perfect venue for local summer entertainment. Parents could take their children to the kiddie park for a couple of hours and spend only a few dollars on rides and ice cream, making the little ones happy. Some kiddie parks were themed, like Wonderland Storybook Park in Wilson with its fairy tale houses and storybook scenes, but most kiddie parks, like Leisureland in Orchard Park, had a typical lineup of kiddie rides, including the Little Dipper roller coaster, a carousel, boat ride, Hodges Handcars, and a helicopter ride.

The life span of kiddie parks was short. By the late 1960s, baby boomers had outgrown these small parks. The large number of families that crowded the neighborhood park declined drastically. With fewer patrons, the parks lost money and were forced to close. Some of the parks that managed to stay open added two or three family rides like a Scrambler or a portable Wild Mouse type of roller coaster in order to appeal to all age groups. Despite their best efforts, they too shut down. The last of the original neighborhood parks, Page's Kiddyland, closed in 2008, ending a Western New York legacy.

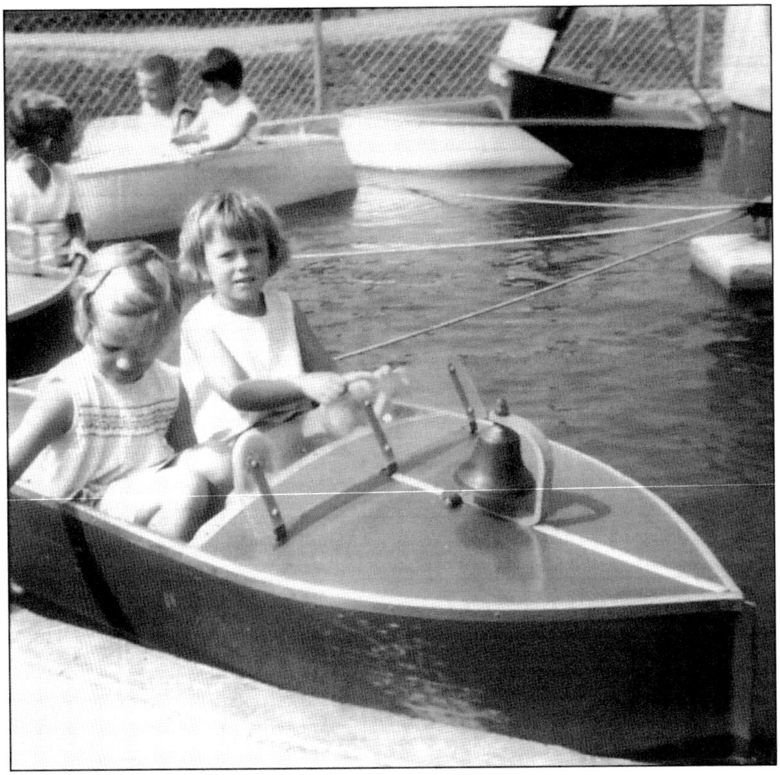

Lalle's Amusement Park opened on Lake Erie's waterfront in Angola in 1906 with a Ferris wheel, carousel, penny arcade, and dance hall. In the late 1940s, kiddie rides were added, attracting families with young children. Diminished interest in the area caused the closing of the park in the early 1970s. (Courtesy of Kathy Loveland.)

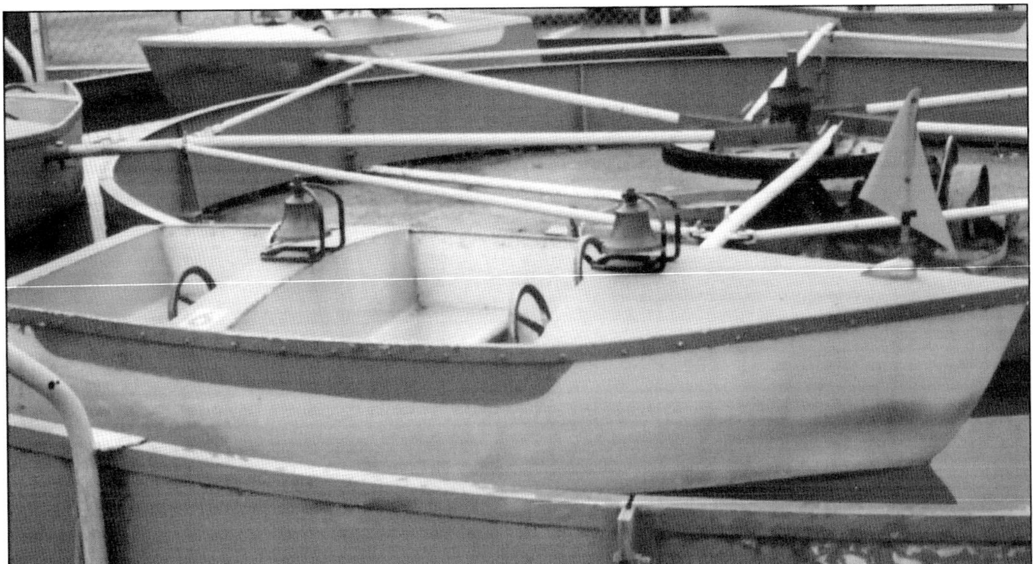

Earl Dealing was born to carnival ride owners in 1916. When they were on the road, his mother would wrap him in a blanket and put him down for a nap in the carousel chariot. At one point, his father owned a movie house, but when it failed, he moved his family to Western New York, where he operated his rides. (Courtesy of Joan Smyth.)

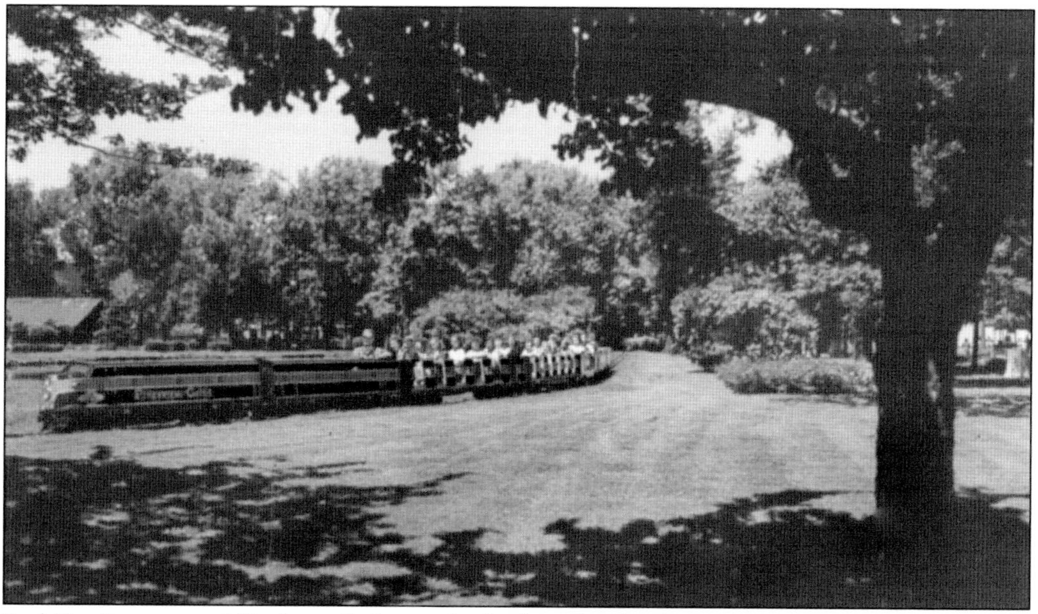

Earl Dealing opened Dealings Rides in the backyard of his home on Niagara Falls Boulevard near Ellicott Creek in 1950. The park had four kiddie rides—boats, cars, a rocket ride, and the Little Dipper roller coaster—as well as a carousel and miniature train. The train ran around the perimeter of the yard through the trees. Earl often opened his park for free to children who were disabled or financially less fortunate. (Courtesy of Joan Smyth.)

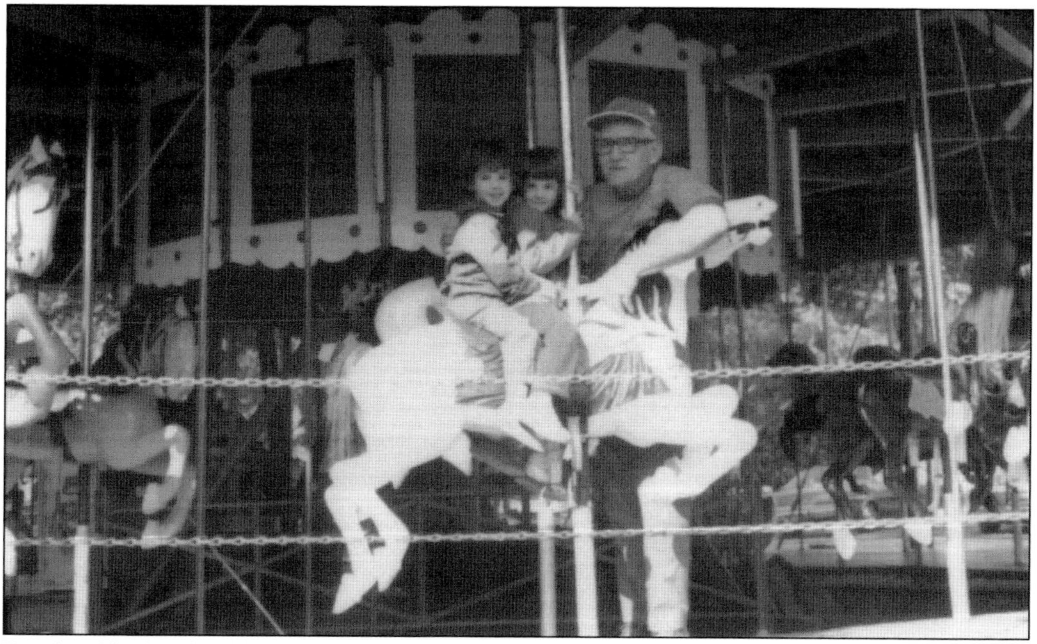

Five local high school boys ran the rides, but Dealing usually operated the carousel himself. The two-row, Spillman Engineering carousel featured jumping horses with real horsehair tails. In 1980, Dealing decided to close his park. There had never been an accident, and he was unwilling to tempt fate further. He is shown here with two young customers, John and Jennifer Stevenson, in 1977. (Courtesy HCFM.)

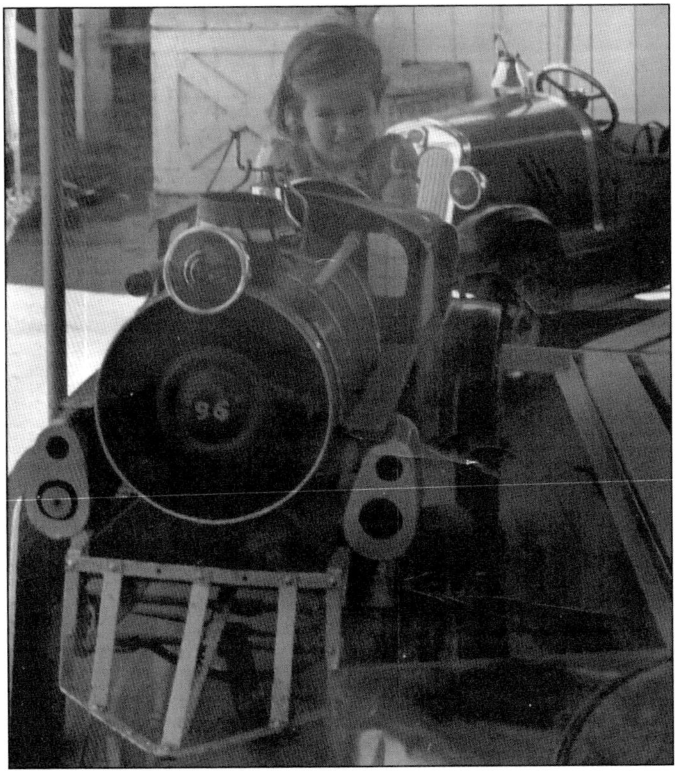

Impresario Harry Altman opened the Glen Casino and Amusement Park in Williamsville next to Ellicott Creek's waterfall in the early 1940s. Some rides and concessions had been operating on the property as early as 1933, including a carousel, kiddie plane ride, and shooting gallery owned by concessionaire Phil Morrot. The Glen Casino featured many famous entertainers, including Sammy Davis Jr., Frank Sinatra, and the Mills Brothers. (Courtesy of Dawn Lewis.)

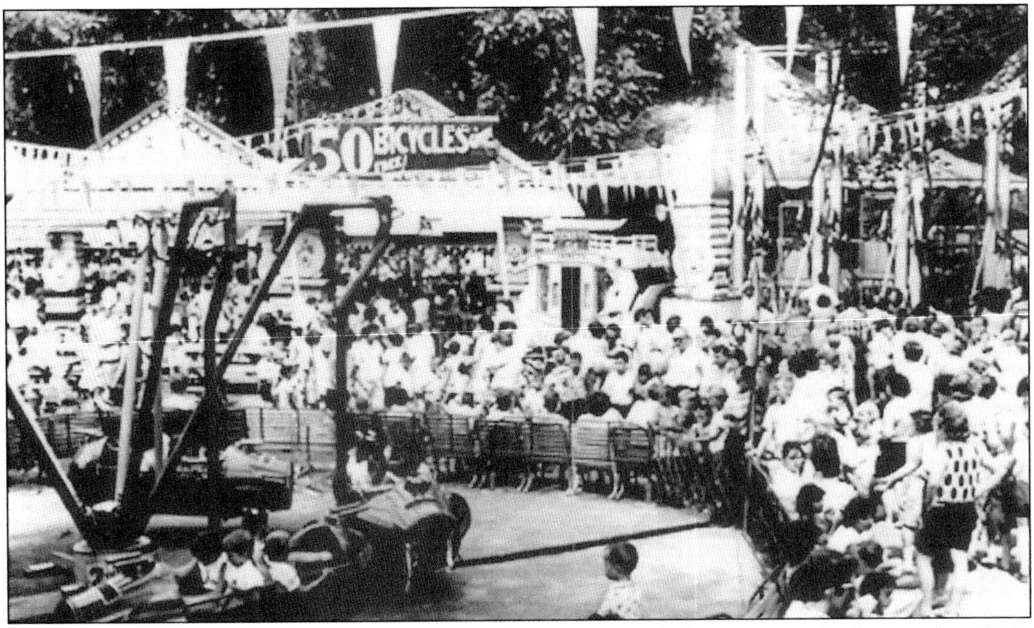

Games, novelty stands, food stands, and kiddie rides packed the 9-acre park during the 1950s and 1960s. On any given summer evening, the midway was crowded with parents and youngsters. Glen Park was one of the most popular kiddie parks in Western New York. In 1966, the Casino was converted into the Inferno, a teen nightclub featuring local and national rock and roll bands. (Courtesy of Dawn Lewis.)

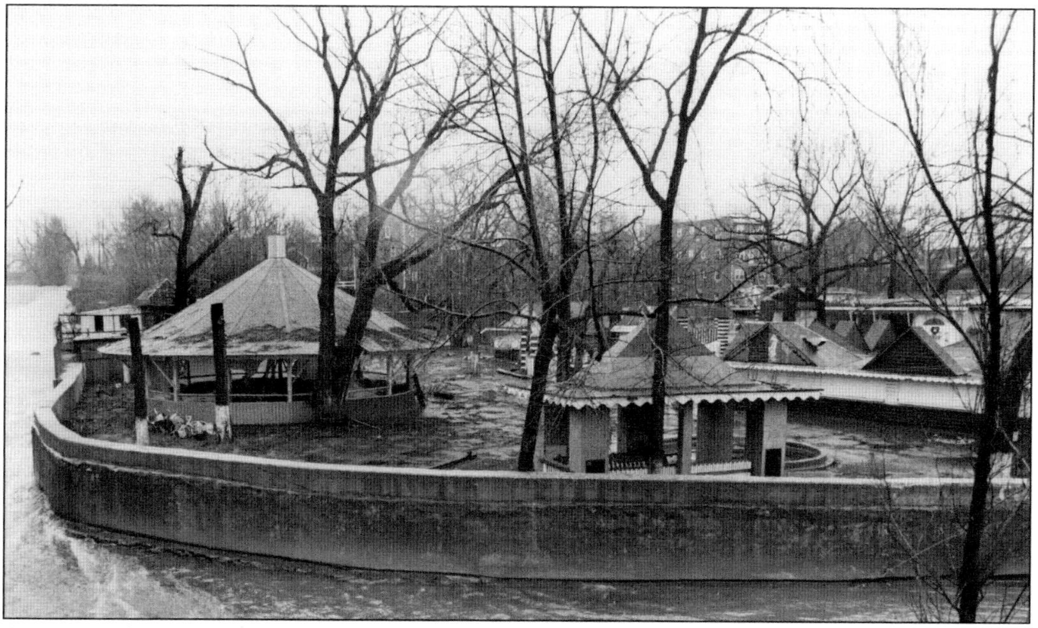

On September 23, 1968, a fire broke out in the Inferno. It wiped out a large portion of the grounds before the fire department arrived. Although the kiddie park was untouched by the fire, it did not reopen the following season. A second fire in 1973 destroyed the remaining buildings. The towns of Amherst and Williamsville jointly created a lovely town park, opening it to the public in 1976. (Courtesy BSCACEC.)

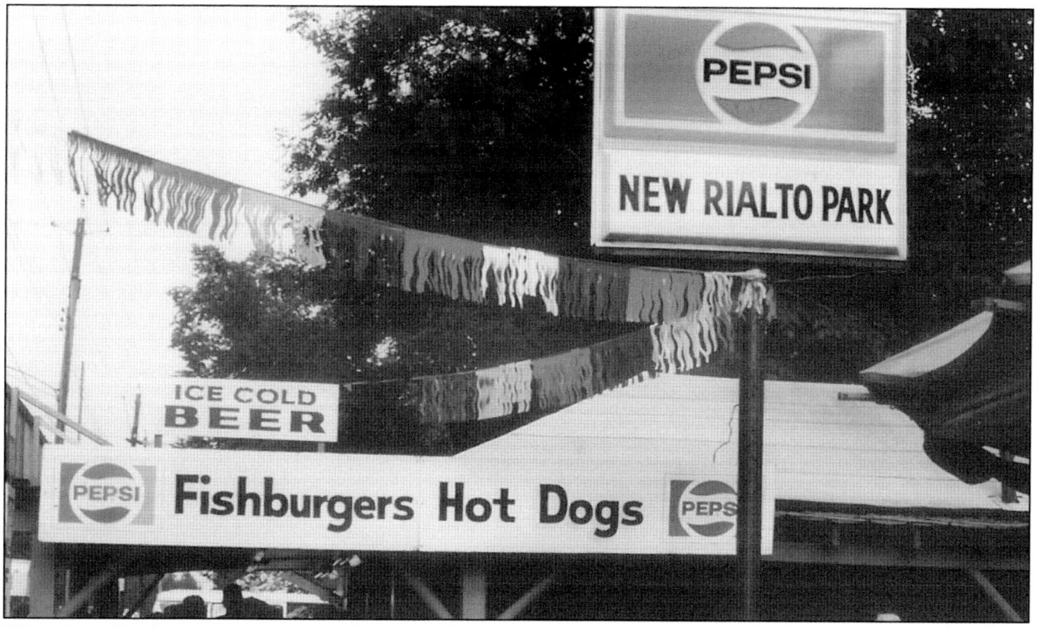

The New Rialto amusement park opened in 1940 on Main Street in Olcott across from Krull Park. Phil Morrot managed the park and also operated his carousel, kiddie plane ride, and Ferris wheel on the grounds. Game and food stands fronted the park. Hot dogs, hamburgers, and french fries were standard amusement park fare, but the New Rialto also offered fresh, handmade fish burgers. (Courtesy of Dan Wilke.)

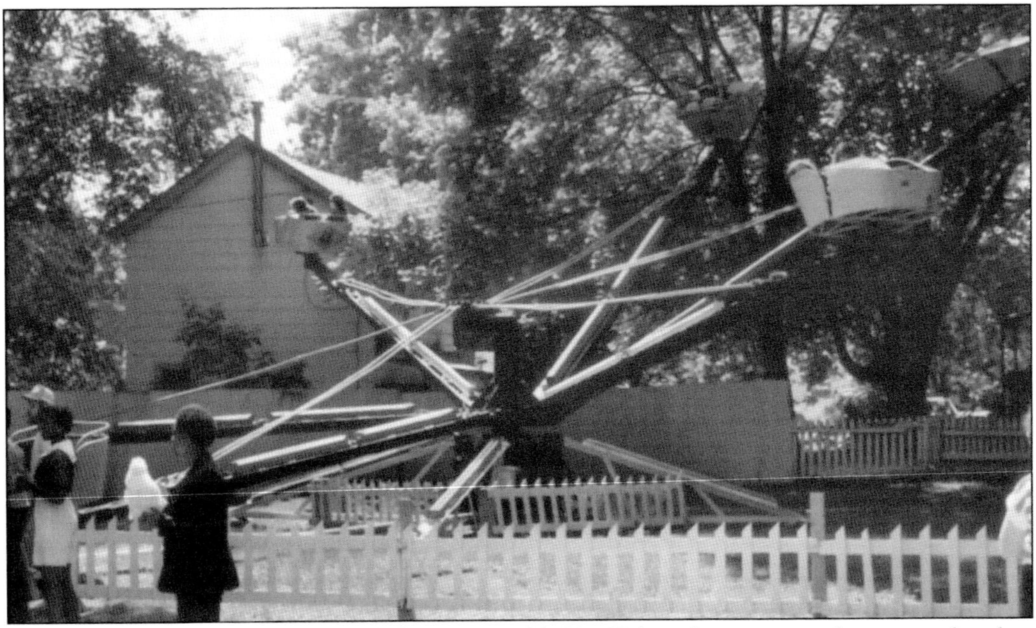

Phil Morrot tried to buy the park following World War II, but the owner at the time refused to sell. After a disagreement over the rent, Morrot packed up his rides and left. A Mr. Myler bought the park in 1947. In the next few years, he added 10 kiddie rides and four major attractions that included a dark ride, a Ferris wheel, and the Octopus, shown here. (Courtesy of Dan Wilke.)

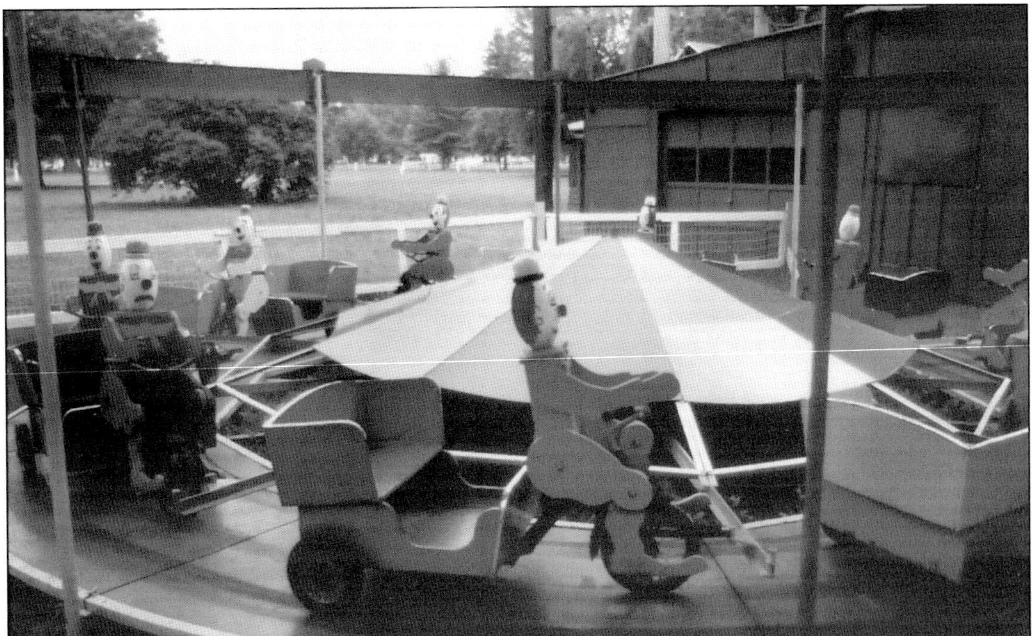

The clown ride was one of the more unusual attractions at New Rialto Park. The clown legs were jointed, creating the illusion that they were pedaling the riders around the track. Other kiddie rides included a car ride, airplane ride, miniature train, boat ride, helicopters, and Skyfighter. A stand facing Main Street housed games of chance. (Courtesy of Dan Wilke.)

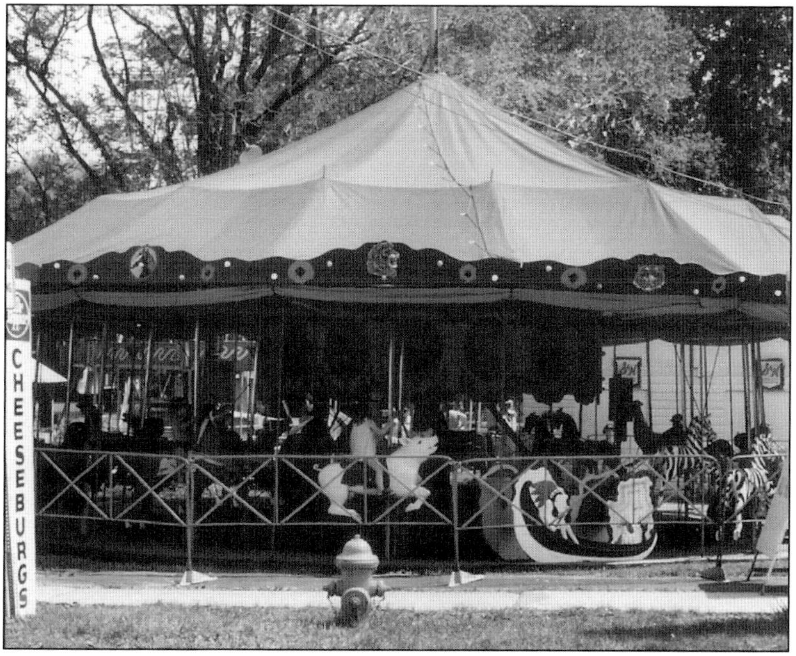

A Herschell-Spillman two-row portable carousel was the centerpiece of the park, placed near the street where it would attract attention. A menagerie, it had horses, pigs, dogs, zebras, and roosters. Two carved chariots, one a portrait of Uncle Sam with a bald eagle and the other—a Native American maiden in a canoe—provided seating for adults. (Courtesy of Dan Wilke.)

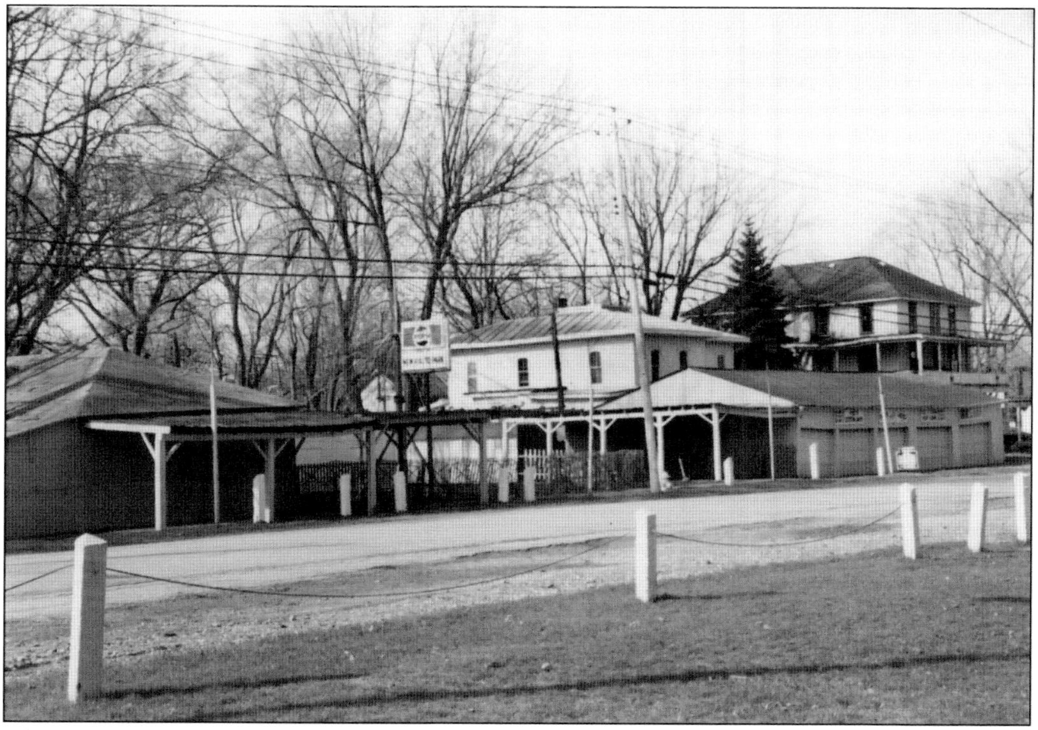

Olcott never enjoyed the large number of visitors it had in the early days before the Great Depression. Patronage at the New Rialto dropped during the 1970s and 1980s. There were many summer days when there was not a single customer in the park. The dark ride was shut down and major rides and some of the kiddie rides were sold off until only the carousel was operating. (Author's collection.)

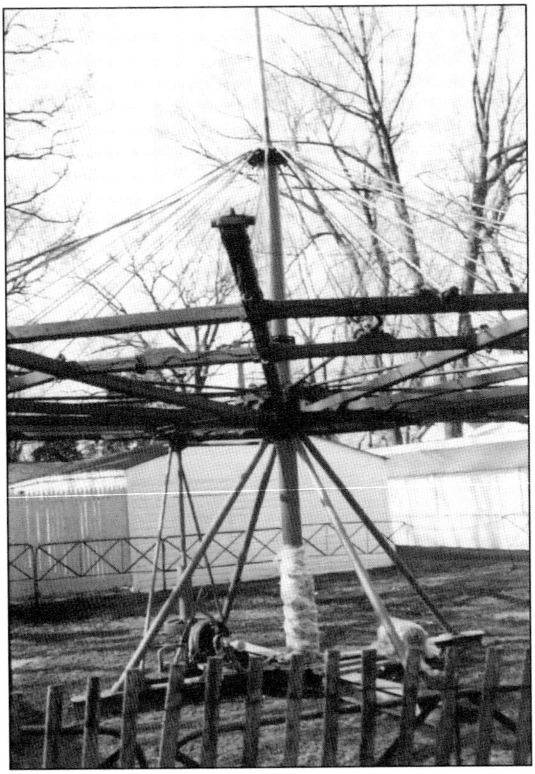

The 1992 season was New Rialto Park's last year of operation. The carousel animals were removed from the machine and placed into storage. Several years later, a fire destroyed a nearby house and took with it most of the park's buildings. Today, the park grounds remain abandoned, the carousel frame deteriorating from age and exposure to weather. (Author's collection.)

When Phil Morrot left New Rialto Park, he took his rides to his property on the banks of Tonawanda Creek in Indian Falls and built his own amusement park, Boulder Park. It debuted on May 28, 1949, with all of Morrot's rides, including the menagerie carousel. Morrot sold the park to Wilbert Stradtman in 1964. Patronage declined, and the park shut down in 1970. (Courtesy of Dan Wilke.)

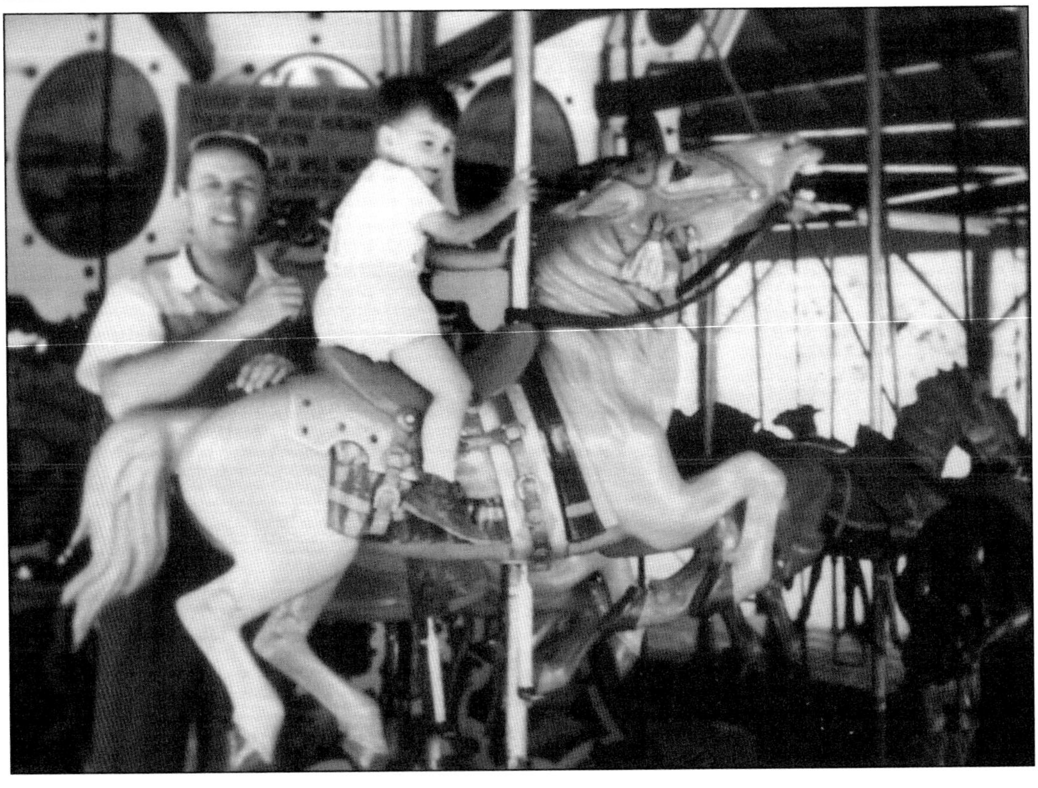

Celoron Park owner Harry Illions bought Liberty Park in 1948. Located along Cayuga Creek on the corner of William Street and Union Road in Cheektowaga, it had a few rides and a picnic grove. Illions added a giant slide, miniature train, and kiddie rides. His heirs sold the park after his death in 1962. A gas station and a few businesses now occupy the land. (Courtesy of C. Thomas.)

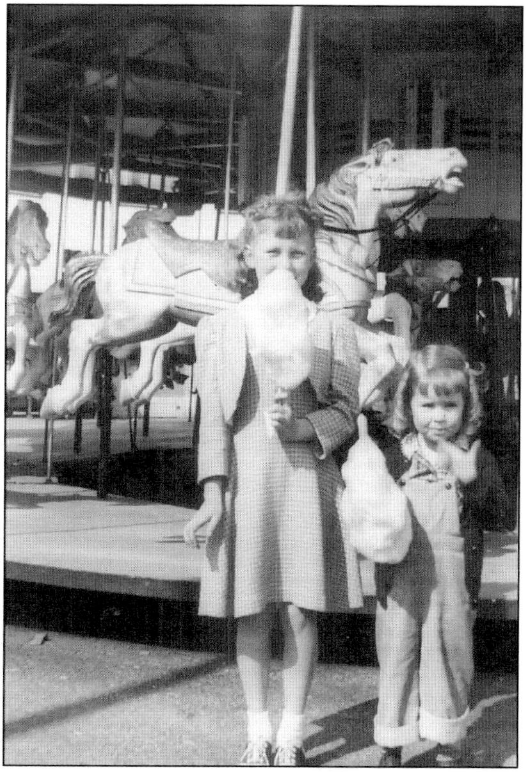

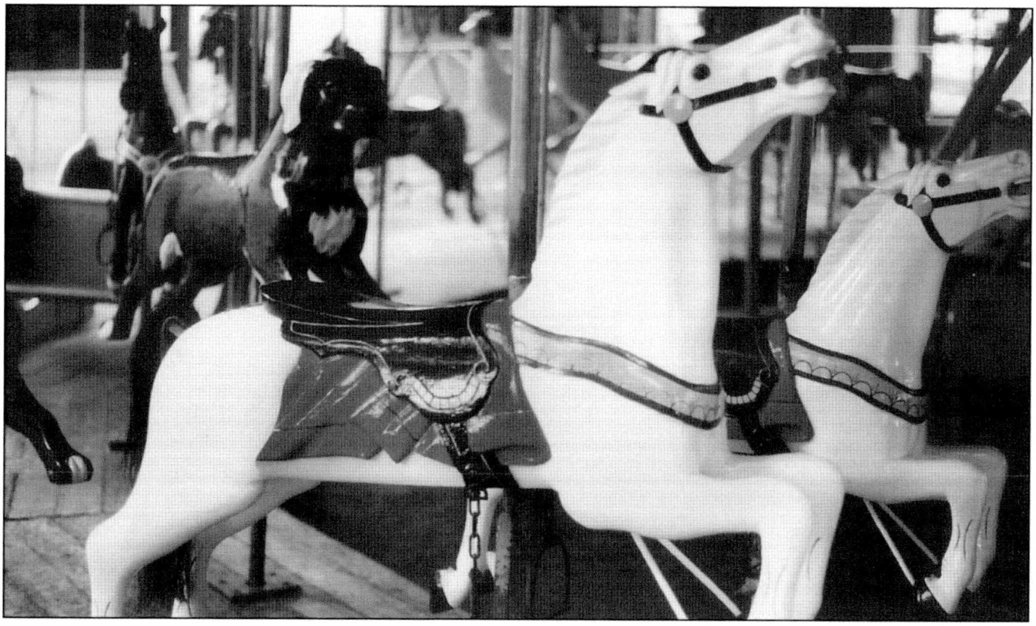

Thruway Plaza was the largest shopping plaza in the country when it opened on Harlem and Walden Roads in 1952. In 1957, the Kiddie Ranch debuted on the property with several kiddie rides and a 1905 two-row Herschell-Spillman menagerie carousel. The other rides were removed by 1960, but the carousel spun at the plaza until 1966. It currently operates at Harbor Place in Baltimore, Maryland. (Courtesy of Dan Wilke.)

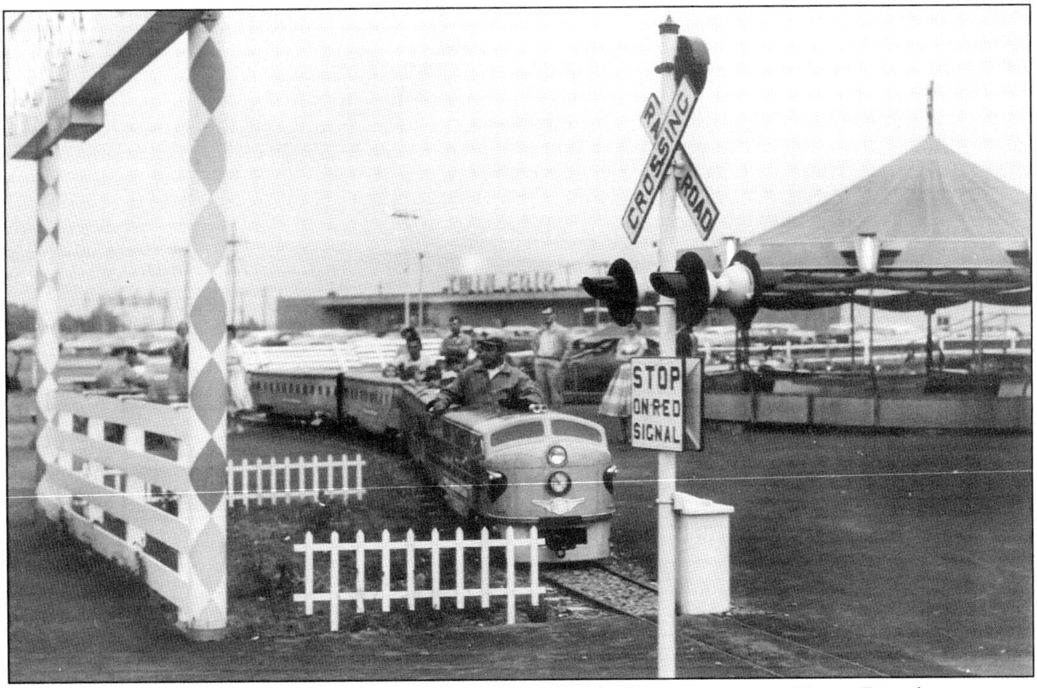

Kiddieland was a favorite stop for youngsters going with their parents to Twin Fair department store on the corner of Dick and Walden Roads in Cheektowaga. All the rides were from the Allan Herschell Company. The miniature train encircled a carousel, boat ride, helicopters, and Skyfighter. Kiddieland existed from 1958 to 1966. (Courtesy of Joan Smyth.)

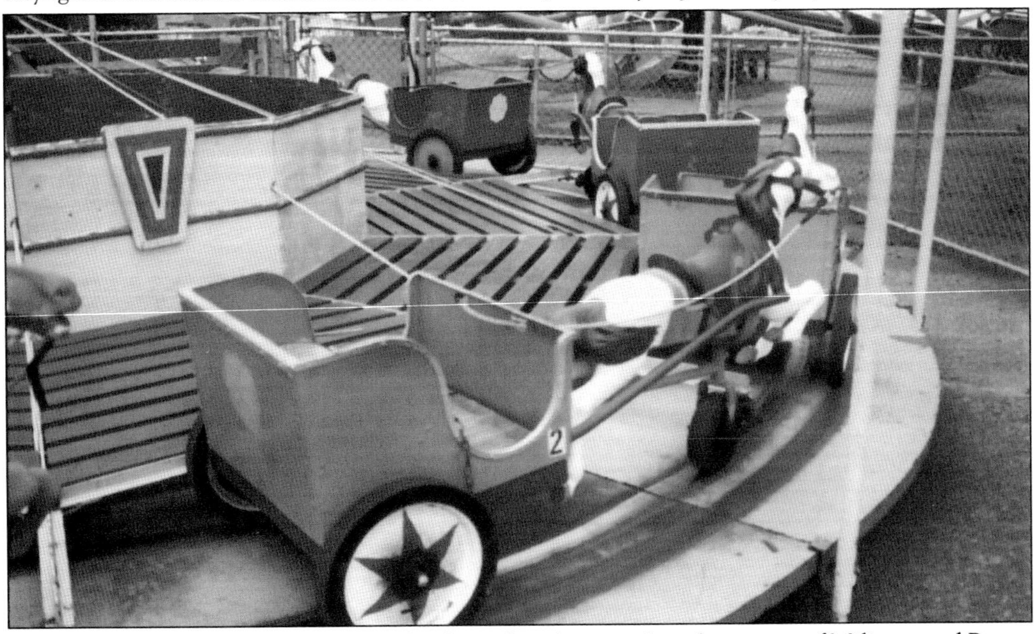

Kiddyland opened in 1964 at Page's Whistle Pig hot dog stand on the corner of Military and Porter Roads in the town of Niagara. It featured several Allan Herschell rides, a kiddie Ferris wheel, and a miniature train. Over time, the park was downsized to five rides, but the park continued to operate until 2008 when the owners retired. (Author's collection.)

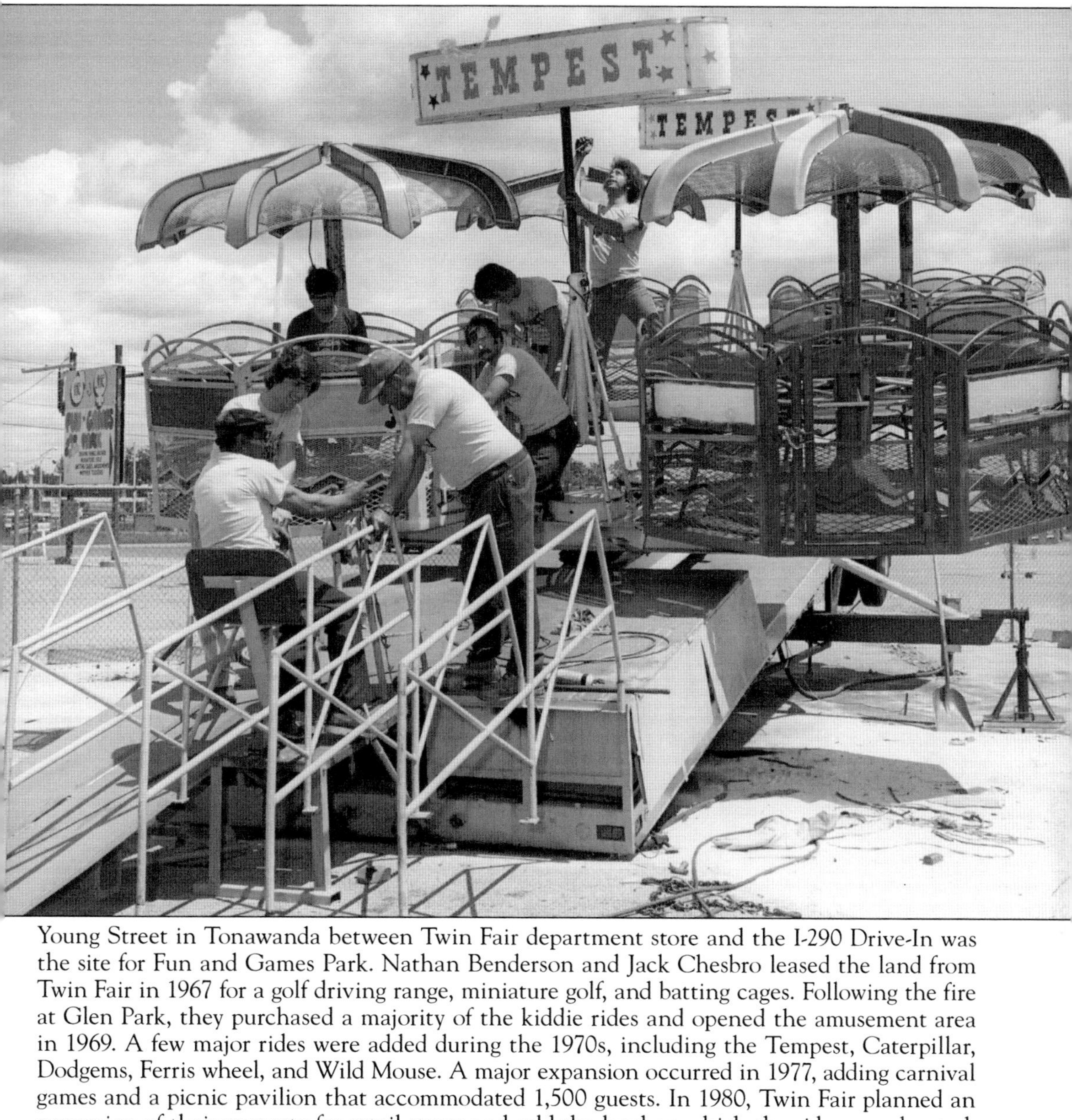

Young Street in Tonawanda between Twin Fair department store and the I-290 Drive-In was the site for Fun and Games Park. Nathan Benderson and Jack Chesbro leased the land from Twin Fair in 1967 for a golf driving range, miniature golf, and batting cages. Following the fire at Glen Park, they purchased a majority of the kiddie rides and opened the amusement area in 1969. A few major rides were added during the 1970s, including the Tempest, Caterpillar, Dodgems, Ferris wheel, and Wild Mouse. A major expansion occurred in 1977, adding carnival games and a picnic pavilion that accommodated 1,500 guests. In 1980, Twin Fair planned an expansion of their property for retail stores and sold the land on which the rides were located. The remainder of the park closed in 1981. The park site is now occupied by a shopping plaza and BJ's Warehouse. (Courtesy BSCACEC.)

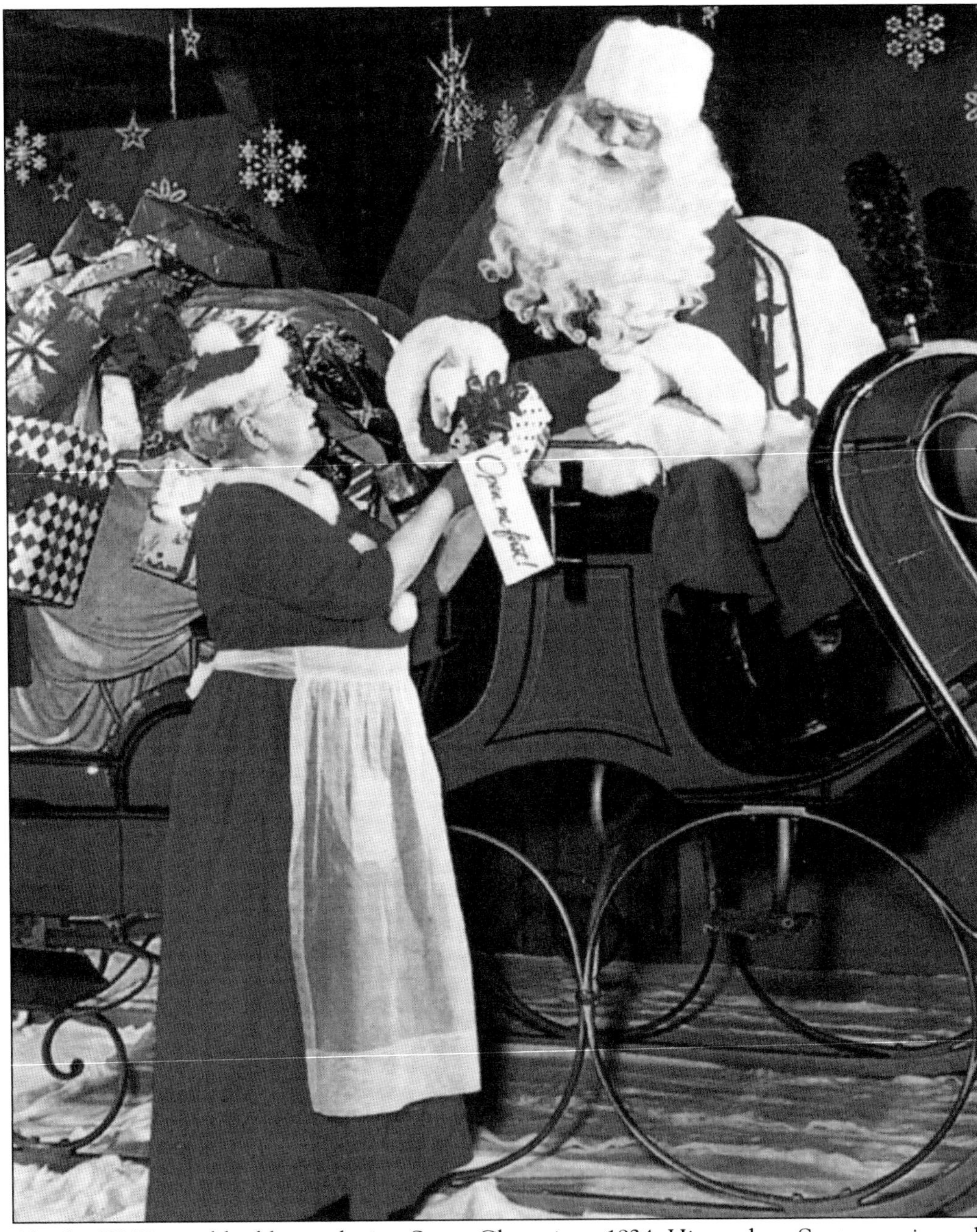

Charles W. Howard had been playing Santa Claus since 1934. His work as Santa was in such high demand throughout New York State he decided to open a Santa Claus School on his farm in Albion to teach other men how to play Santa Claus and help them with their Santa duties. Howard, in this photograph with his wife, Ruth, as Mrs. Claus, portrayed Santa Claus for many years in Macy's Thanksgiving Day parade. His dream to create a Christmas shrine to honor Santa Claus came true when he opened Christmas Park on his farm in 1953. There were many facets to Christmas Park, from the playground, petting farm, and Santa's Gold Mine to a toy shop, gift shop, and Mrs. Claus's Kitchen restaurant. Coins were collected from a wishing well to create a good Christmas for less fortunate children in the area. (Courtesy C. Thomas.)

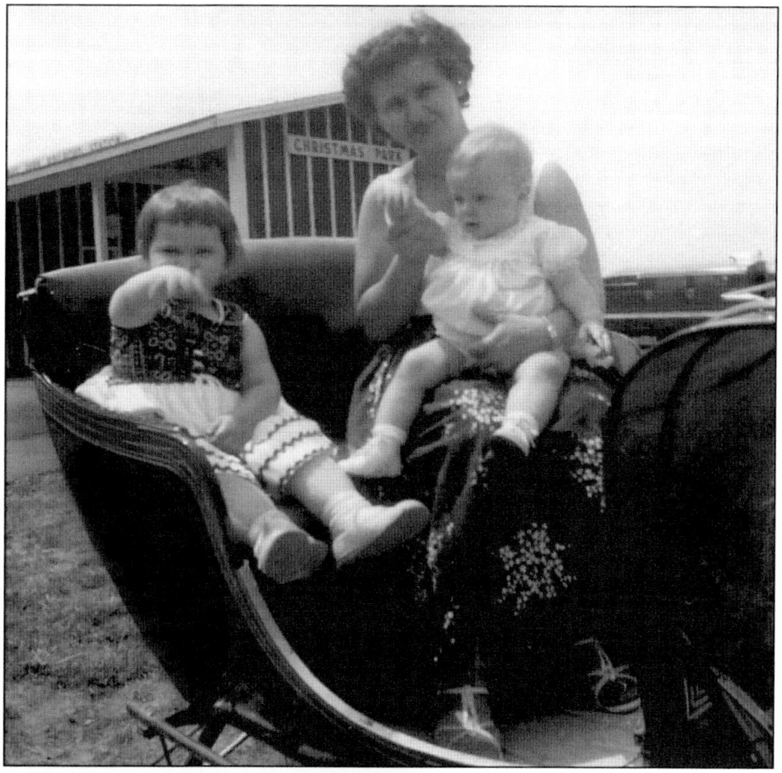

Howard had a collection of antique sleighs, which he placed throughout the park, but his favorite he kept only for display. Made prior to the Civil War by the Perrin Carriage Company of Buffalo, it had silver fittings, gold striping, and velvet upholstery. Virginia Jankowiak and her daughters, Rose Ann, left, and Marcia, seated on her mother's lap, pose for this photograph taken by their father, Richard Jankowiak, in 1961. (Author's collection.)

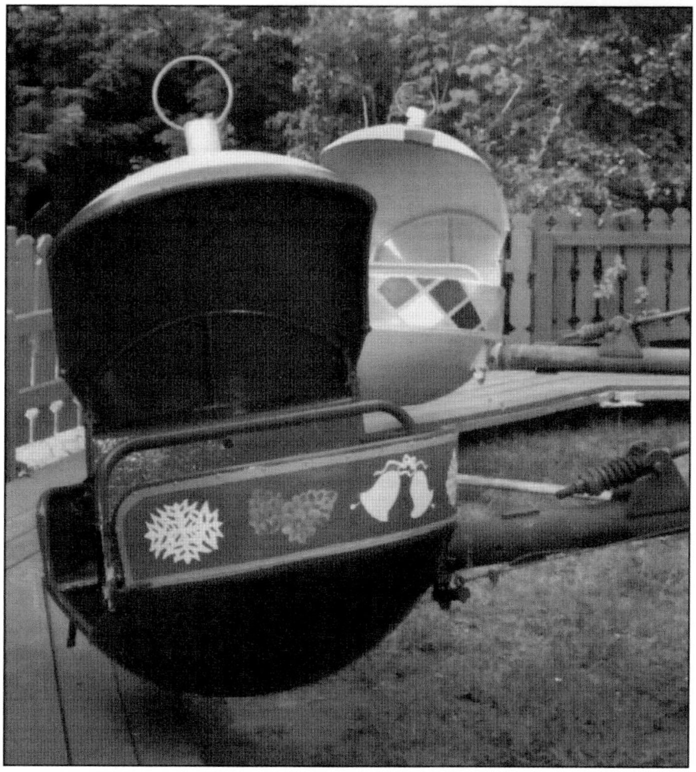

There were only three rides at Christmas Park, the live pony ride, the miniature train, and the Christmas Tree ride, which was a specially made Allan Herschell helicopter ride converted into ornaments that circled a large Christmas tree. The Railmaster, a diesel-operated miniature train, circled the farm, passing through the evergreen plantation, an igloo-shaped tunnel, and past displays like the life-size Nativity. (Author's collection.)

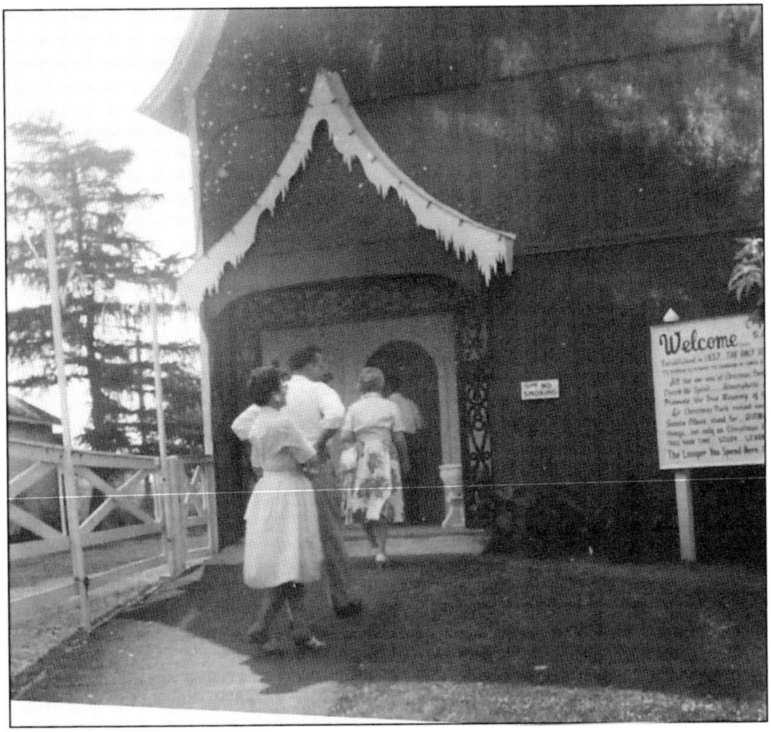

The L-shaped barn held displays of Christmas past, Christmas around the world, and animated reindeer and elves. There was also a stable with live reindeer. The entire barn area was decorated with hundreds of twinkling colored lights. Christmas music continually played inside the buildings and out. Man-made snow, appearing as white dots in this photograph, drifted down on visitors entering the barns. (Author's collection.)

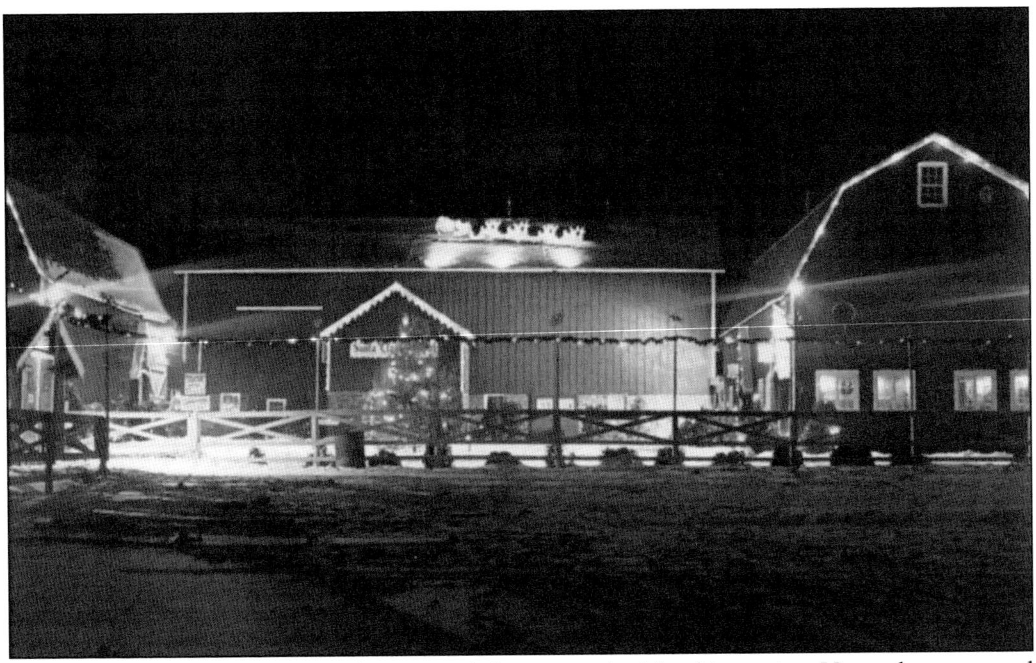

Howard died in 1966 due to complications of a heart attack. After his passing, Howard was entered into the 1966 United States Congressional Record as the Dean of Santa Claus. The park went bankrupt following his death, and everything was sold at auction in 1968. Christmas Park and Howard's dream melted away. (Courtesy C. Thomas.)

Five

A Park is Reborn

Burt Flynn opened Olcott Amusement Park in 1947 on Main Street just a block from the New Rialto. A slight resurgence in the area during the 1950s made the park a popular daytime destination for picnickers looking for a distraction for their kids. That popularity began to decrease in the following decades. Olcott Amusement Park closed in 1986. All the rides were sold in an auction, the carousel roundhouse was boarded up, and the park property was abandoned.

In 1999, a small committee was formed from the Krull Olcott Development Committee under the chairmanship of Dr. Rosemary Sansone. The committee's purpose was to restore the old carousel roundhouse with the possibility of getting a carousel to operate inside. Fundraising began, and the committee grew to include Jane Voelpel, Tom Kelley, and Kelly Artieri. The Eastern Niagara Chamber of Commerce helped with the restoration project.

As few photographs existed of the roundhouse when Olcott Amusement Park was in operation, a call for photographs of the roundhouse went out to the carousel community. Jack Campbell from Culver, Indiana, contacted the committee. He did not have photographs of the roundhouse, but did own a kiddie car ride from the New Rialto as well as four other vintage kiddie rides and a restored carousel. By then, the committee had grown, and fundraising was underway to purchase a carousel similar to the one that once operated there.

A contract between the two parties was signed. Campbell's rides came to Olcott Beach, and a park was reborn.

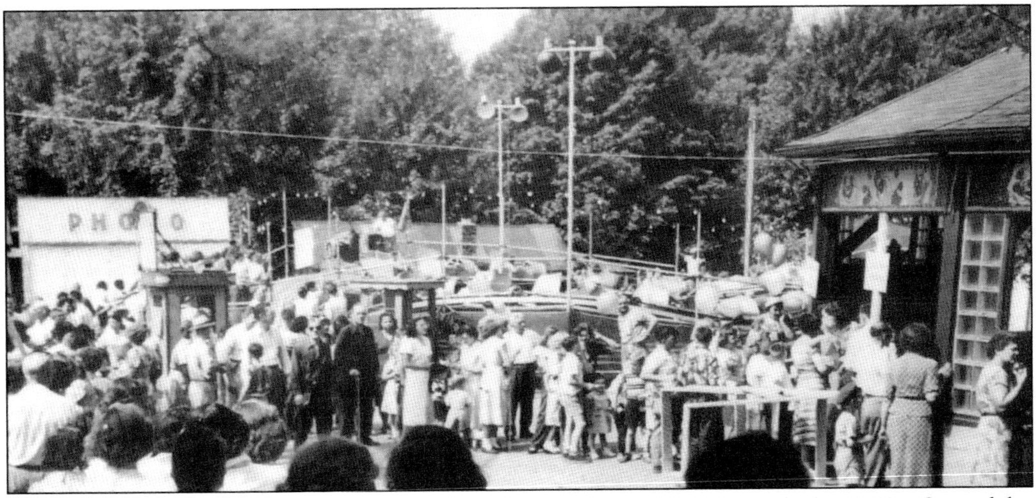

Olcott Amusement Park was a busy place from its opening in 1947 through the 1960s. One of the few adult rides in the park was the Allan Herschell Caterpillar, center, which was replaced with bumper cars during the 1970s. The roundhouse, in its original state, is on the right. (Courtesy of Jane Smyth.)

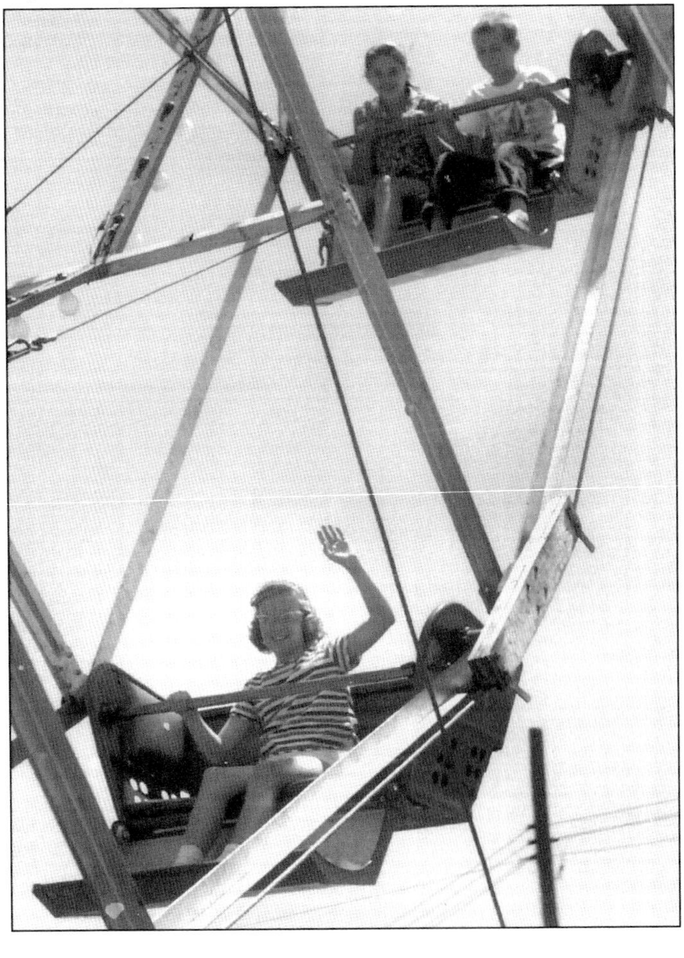

The Ferris wheel was popular as patrons of all ages could ride and see the lovely view of Olcott and Lake Ontario from the top. Three unidentified children enjoyed their ride on the Ferris wheel during the 1950s. Besides a food stand, photograph booth, and several game booths, the park offered a carousel and three kiddie rides: the Skyfighter, a boat ride, and a car ride. (Author's collection.)

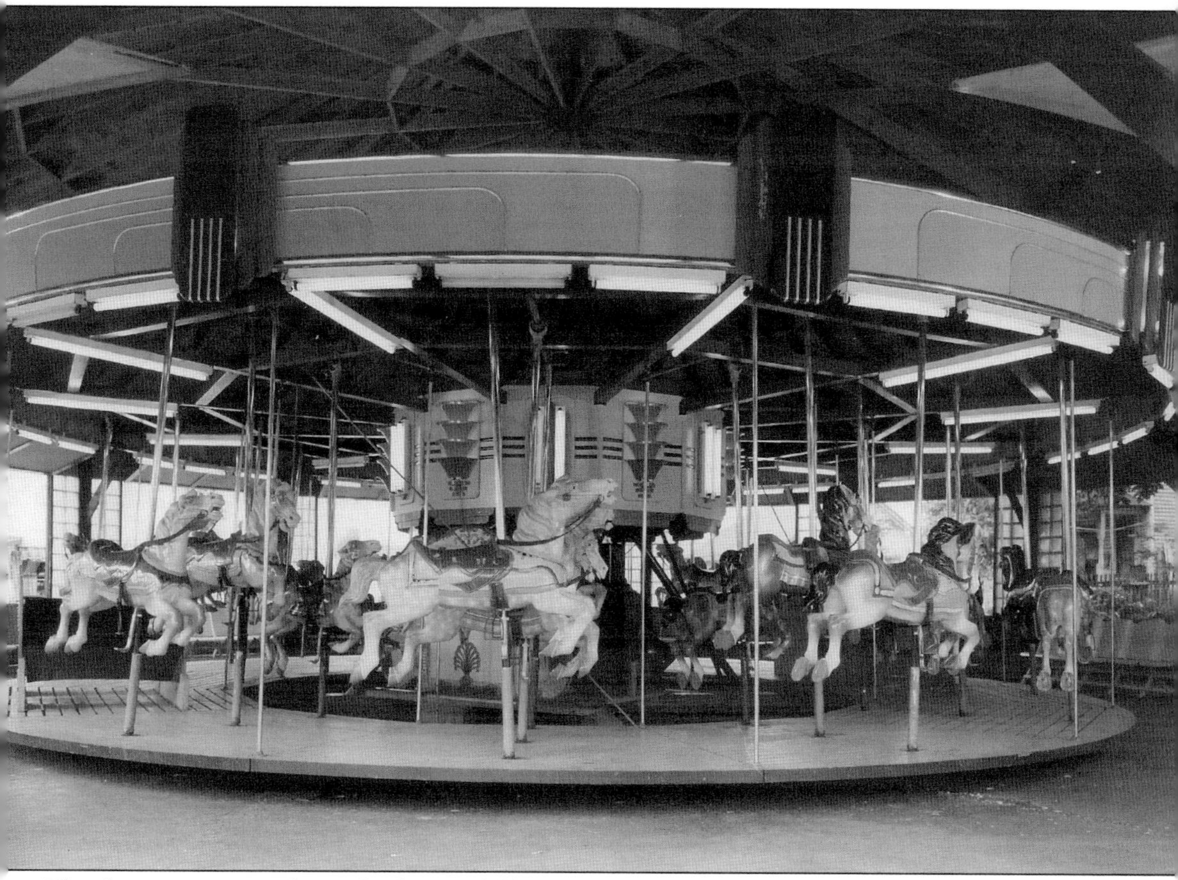

The three-row carousel was the heart of Olcott Amusement Park. It was manufactured by the Allan Herschell Company in North Tonawanda who had revolutionized the carousel industry by introducing cast aluminum horses during the 1920s. The horses were nicely painted as dapples, pintos, palominos, and chestnuts. Their saddles and blankets were finished off with hand-painted scrollwork and pin striping. The art deco designs on the roundingboards, shields, and inside panels were also typical of the Allan Herschell Company's aluminum carousels, giving them a bright, simple, and clean look. The entire carousel was outfitted with fluorescent lights. The roundhouse had overhead doors that, once opened, allowed in plenty of light and lake breezes. Folding theater-style chairs were set around the perimeter of the roundhouse where parents relaxed and watched their children ride. Brassy marching music from a Wurlitzer band organ accompanied the ride. (Courtesy of Joan Smyth.)

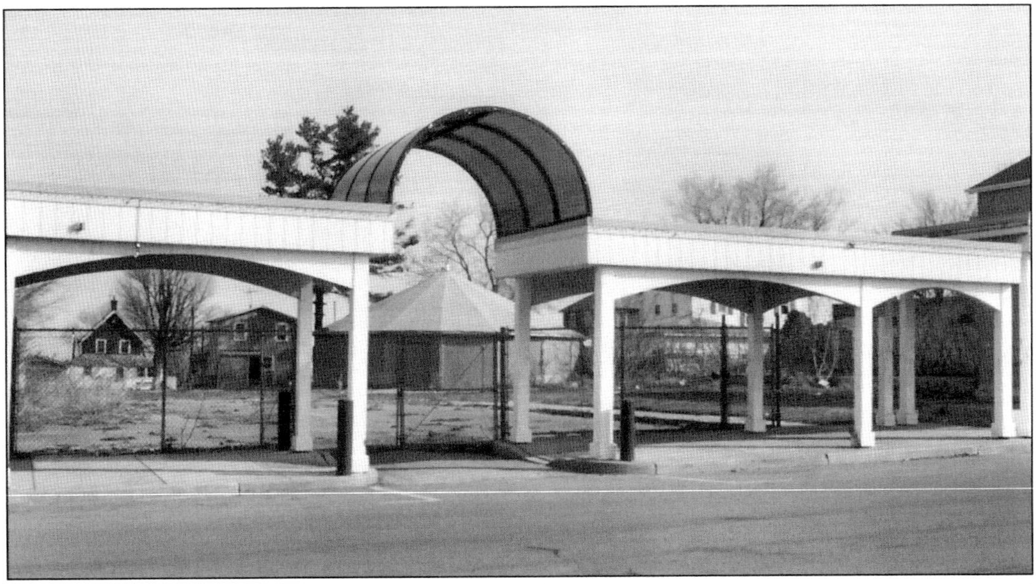

When Olcott Amusement Park closed in 1986, all the rides, including the carousel, were auctioned off. The roundhouse was boarded up, and the park property was abandoned. The bumper car building and other small structures were demolished. The shuttered park was a visual testimony to the economic depression of the hamlet. (Author's collection.)

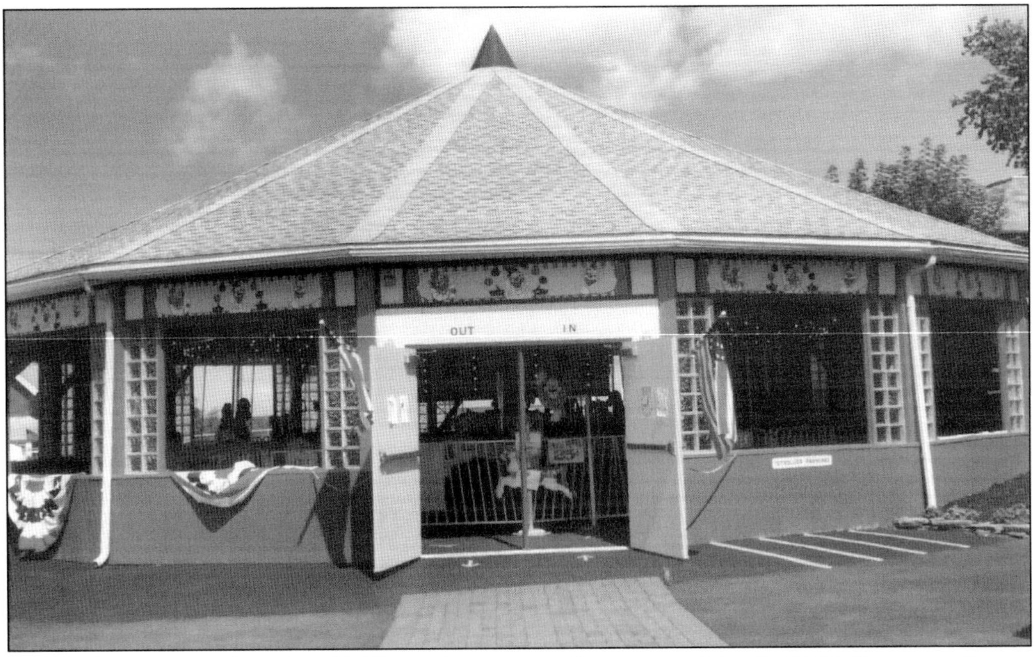

Carousel Park opened on the old Olcott Amusement Park site on May 17, 2003. The roundhouse had been restored to its original condition. It had a new roof and block-glass sections in the walls. A local artist recreated the clown paintings on the upper rim just below the roof. Inside spun a new carousel, restored to original factory colors. (Author's collection.)

The two-row Allan Herschell Company carousel is from the same era as the original carousel, having the identical style horses and art deco trim on the roundingboards. The shields are the same art deco style, with one difference—they are mounted with fanciful character heads like the Viking. (Author's collection.)

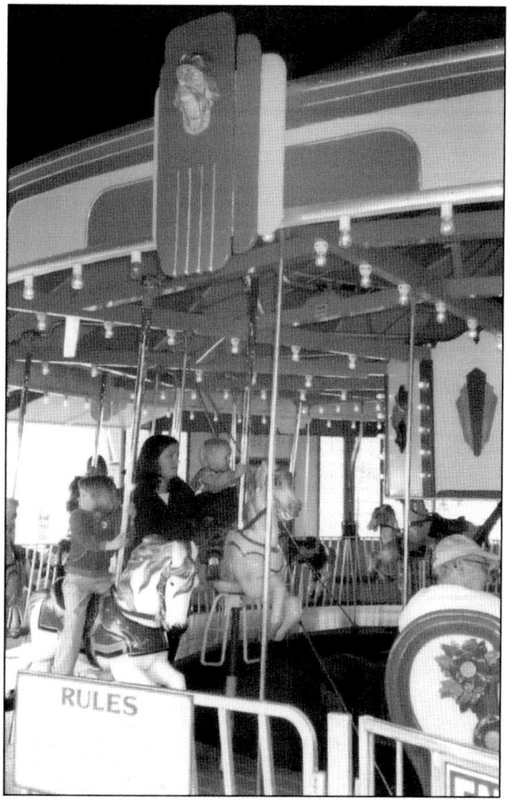

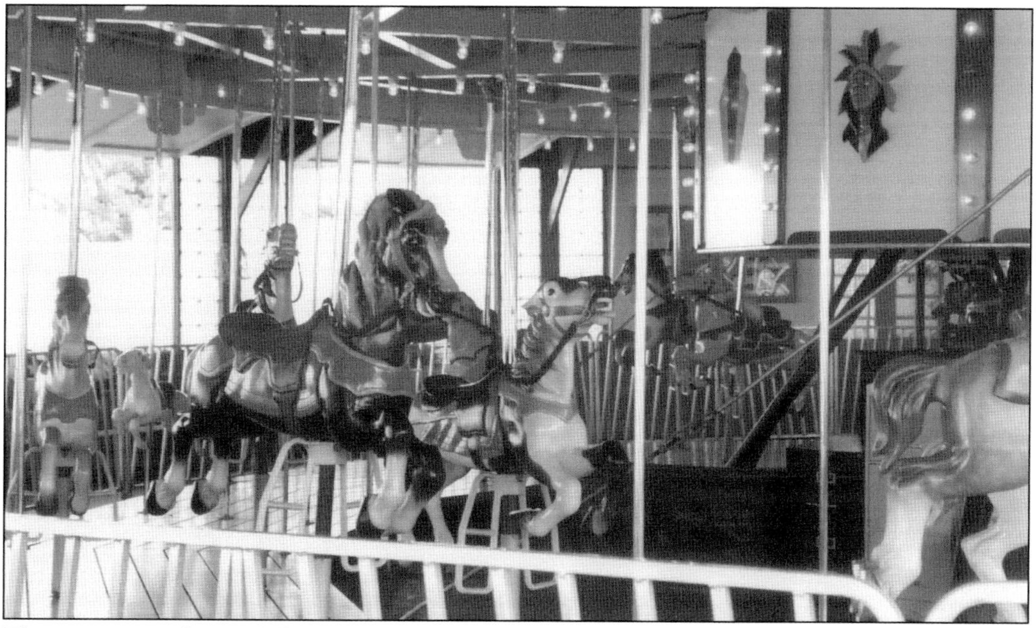

The center panels are different, featuring a Native American chief bust on every other panel. One chariot is on board along with a stationary row of kiddie ponies. Incandescent lights give the carousel a romantic feel. A Wurlitzer band organ, set in its own trailer outside the roundhouse, pumps out brassy, fun music all day long. (Author's collection.)

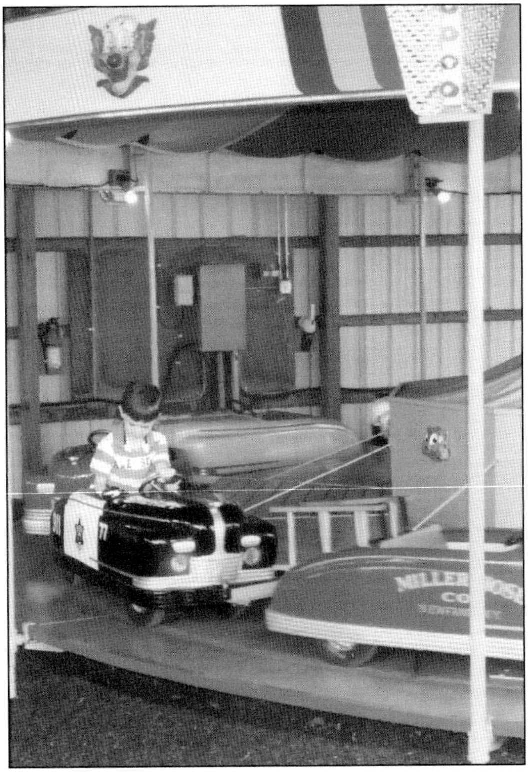

Carousel Park offers the carousel and vintage kiddie rides for 25¢ per ride. The kiddie rides are sheltered under a colonnade, along with Skeeball games. Ice cream and fast food fare are for sale at the snack stand. Whimsical landscaping adds to the fun atmosphere of the park. (Author's collection.)

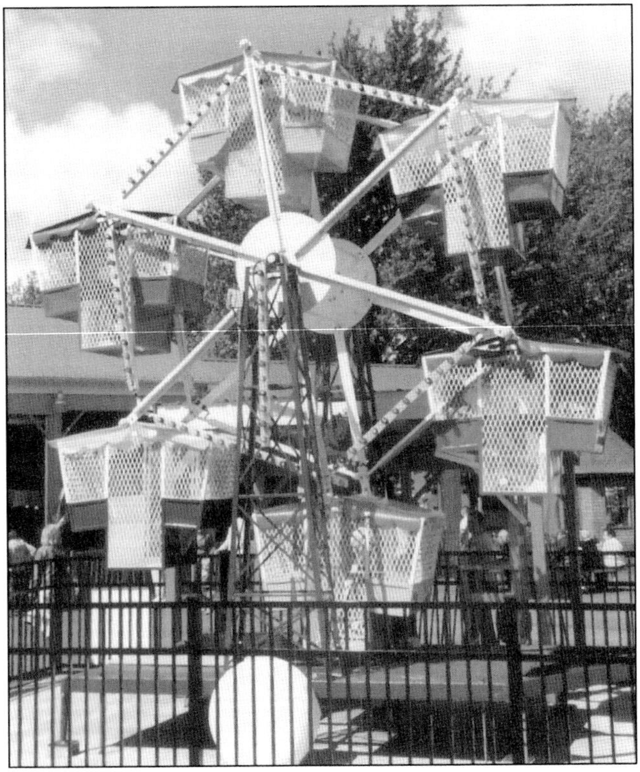

The Ferris wheel was purchased at the Page's Kiddyland auction. It was sandblasted, painted, and assembled on Carousel Park's grounds in 2009. A replica of Olcott's original Rustic Theater was built for concerts and performances. Run strictly by volunteers, Carousel Park has revitalized the neighborhood and brought interest to Olcott once again. (Author's collection.)

Six

FANTASY ON THE ISLAND

A random remark made to builder-developer Lawrence A. Grant led to the creation of Western New York's first theme park, Fantasy Island. It was 1959, and Grant was on the construction site for a shopping plaza on Grand Island Boulevard on Grand Island when the project's architect mentioned that the land across the road would be the perfect location for a theme park.

Grant ran with the idea, and by December, he had formed a corporation called Fantasy Land, Inc., and brought on board seven of the region's businessmen including wholesale jeweler Gerald Birzon who is credited with developing the park's theme and design. The corporation changed its name to Fantasy Island, Inc., since the original name conflicted with one of the areas in Disneyland. A loan for $500,000 dollars was secured from the Small Business Investment Corporation (SBIC) of New York City. SBIC held 30 percent of Fantasy Island stock in exchange for the loan.

Twenty acres of land were procured for the new theme park. Plans called for five themed areas and a central mall entryway that included colorful flower gardens and a picturesque fountain. Shops, exhibits, and shows were planned throughout the park and included refreshment stands like the Gingerbread House, Fort Frankfurter, and the Pink Poodle Restaurant.

Fantasy Island has experienced numerous changes and troubles since it opened in 1961. Despite many roadblocks, it has expanded and developed into a family-oriented park that caters to all ages and tastes with exciting thrill rides, shows, and a kiddie area that harkens back to its roots.

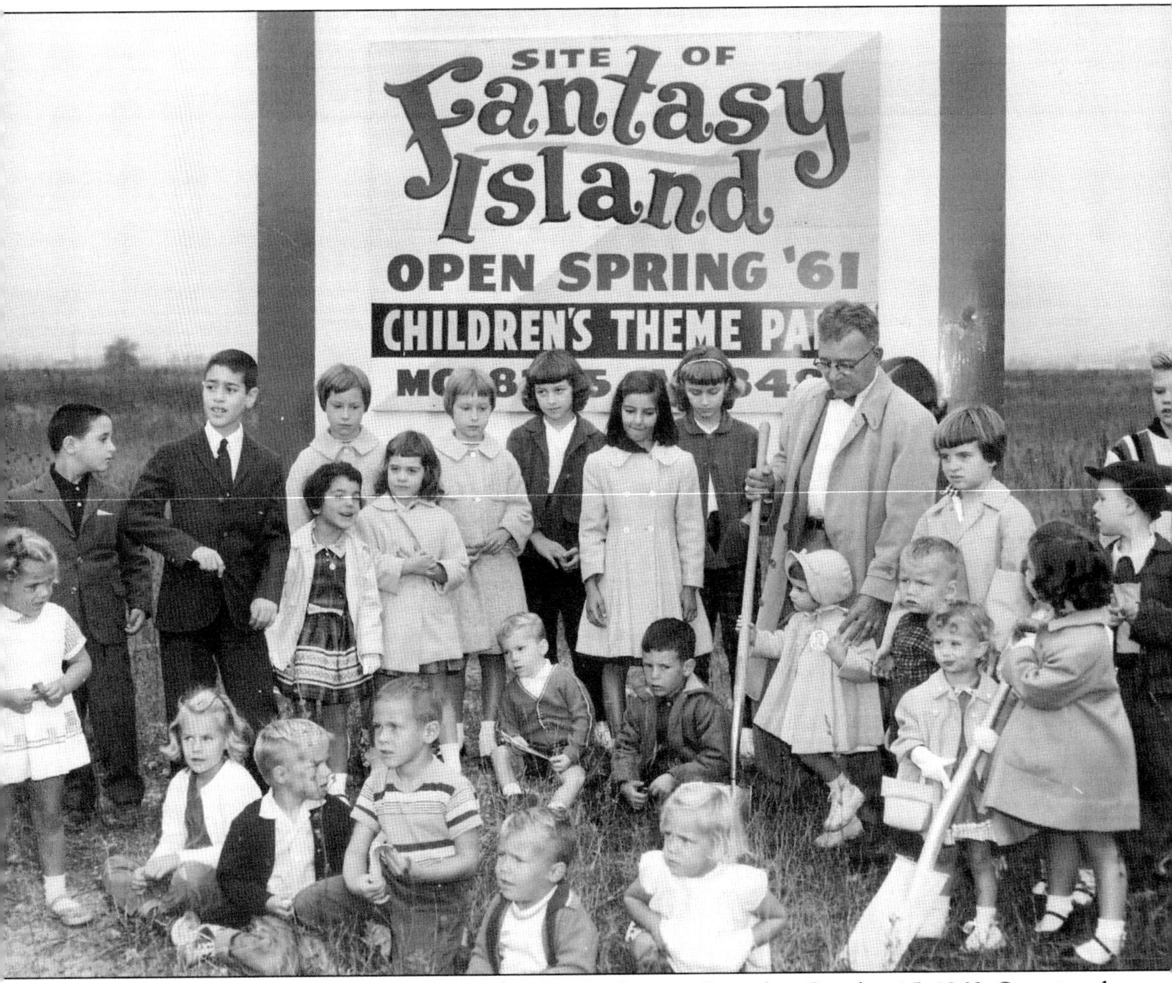

Formal ground breaking for Fantasy Island took place on Saturday, October 15, 1960. Opening day was planned for June 17, 1961, only nine months away. To generate excitement for the new park, publicity photographs were taken of local children gathered around the announcement sign. The gentleman in the crowd is Grand Island supervisor George J. Burgstahler. His granddaughter Amy Rothenburg is standing directly in front of him wearing a bonnet. Construction began immediately after this photograph was taken. Eight acres of the 20-acre package were to be developed into a parking lot for 800 vehicles, and the remaining 12 acres were reserved for the park. Admission price was set at $1 for adults and 50¢ for children under 12. Books of ride tickets, called Whimsies, were 12 for a dollar. Each ride required three to four Whimsies. (Courtesy MFI.)

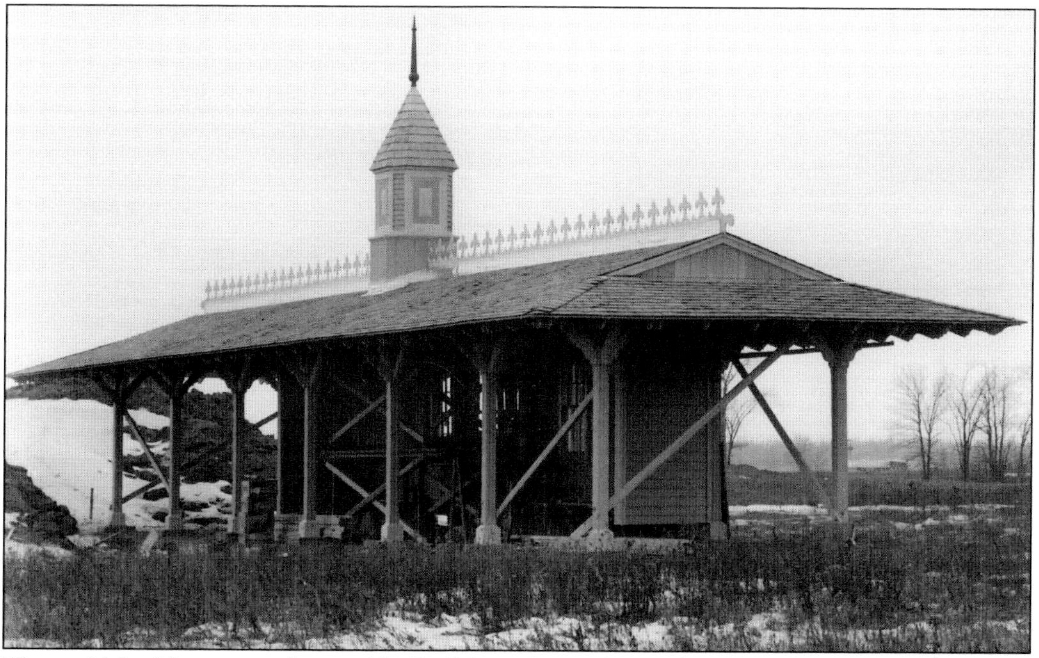

The park's buildings were designed by Buffalo architect firm Milton Milstein and Associates and were designed to reflect the themed area in which they were located. The train station was one of the first buildings erected. Workers scrambled through the winter, fighting freezing temperatures, ice, and snow to build the park. As construction was additionally hampered by a rainy spring, the original opening date was pushed back two weeks. (Courtesy MFI.)

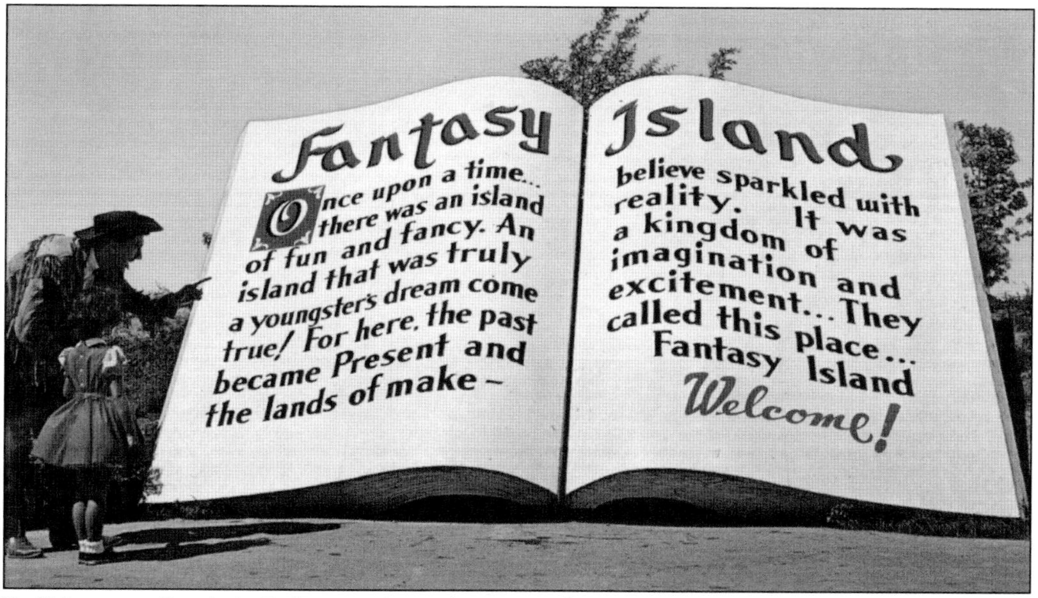

Buffalo mayor Frank A. Sedita proclaimed opening day as Fantasy Island Day. It was a windy but sunny day, perfect for the 500 invited guests. Children were awed as they entered Fantasy Island and were greeted by storybook characters, the Fantasy Island Princess, and a giant storybook. At the end of the entrance mall was the Happy Birthday House shaped like a giant two-tiered birthday cake topped with candles. (Author's collection.)

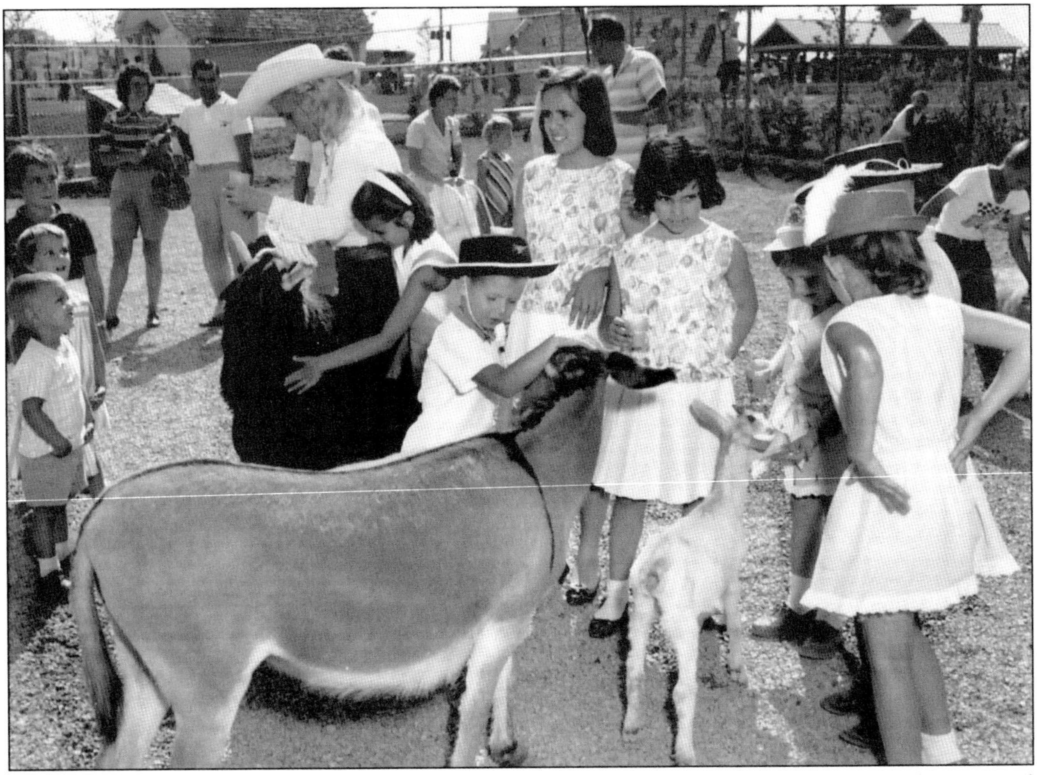

Just behind the Pink Poodle Restaurant, visitors came to the first of the five lands, Animal Kingdom. Within the fenced area were free-roaming goats, sheep, and burros children could feed and pet. Children could also visit the Big Red Barn where horses were stabled. Annie Oakley, in the cowgirl hat, shows children how to properly feed a goat. (Courtesy MFI.)

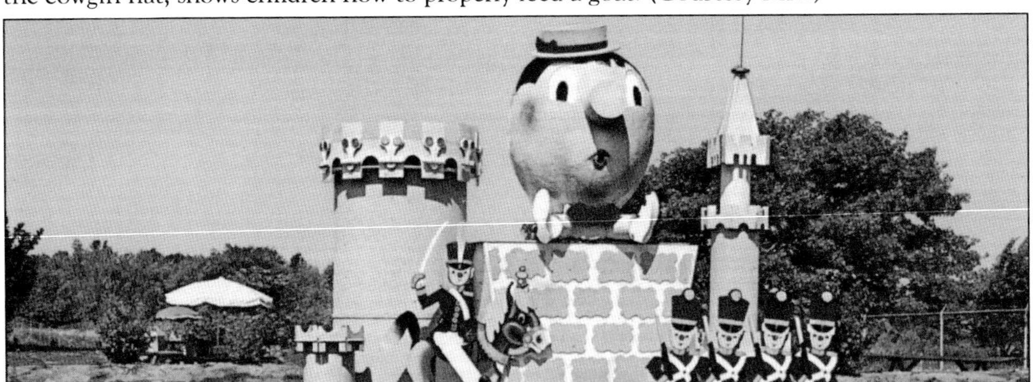

The Garden of Fables was home to classic storybook characters. Children entered through a large dollhouse where dolls of all nations could be purchased. A winding path led through the garden past exhibits and storybook houses. Vincent Staley was hired to do all the park artwork, which was bright and fanciful, appealing to young children. (Author's collection.)

The exhibits included Jonah and the Whale, Gulliver, the Crooked Man, Old Woman's Shoe, and Humpty Dumpty. Jack and the Beanstalk was one of the animated exhibits. The giant at the top rotated slowly, creating the illusion that he was peering down at visiting children. This original exhibit is still at the park, although the giant no longer turns. (Author's collection.)

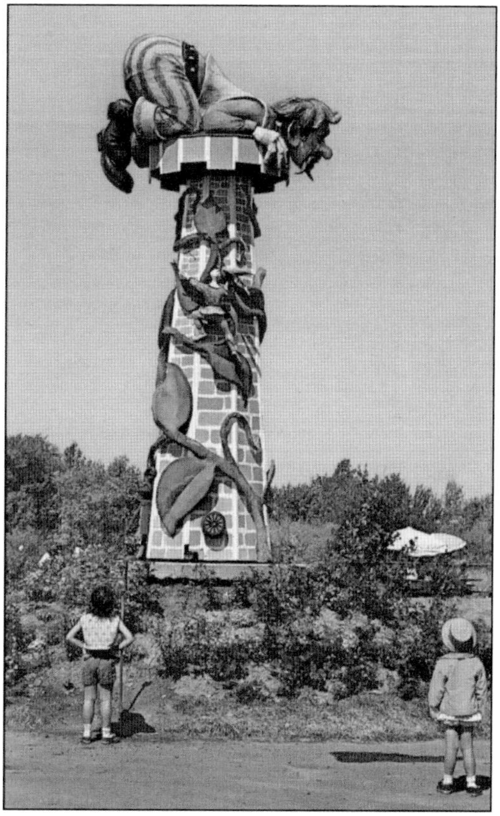

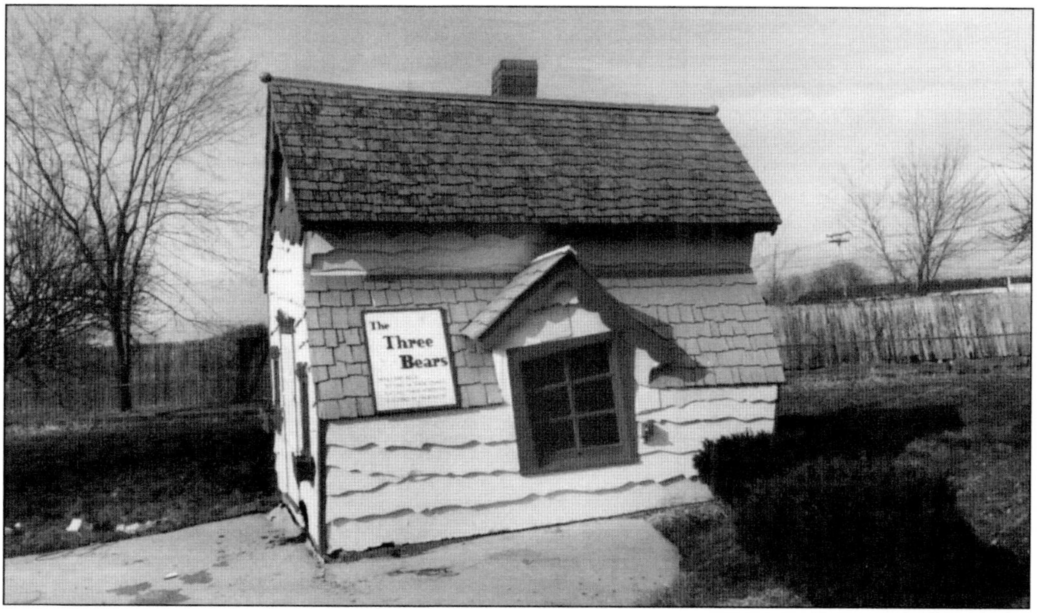

Small storybook houses had windows children could look through to see the characters inside. A push of a button (to the right of the window) animated the characters accompanied by a song, bringing them to life. The three bears turned their heads and moved their arms. Nearby, blackbirds sprang up from a pie at the Song of Sixpence house. (Courtesy MFI.)

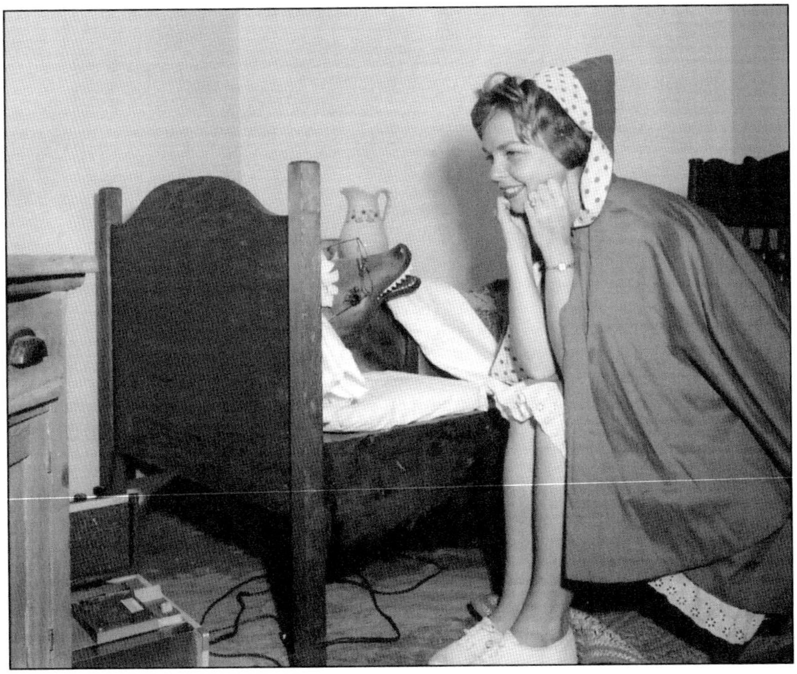

Live characters were portrayed by local high school students. Little Red Riding Hood stopped for a moment for a publicity photograph with the big bad wolf, who pretended to be grandma. Realistic furniture, curtains, and wallpaper added to the authenticity of the houses. The audio machine is hidden on the floor between the bed and the dresser. (Courtesy MFI.)

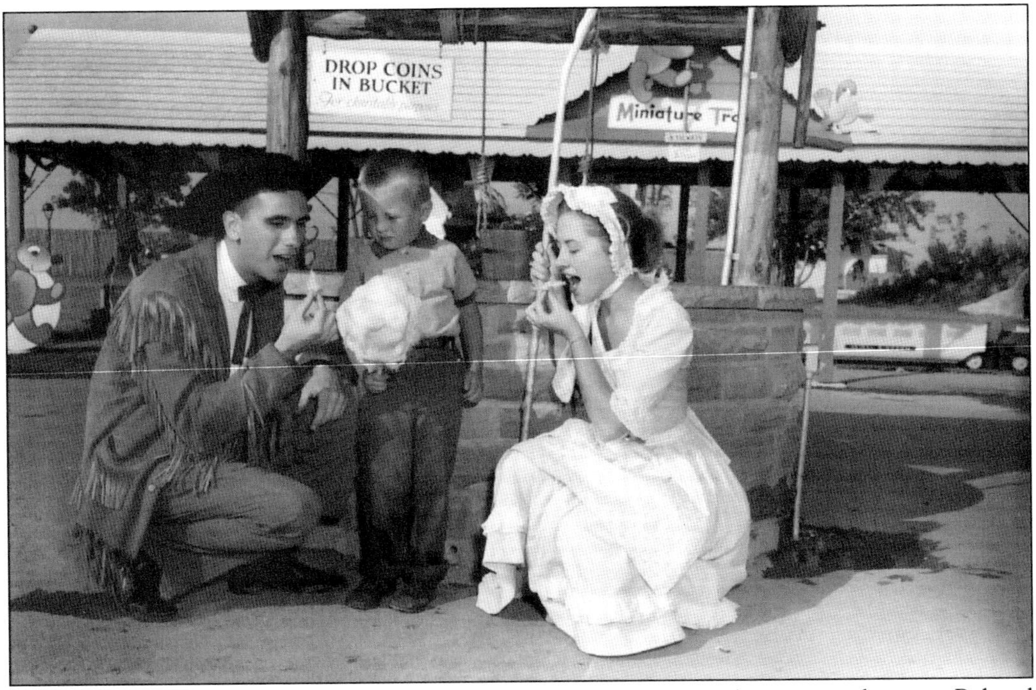

Money collected from the wishing well went to various children's charities in the area. Behind the wishing well is the 12-gauge miniature train, which chugged in a circle in the center of the Garden of Fables, passing through a miniature tunnel. This unidentified little boy is close to tears as Cactus Pete and Little Bo Peep share his cotton candy. (Courtesy MFI.)

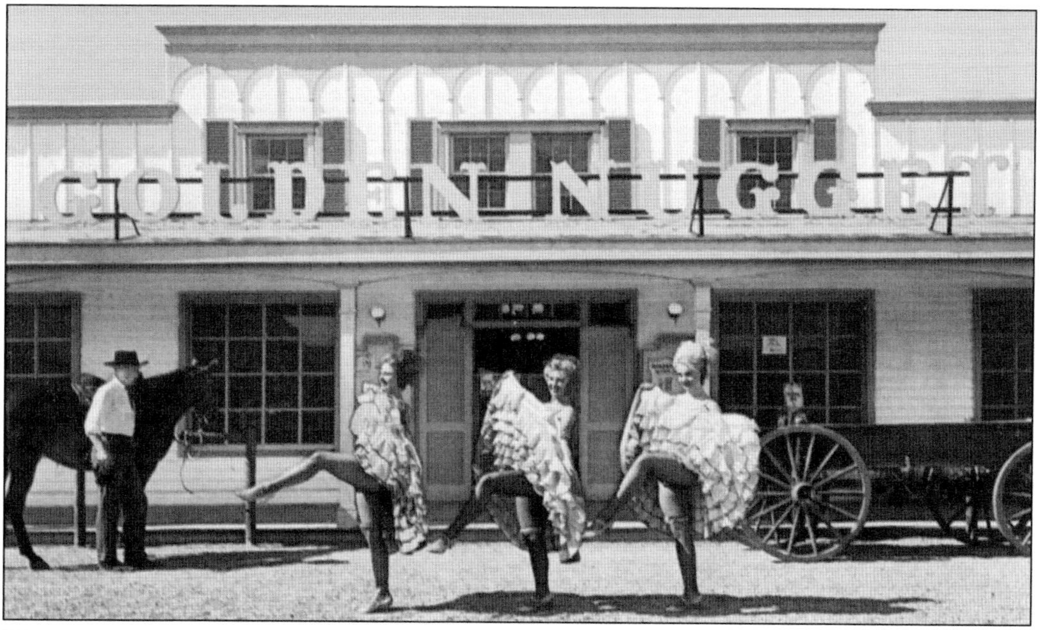

Western Town was a reproduction of an 1850 Wild West town street. Buildings flanking the street included a stagecoach stop, newspaper office, jail, livery stable, general store, trading post, and Boot Hill Cemetery. The Golden Nugget Saloon served up root beer floats while high-kicking cancan dancers entertained the customers. (Author's collection.)

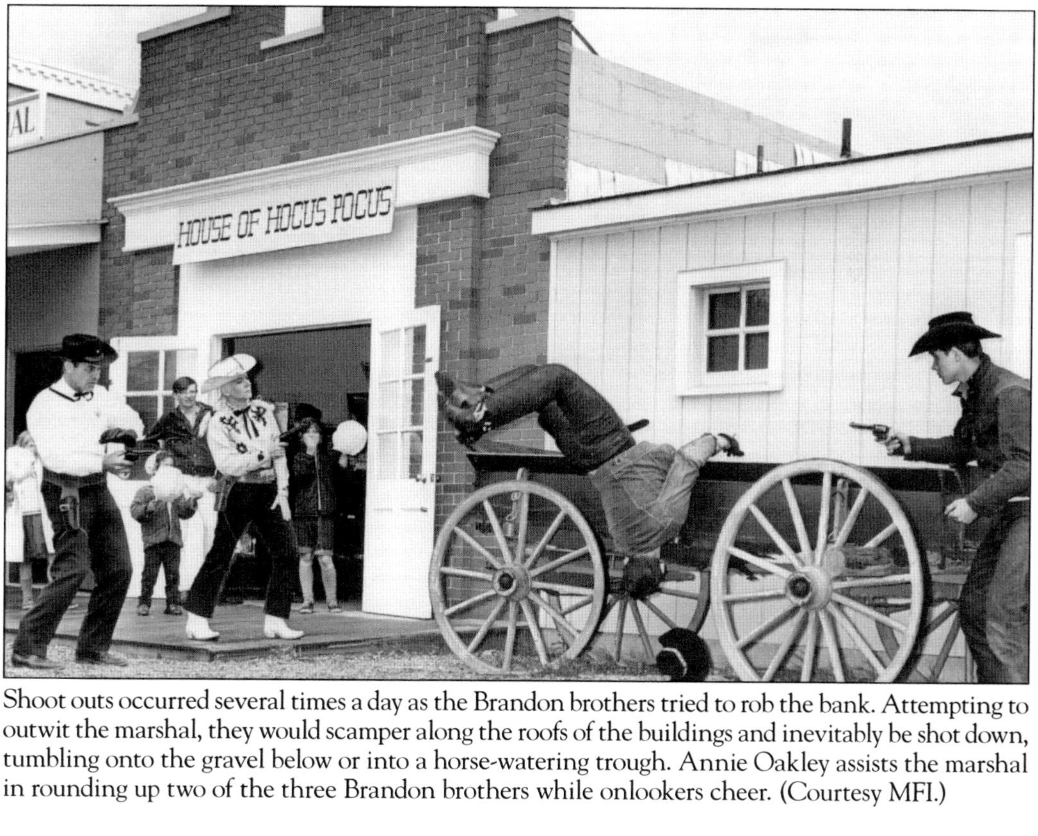

Shoot outs occurred several times a day as the Brandon brothers tried to rob the bank. Attempting to outwit the marshal, they would scamper along the roofs of the buildings and inevitably be shot down, tumbling onto the gravel below or into a horse-watering trough. Annie Oakley assists the marshal in rounding up two of the three Brandon brothers while onlookers cheer. (Courtesy MFI.)

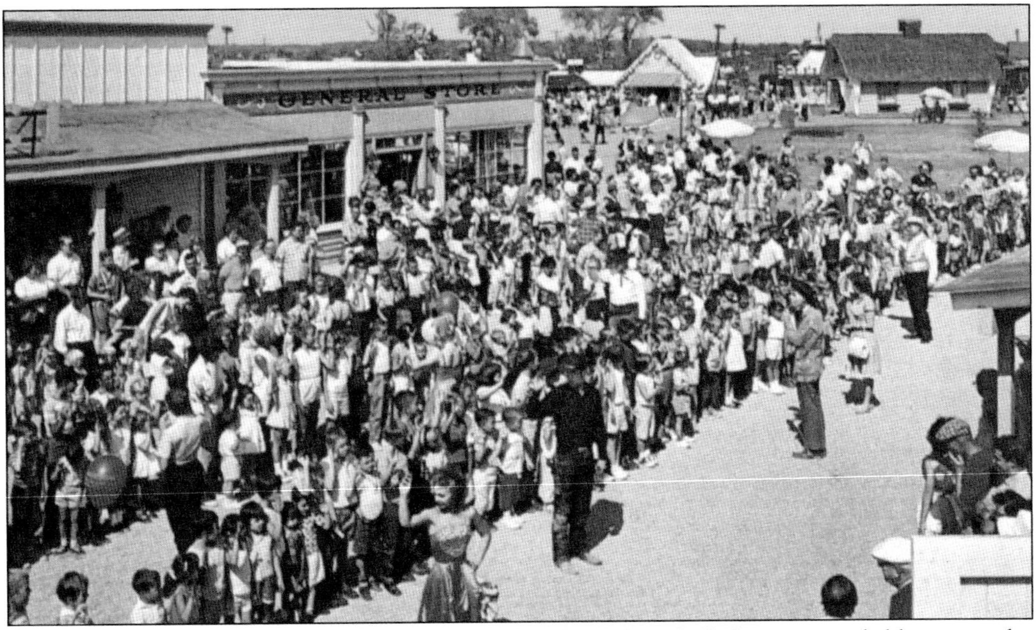

Once the Brandon brothers were in jail, the town folk gathered all the visiting children into the street for the deputizing ceremony. After taking an oath to uphold the law, listen to their parents, and always do their homework, children were given a small tin star to wear. (Author's collection.)

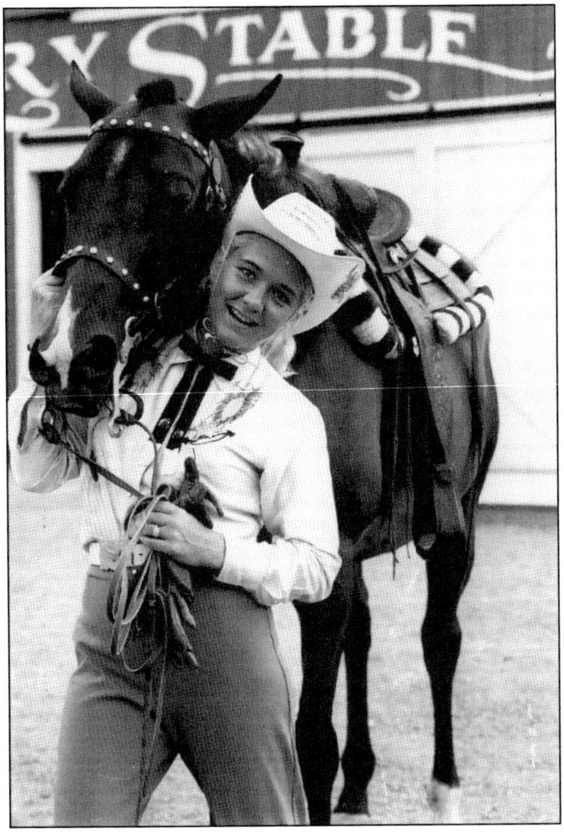

Horses were kept at the Livery Stable. Some of the more exciting shoot outs involved the marshal and his deputy chasing the bank-robbing Brandon brothers on horseback through Western Town past the Indian Village into the undeveloped area of the park. Annie Oakley and her horse often entertained visitors with trick-riding demonstrations. (Courtesy MFI.)

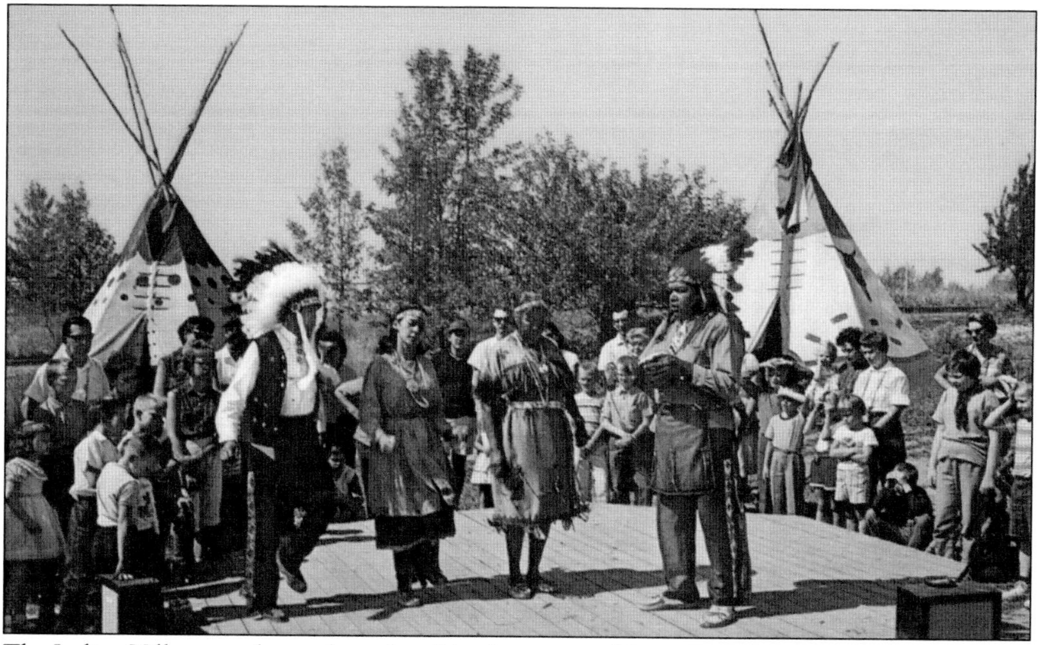

The Indian Village was located on a knoll in the center of the river and was reached by an arched bridge. Native Americans from the Seneca reservation demonstrated dancing, bead making, wood carving, and talked about the life in an early native village. Children were encouraged to join in the dances. (Courtesy MFI.)

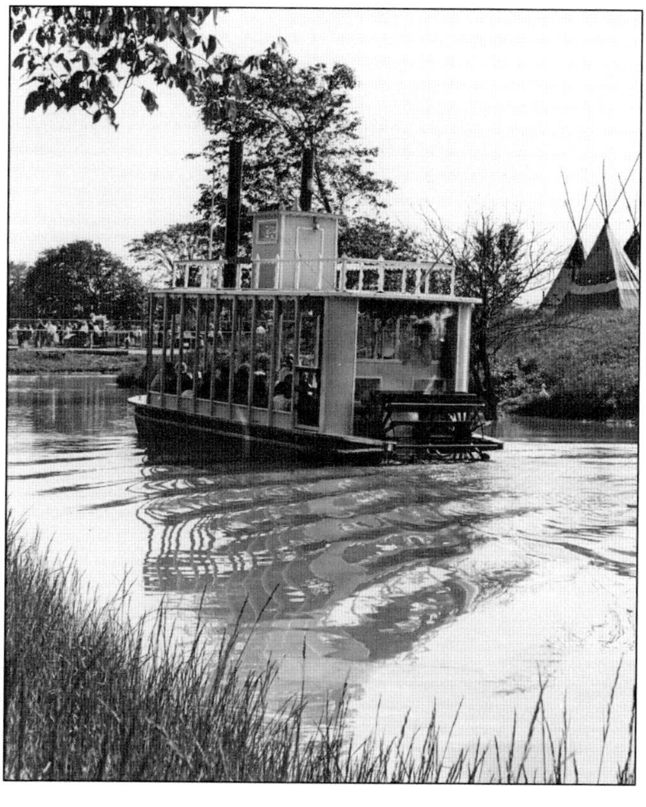

The Mississippi River paddleboat made many trips on the river around the Indian Village encampment every day. It was originally called the *Mark Twain*, but that name was changed to Cap'n Bill's Ol' Mississippi Paddlewheel Steamboat. The boat operated until the mid-1980s, when continual maintenance issues rendered it unsafe. (Courtesy BSCACEC.)

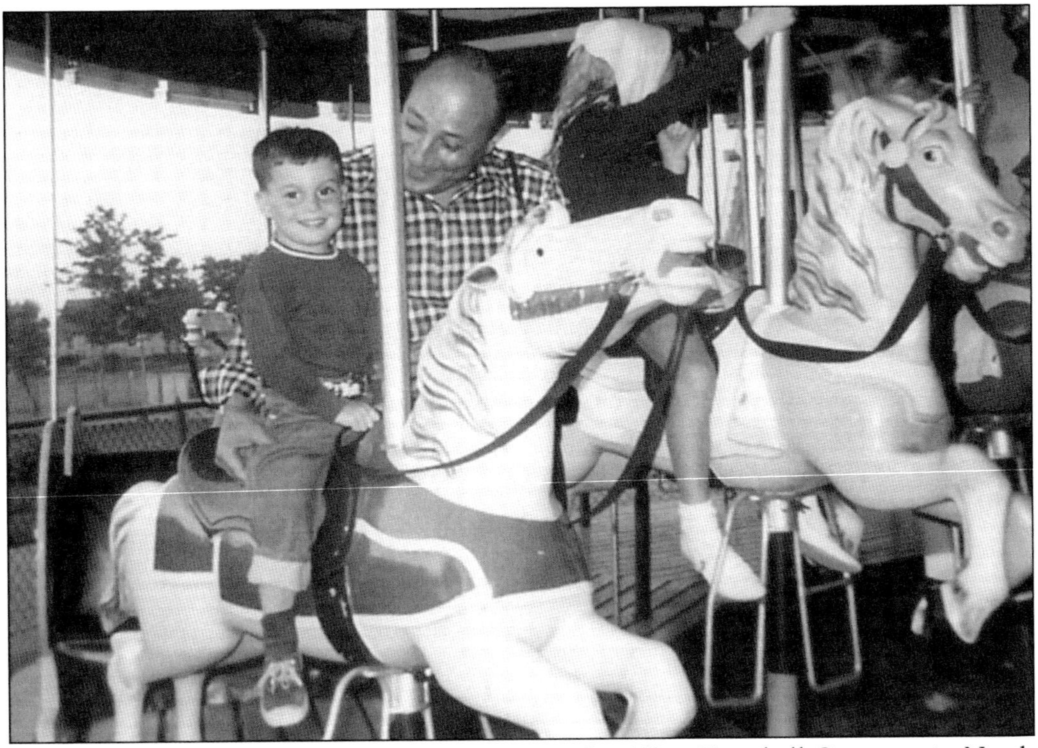

Action Town had a full kiddie ride package from the Allan Herschell Company in North Tonawanda that included helicopters, tractor ride, boats, roadway, pony-cart track, and a three-row aluminum carousel. Here, Murray Mintz (center) and his son Rich take a ride on the carousel. (Courtesy of Rich Mintz.)

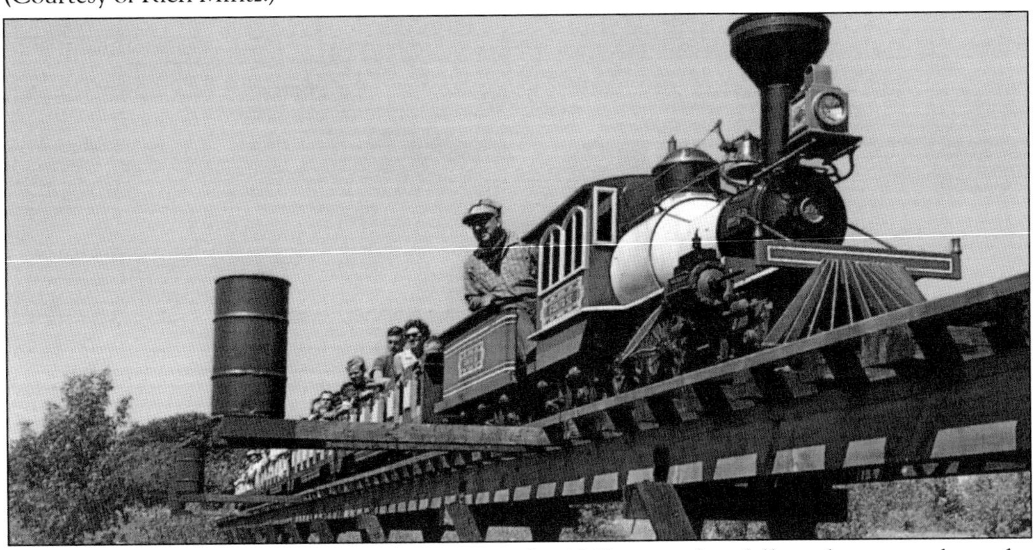

Also from the Allan Herschell Company was the 1865 train that followed a route along the north end of the park. It passed through a tunnel behind the Big Red Barn and crossed a trestle that spanned the creek. The Brandon brothers often held up the train, but the marshal and his deputy always stopped their dastardly deed before they could steal passengers' jewels and money. (Courtesy MFI.)

Buffalo television station, WGR Channel 2, broadcasted a live *Fantasy Island* show on Saturday mornings at 9:00 a.m. during the park's opening year. Clyde V. "Buddy" Farnan Jr., Fantasy Island's first general manager, produced and starred in the show as the hero, Buckskin Joe. Farnan left Fantasy Island in 1965 to manage Funtown Park in Atlanta, Georgia. (Courtesy MFI.)

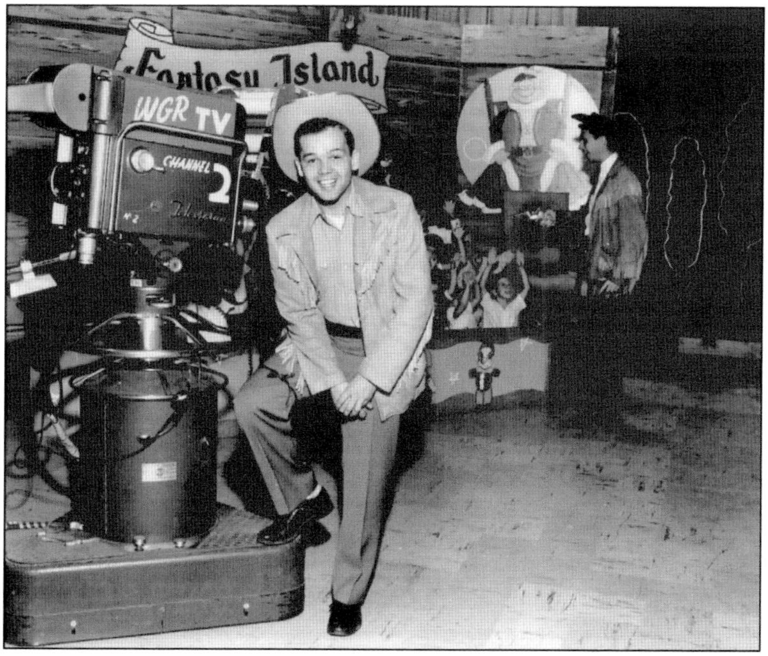

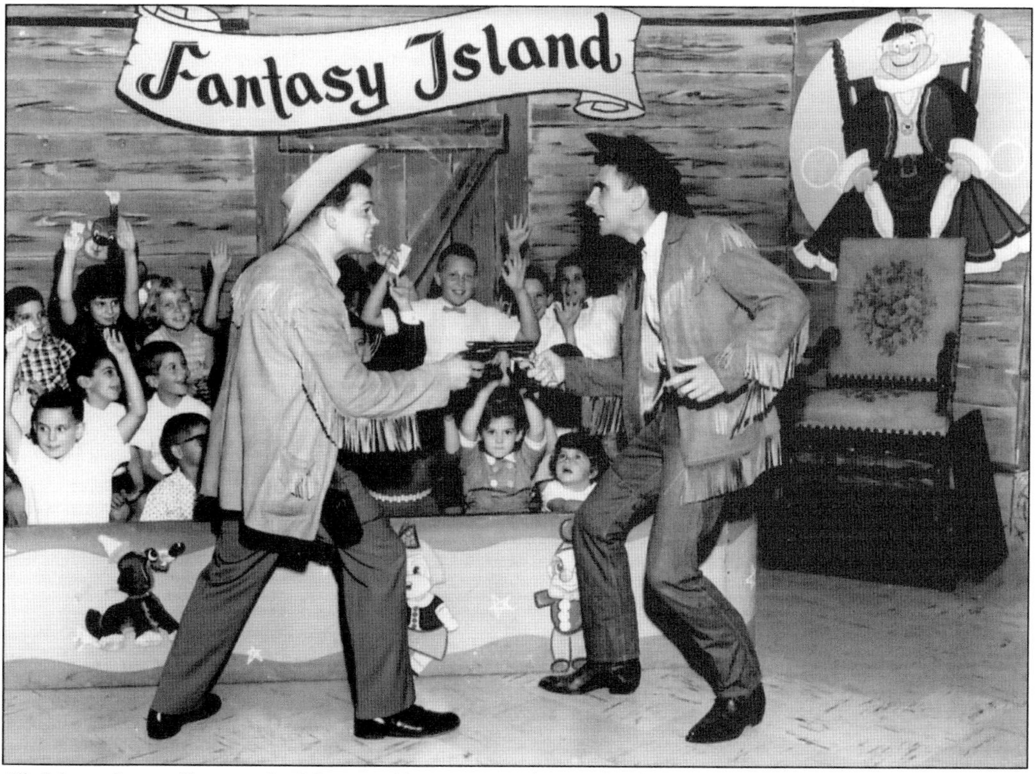

Children from all over the Niagara Frontier made up the live audience. Each child received a free admission ticket to the park. The one-hour show focused on the characters at Fantasy Island. Buckskin Joe would keep bad guy Cactus Pete in line and interact with puppets. Storybook characters like Old King Cole and Bo Peep also made appearances. (Courtesy MFI.)

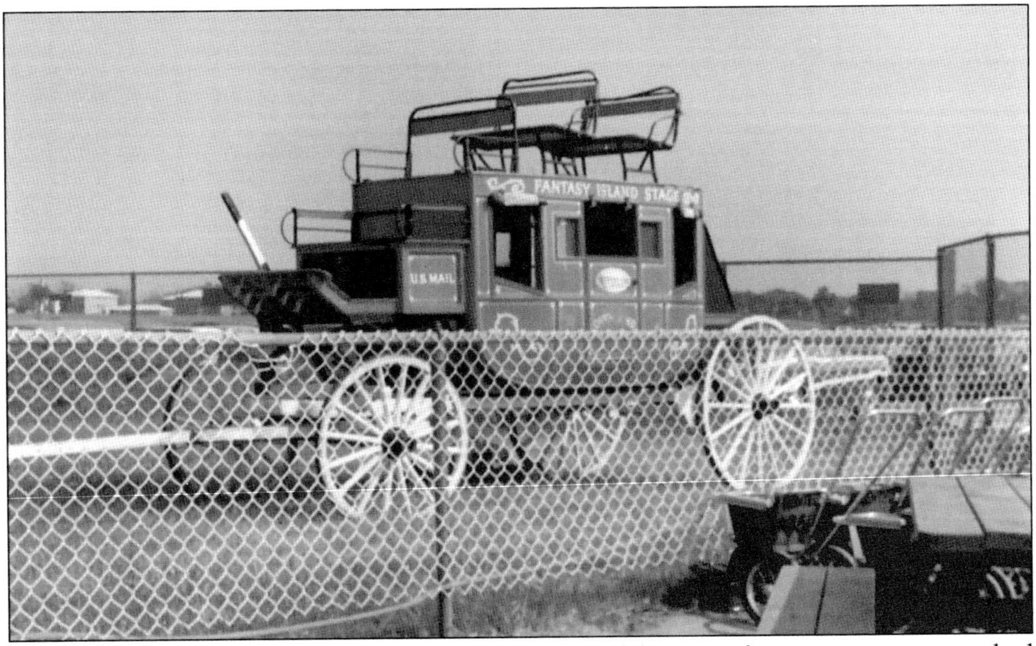

Despite all it had to offer, Fantasy Island did not do as well during its first season as investors had expected. Changes were made in 1962. A pay-one-price policy was inaugurated. Rides, shows, and attractions were all included in the admission. Gate attendance increased. New rides were added, including a stagecoach ride that went deep into the farthest area of the park. (Courtesy MFI.)

Improvements continued the following season. A new entrance gate with admission booths was acquired from the 1961–1962 Seattle World's Fair. The Magnetic Mine was introduced. The attraction's floor appeared level, but when visitors entered, they found themselves "pulled" down to one side of the mine. The floor was actually built at a 30-degree angle. (Author's collection.)

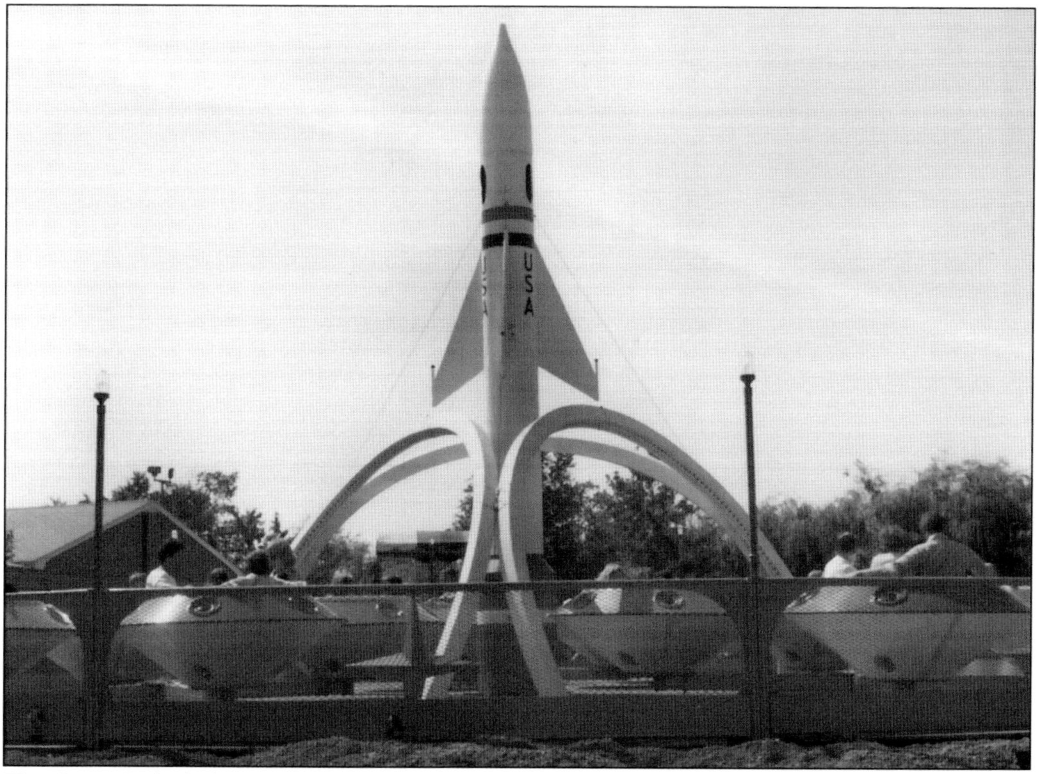

The Space Whirl also came from the 1961–1962 Seattle World's Fair. Flying saucers whirled around a central stationary rocket ship. The ride was placed at the end of the main mall, opposite the Birthday House, and was popular for many years. Riders were spun in three different directions during the ride. (Courtesy MFI.)

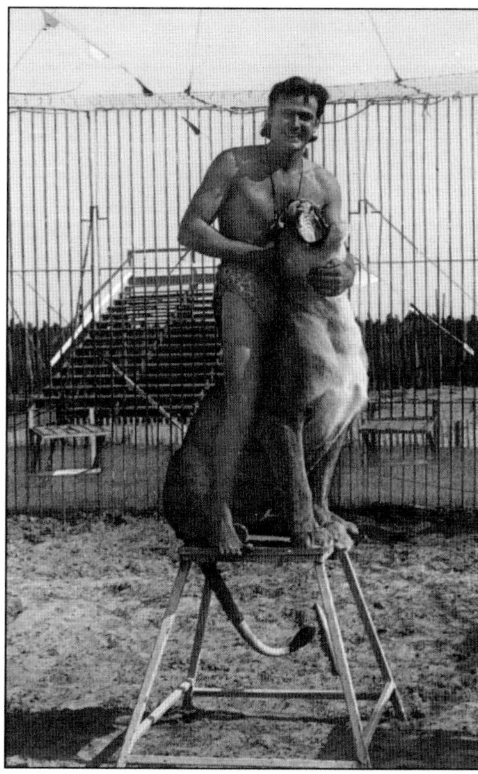

In 1966, Fantasy Island went wild with the arrival of famous French lion tamer Tarzan Zerbini. His wife, Jackie, was a trapeze artist who worked without a net. These spine-tingling shows were featured in a 2,500-seat outdoor arena. That same year, SBIC turned over all park stock to local investors. (Author's collection.)

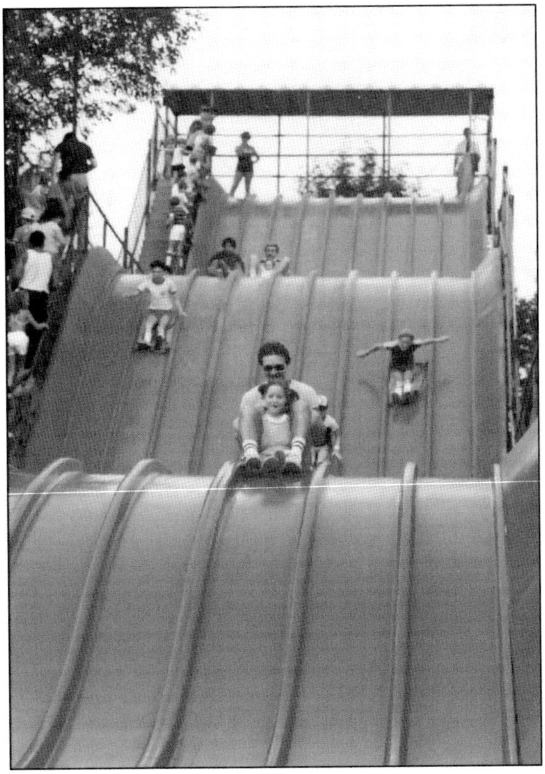

Fantasy Island owners continued to expand the park over the next few years, obtaining more land, adding more picnic facilities and new rides like the Little Dipper roller coaster and the Giant Slide. A miniature golf course was added next to the Magnetic Mine. By 1970, the park's annual gross income reached $500,000 dollars. (Courtesy MFI.)

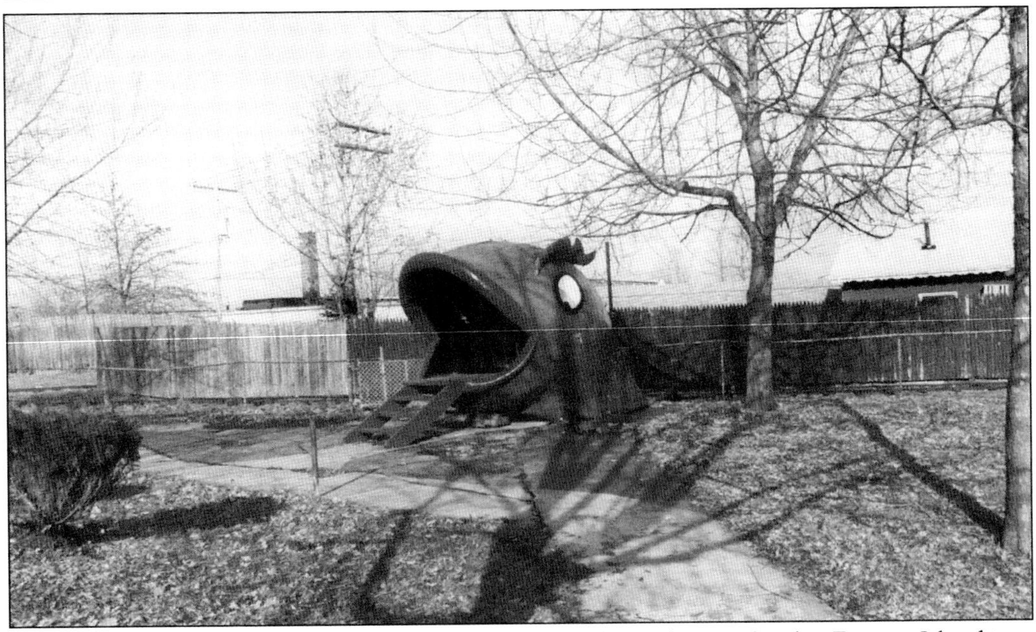

In the winter of 1972, blueprints were drawn up for grandiose plans to develop Fantasy Island into a Disneyland-type attraction. The design encompassed 150 acres of land spanning either side of the New York State Thruway and was to have areas with themes of old Buffalo and Montreal, non-thrill rides, and a long pedestrian bridge crossing over the thruway. The original themed areas were included in the plan. (Courtesy MFI.)

Those ambitious plans never materialized, but by 1974, park investors did purchase enough land to bring the park's holdings to 85 acres, a half-mile of which ran along the New York State Thruway. The Wildcat roller coaster, created by well-known roller-coaster designer Anton Schwarzkopf, was one of the first adult rides added to the park. (Courtesy MFI.)

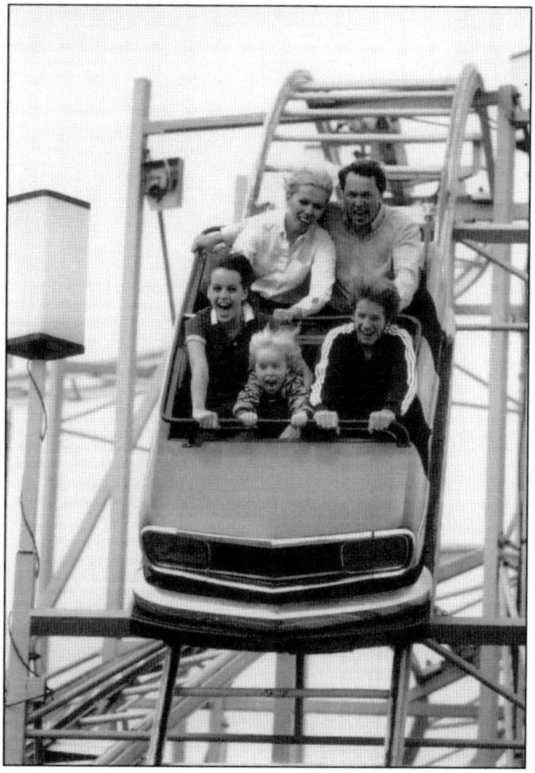

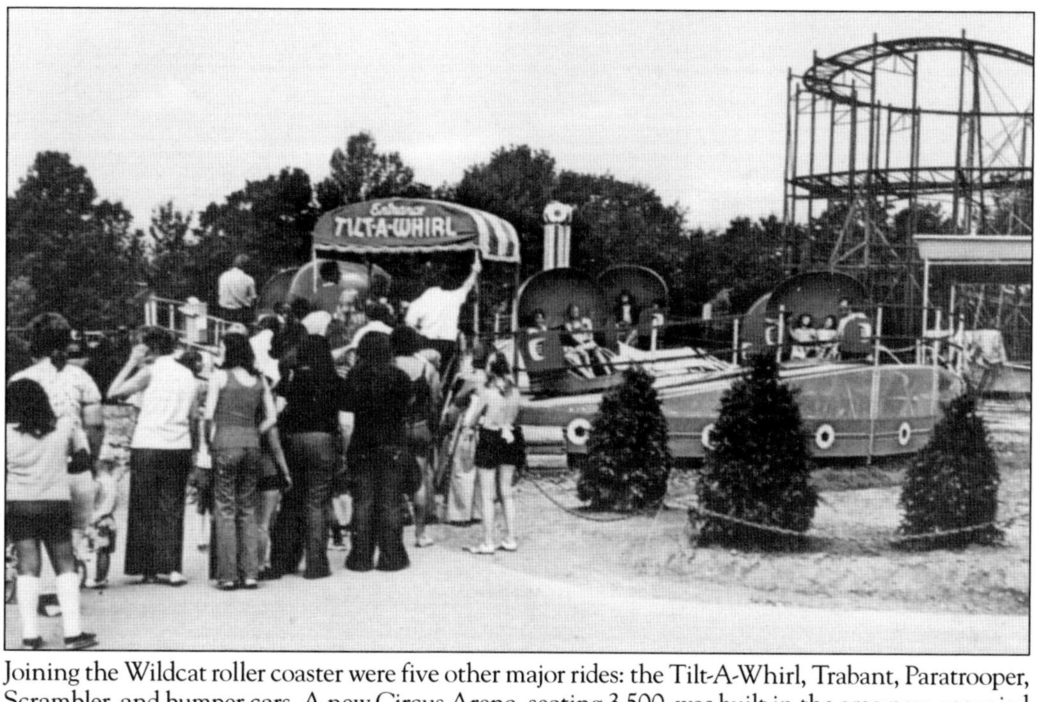

Joining the Wildcat roller coaster were five other major rides: the Tilt-A-Whirl, Trabant, Paratrooper, Scrambler, and bumper cars. A new Circus Arena, seating 3,500, was built in the area now occupied by the water park. A large game building and shooting gallery and new picnic shelters completed the new area. (Author's collection.)

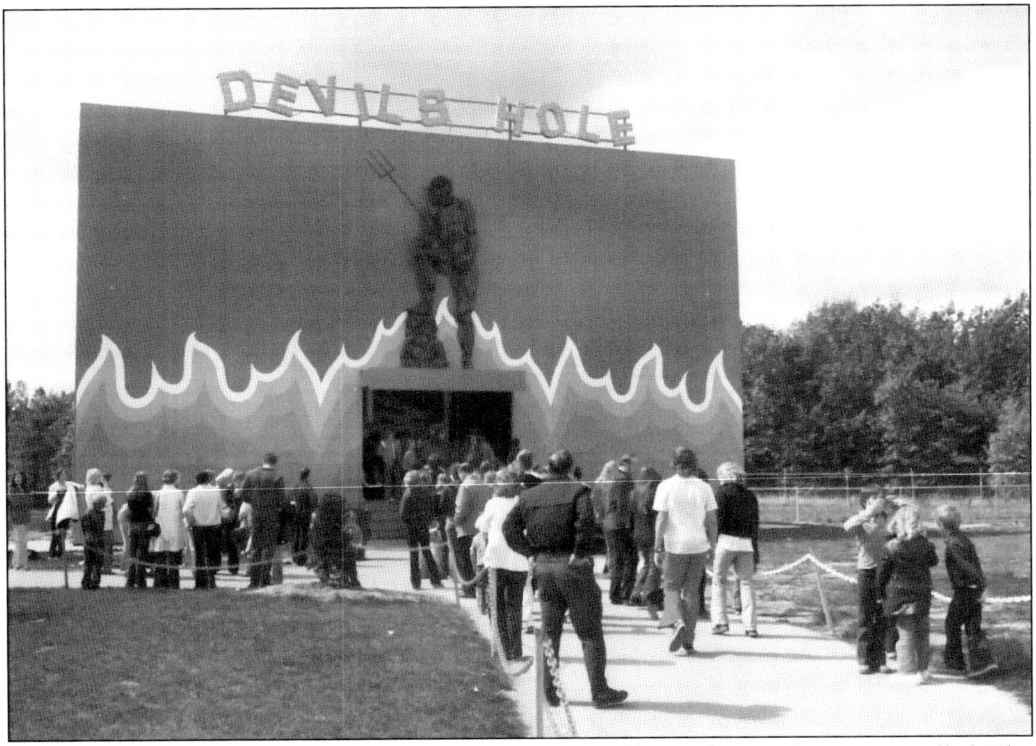

For the 1975 season, five more acres were developed and additional new rides were installed. The Devil's Hole, a very popular ride with teenagers, had a massive facade of flames and a giant devil statue hovering over the entrance. Inside, passengers stood against the walls of a giant barrel. As the barrel began to spin, the floor would drop down, and centrifugal force would keep riders suspended against the wall. (Courtesy MFI.)

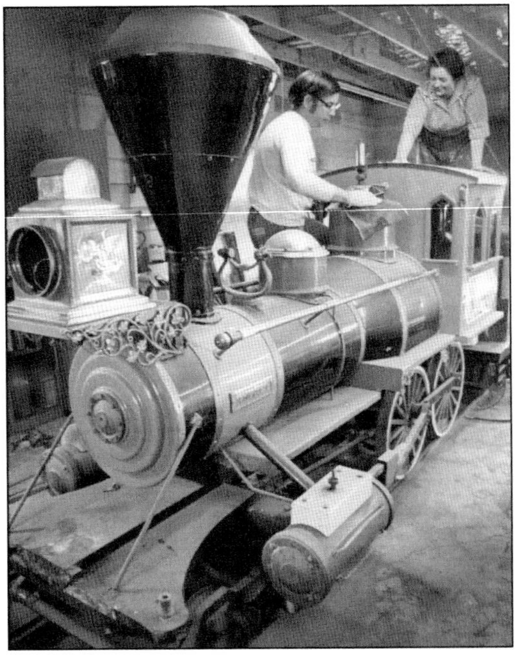

The 1865 train was replaced with a larger iron horse–style train, which had previously run at Beaver Island State Park on Grand Island. A second iron horse was added to the Fanta Se Railroad in 1974. Jim Menke (left) and Elizabeth Moyer (right) polish up one of the engines for the season. Menke was the park's puppeteer for many years. (Courtesy BSCACEC.)

Although the 1975 season was successful, the years following were less so. Expansion slowed as Western New York's economy began to decline. Efforts were made to attract customers with admission discounts and a new animated bear show. In this photograph, park president and general manager James H. Searns oversaw the assembly of the Rampage ride in 1979. (Courtesy BSCACEC.)

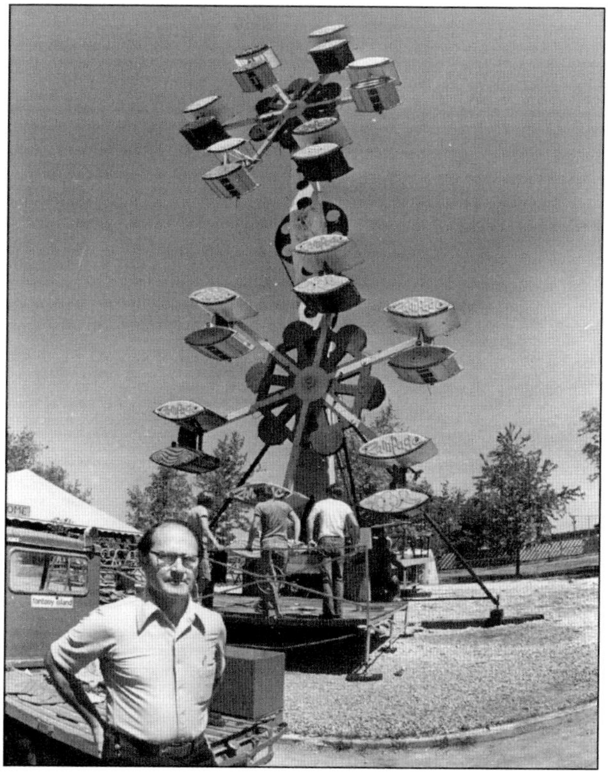

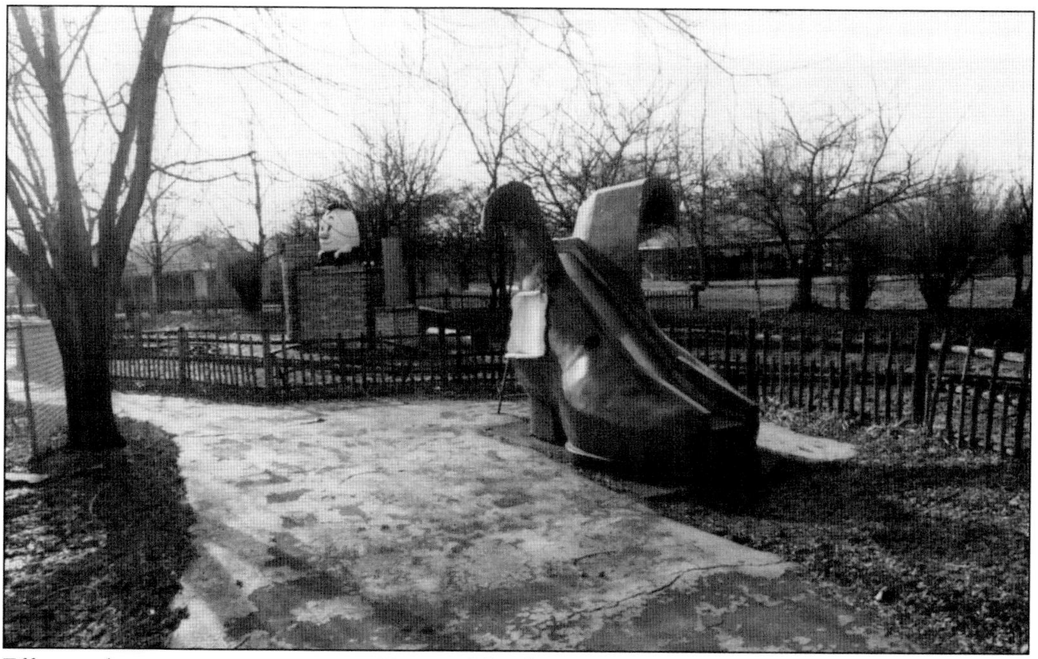

Efforts to keep patrons returning to Fantasy Island were not enough during those tough economic times. The park was unable to turn a profit, and upkeep slipped. Peeling paint and cracked walkways were unattractive to visitors. The Garden of Fables exhibits looked worn and outdated. The park filed for bankruptcy in 1982 and remained closed that season. (Courtesy MFI.)

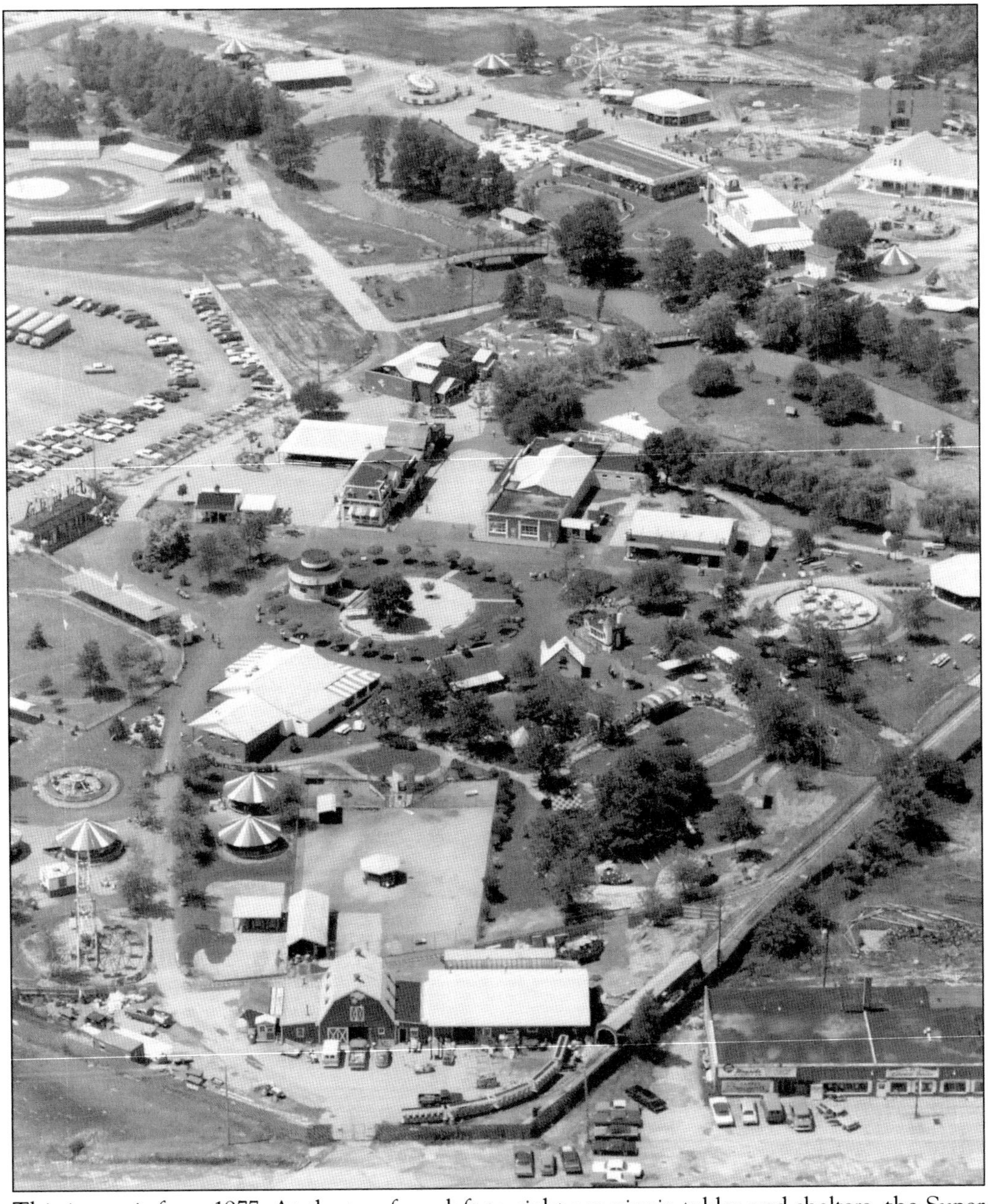

This image is from 1977. At the top from left to right are picnic tables and shelters, the Super Spiral, snack stand, restrooms, Paratrooper, game booth, Scrambler, Devil's Hole, another game building, and Tilt-A-Whirl. In front of the snack stand are the bumper cars, a games stand, observation tower, and the Giant Slide. The outdoor arena is in the upper left of the image. The broad walkway directly behind the arena was part of the old stagecoach route. In the center from left to right are the train station, the Birthday House, now a performance stage, Garden of Fables, Little Dipper roller coaster, and the Space Whirl. At the bottom from left to right are Action Town, Animal Kingdom, and the Big Red Barn, which had been converted into a maintenance building. The train route no longer ran behind the barn and through a tunnel, but between the barn and Animal Kingdom instead. (Courtesy MFI.)

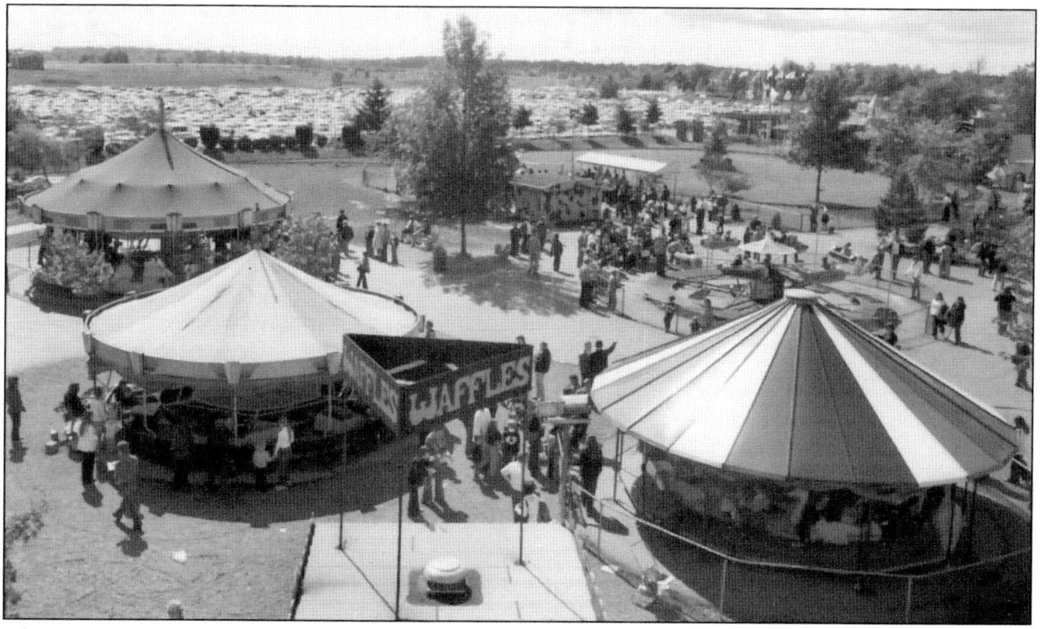

Chemical Bank, the park's largest creditor, took over the park and put it up for sale in 1982. Charley Wood, owner of the Great Escape and Gaslight Village in Lake George, New York, purchased Fantasy Island. Wood, born and raised in Lockport, had always wanted to build an amusement park in Western New York. On November 23, 1982, he held a festival in Buffalo celebrating the purchase. (Courtesy MFI.)

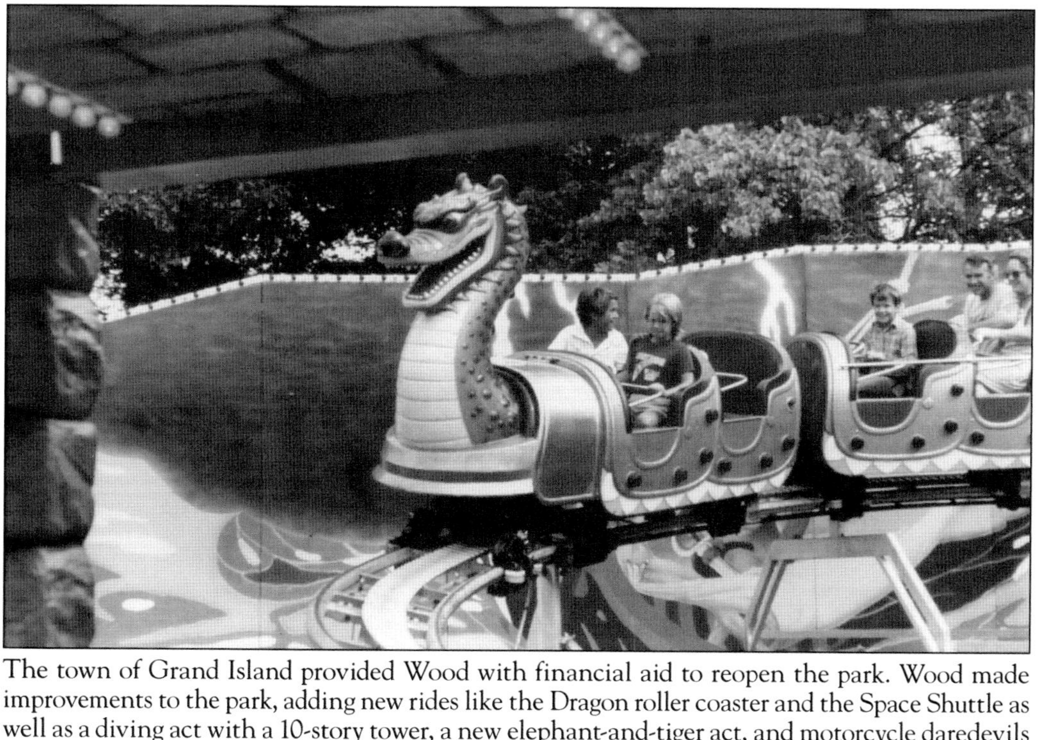

The town of Grand Island provided Wood with financial aid to reopen the park. Wood made improvements to the park, adding new rides like the Dragon roller coaster and the Space Shuttle as well as a diving act with a 10-story tower, a new elephant-and-tiger act, and motorcycle daredevils who rode their bikes inside the Globe of Death. (Courtesy MFI.)

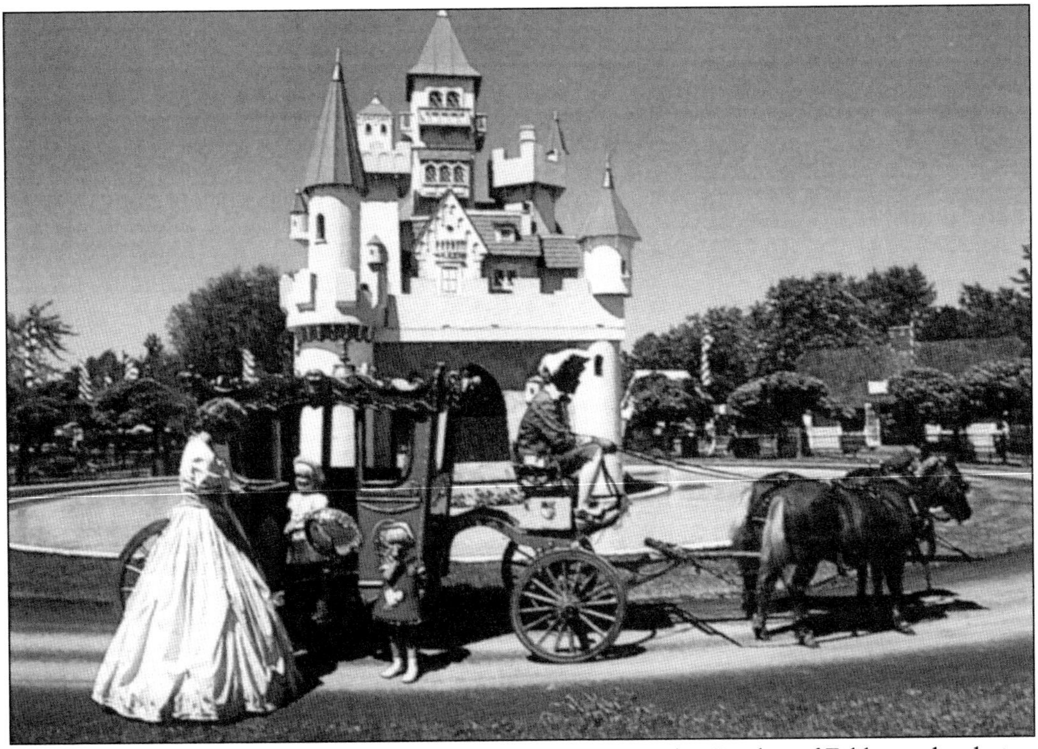

Wood called upon his friend, artist Arto Monaco, to restore the Garden of Fables and redesign the area once occupied by the Birthday House. Monaco created a fanciful castle surrounded by a moat and brought in the Coronation Coach and his whimsical trackless train from his own defunct park, The Land of Makebelieve. Here Cinderella prepares to take a coach ride with two young visitors. (Author's collection.)

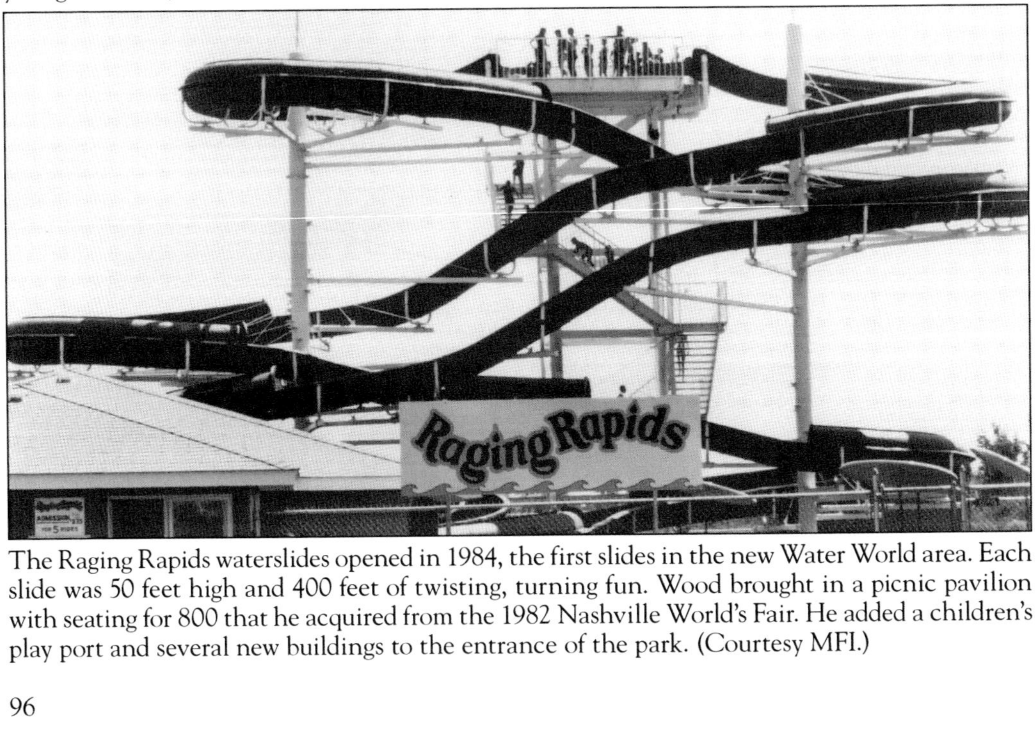

The Raging Rapids waterslides opened in 1984, the first slides in the new Water World area. Each slide was 50 feet high and 400 feet of twisting, turning fun. Wood brought in a picnic pavilion with seating for 800 that he acquired from the 1982 Nashville World's Fair. He added a children's play port and several new buildings to the entrance of the park. (Courtesy MFI.)

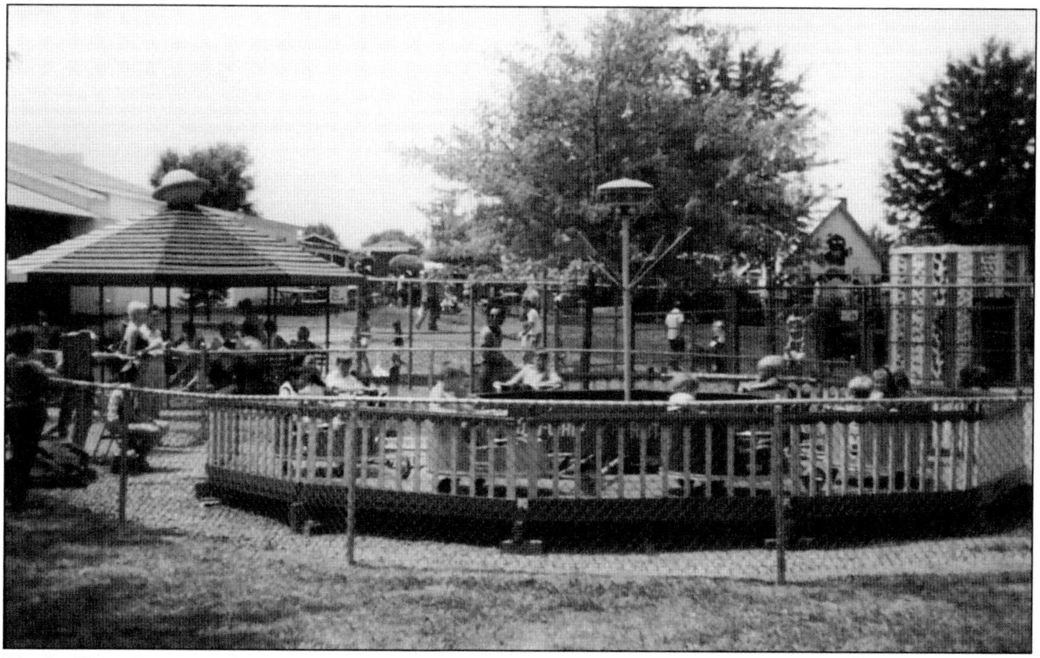

Under Wood's ownership, Fantasy Island was revitalized. With his son-in-law Tom Wages as general manager, Wood continued to make improvements, expand Water World, and obtain further acreage. Then, unexpectedly, in 1989, Wood struck a deal with International Broadcasting Corporation (IBC) and turned over ownership of Fantasy Island and Great Escape to them. (Courtesy MFI.)

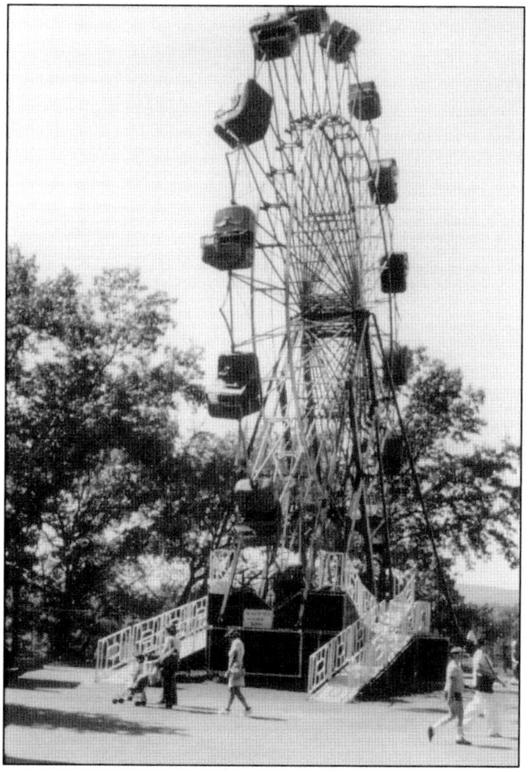

IBC added the Sky Diver, the Balloon Race, and kiddie bumper cars. The park continued to do well, but in 1990, everything began to fall apart. In June, a diver broke his back during a stunt. In August, three workmen and one patron were injured when the Yo-Yo broke down. Another accident involving two young children on the Little Dipper resulted in the removal of that ride. (Courtesy MFI.)

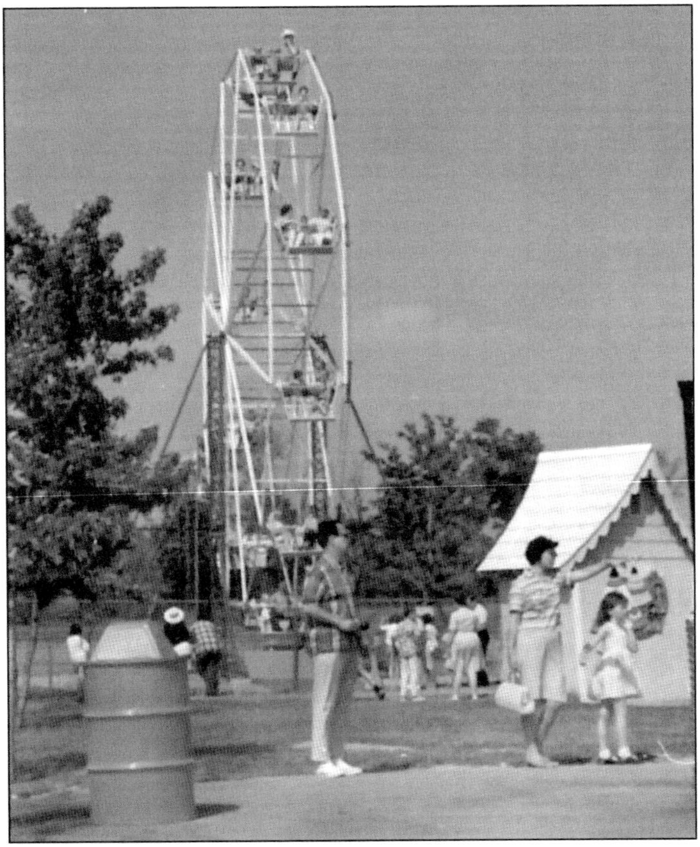

The following summer, a 14-year-old boy fell to his death when a car on the Ferris wheel broke away. Less than two weeks later, another accident occurred when two bolts sheared off an empty car on the Flying Bobs. It broke loose and fell several feet, pulling down the center paneling and knocking off several pieces of scenery. Amazingly, no one was injured. The New York State Labor Department inspected all the rides at the park and declared them safe, but employees cited other problems to the press. Parents feared their children would be injured, and attendance dropped drastically. IBC filed for bankruptcy. (Courtesy MFI.)

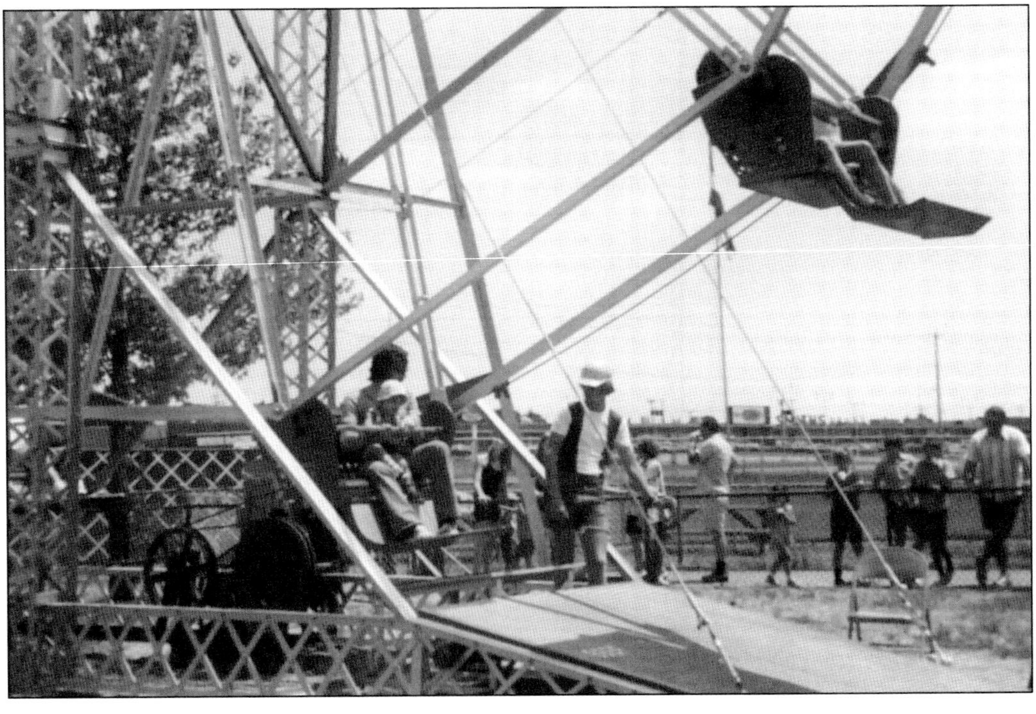

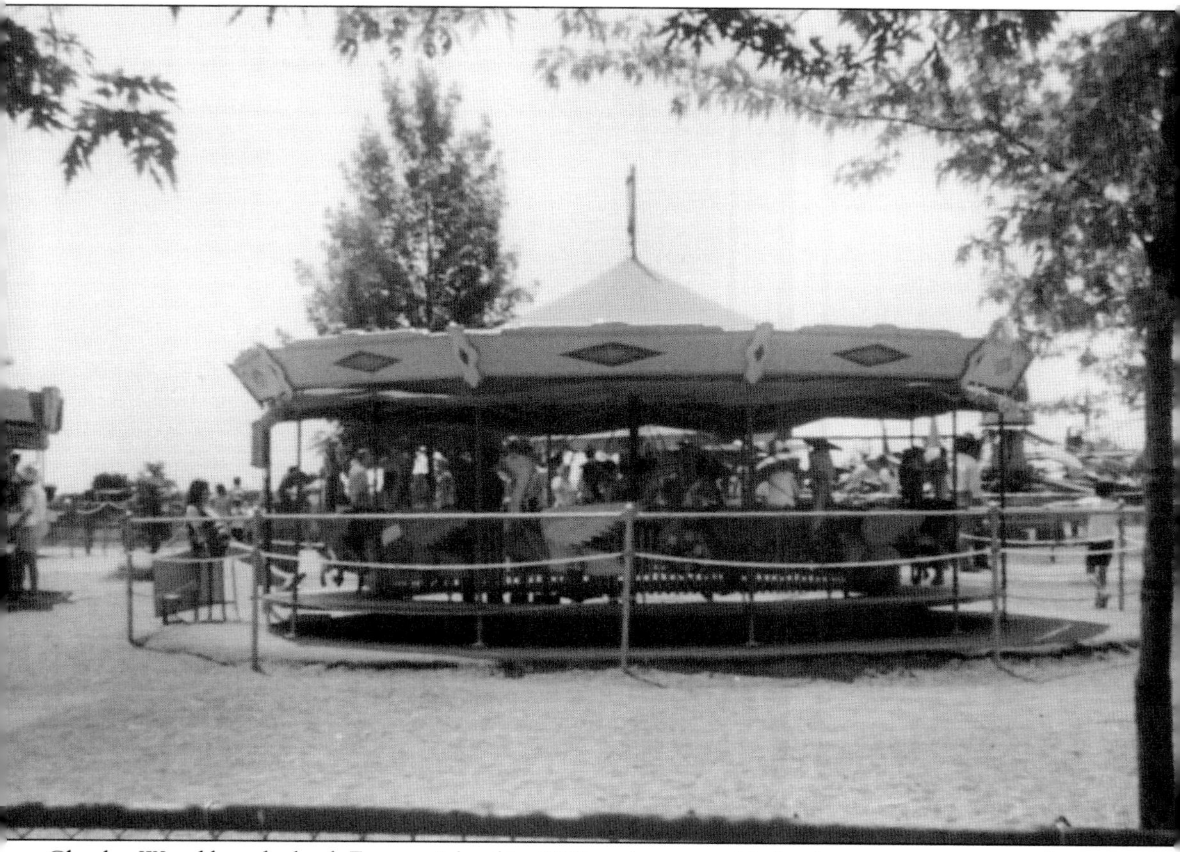

Charley Wood bought back Fantasy Island in 1992 and reopened it for the summer season under a new name, Two Flags Over Niagara. He hoped the moniker would inspire Western New Yorkers to forget the tragedies of the past two years and return to the park, but customers were still fearful, and admissions remained down. At the end of the season Wood put the park up for sale. He operated it through 1993. He said he would continue operating the park until a buyer could be found. Wood did very little to improve the park while waiting for a buyer. It continued to look and feel rundown. IBC had removed the rides where the accidents had happened and had sold several others, like kiddie favorite the Blue Goose, to pay off debts before filing for bankruptcy. There were large gaps throughout the park. (Courtesy MFI.)

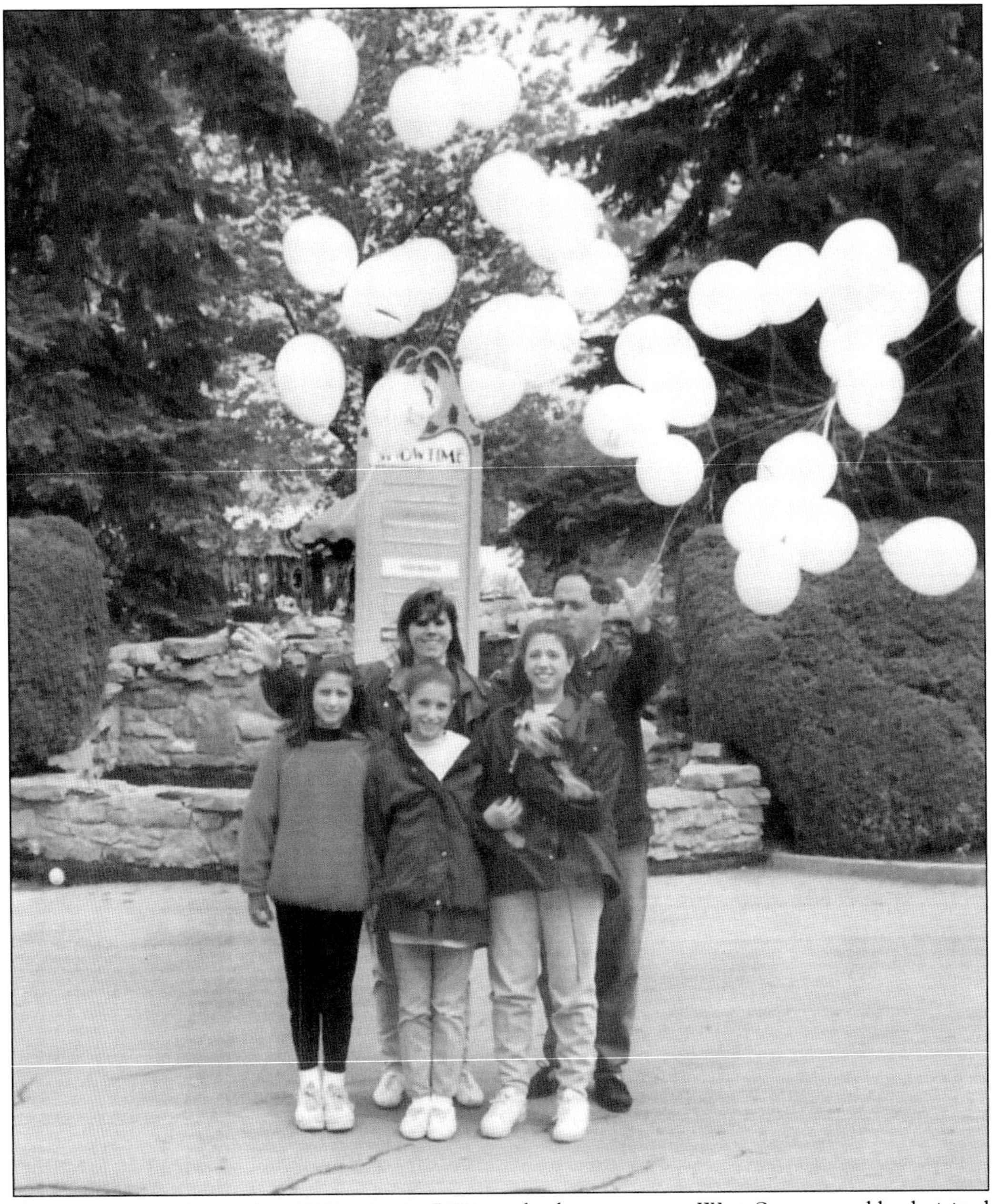

A buyer stepped forward in 1994. Martin DiPietro had grown up in West Seneca and had visited many of the area's amusement parks. At age 17, he discovered he had a talent for winning carnival games. Eventually he purchased his own carnival company, Martin's Shows. The opportunity to own Fantasy Island was one he could not pass up. His first task was to clean up the park and its tarnished reputation. He began with returning the original name—with one difference: it was now Martin's Fantasy Island. He invested money into painting and cleaning up the park, replacing old rides with more modern ones, and rearranging others. His plan was to appeal to all age groups, but specifically families. DiPietro launched balloons to celebrate the day he became owner of the park. He is shown here with his wife, Sue, his dog, Rigatoni, and, from left to right, daughters Alicia, Jennifer, and Heidi. (Courtesy MFI.)

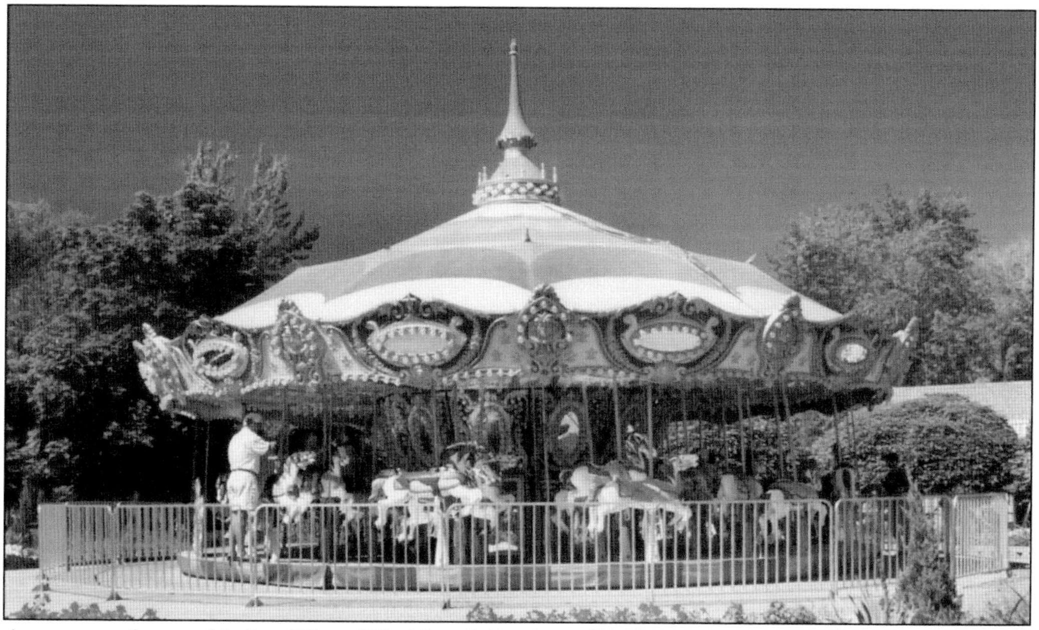

A wave pool was added to Water World and Garden of Fables was resurrected as Fableland with new animated displays like Aladdin and Pinocchio. A fancy fiberglass carousel replaced the castle, creating a focal point for the park. A giant Ferris wheel was placed at the back of the park, visible from the New York State Thruway. (Courtesy MFI.)

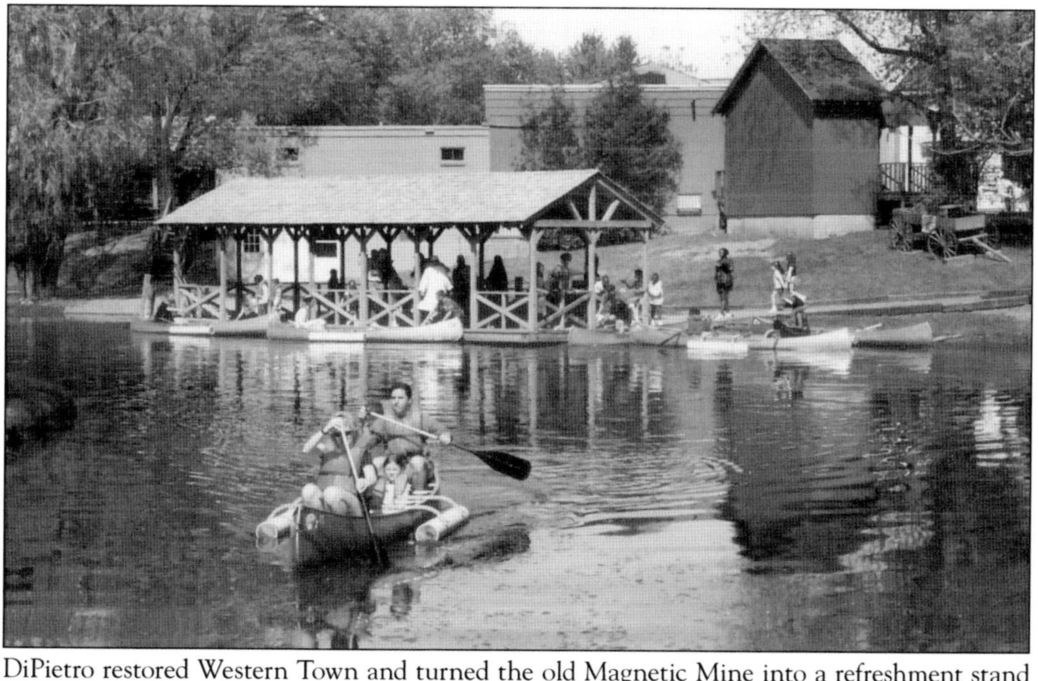

DiPietro restored Western Town and turned the old Magnetic Mine into a refreshment stand and old-time photograph booth. He added canoes, utilizing the old Mississippi boat ride loading platform. Visitors paddled the canoes around the island where the Indian Village had once been. The village was recreated, using fiberglass figures and a teepee. (Courtesy MFI.)

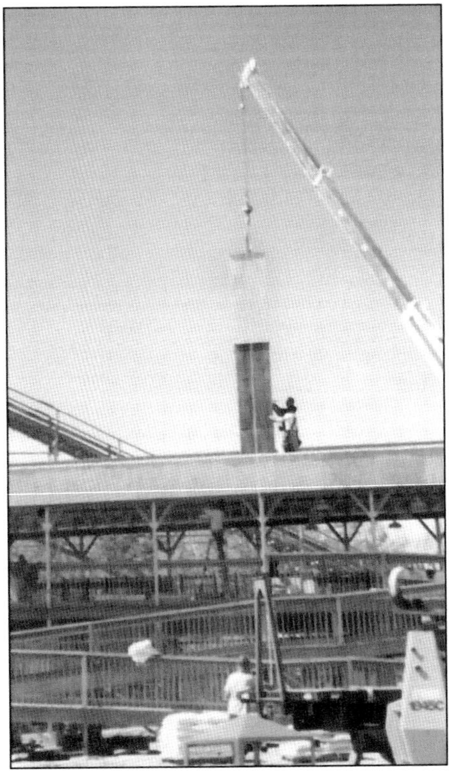

The fall of 1998, one of DiPietro's dreams began to take shape. Footers were poured for the new wooden roller coaster, the Silver Comet. Over a frigid winter, workers from Custom Coasters, Inc., erected the galvanized steel supports and laid the Douglas fir wood track. The station was a recreation of the old art deco station of Crystal Beach's Comet roller coaster. (Author's collection.)

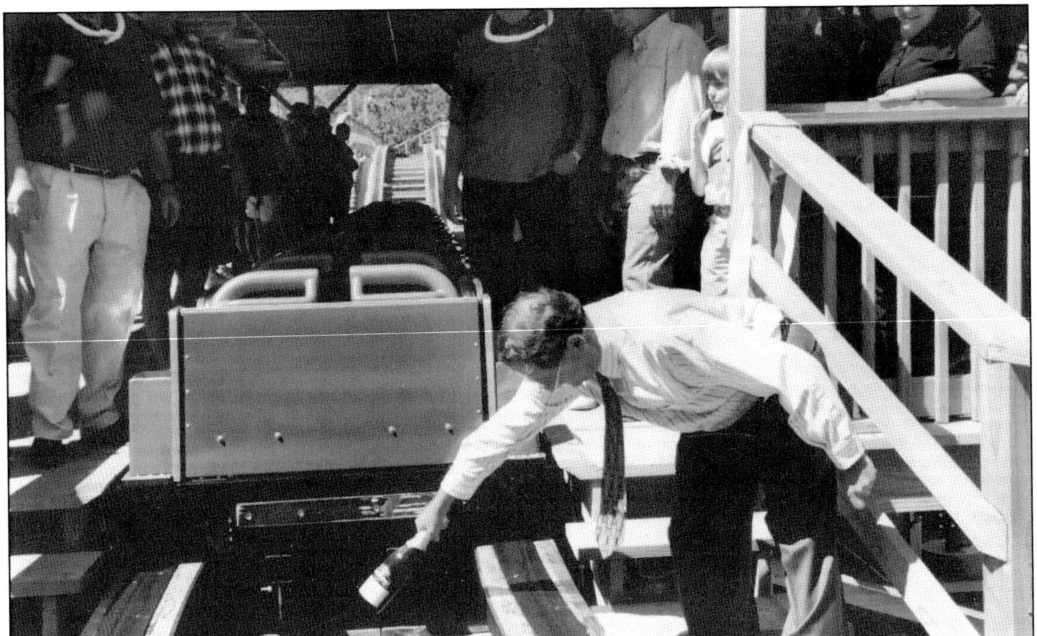

On May 11, 1999, the Silver Comet took its first test run. Workers and observers cheered as the train, loaded down with sandbags, made it all around the course without stalling. Memorial Day weekend, the Silver Comet officially opened to the public. DiPietro christened the roller coaster with a bottle of champagne. (Author's collection.)

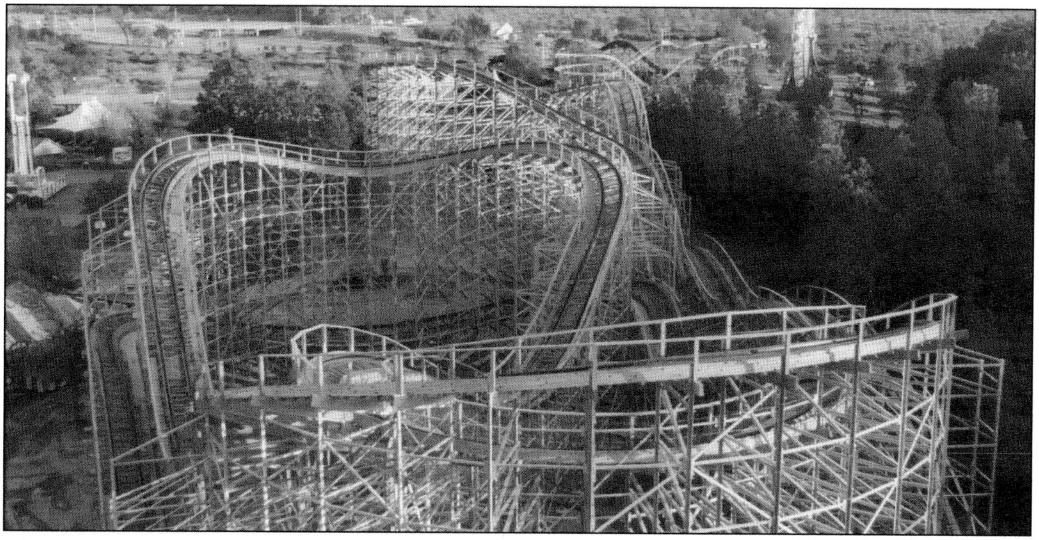

The Silver Comet's first hill rises 95 feet in the air. Riders can catch glimpses of Canada, Buffalo, and Grand Island as the train reaches the top. The out-and-back, twister configuration packs a punch with quick drops and a speedy swoop turn. The train gains momentum through the ride, ending with an out-of-control finish into the brake run. (Courtesy MFI.)

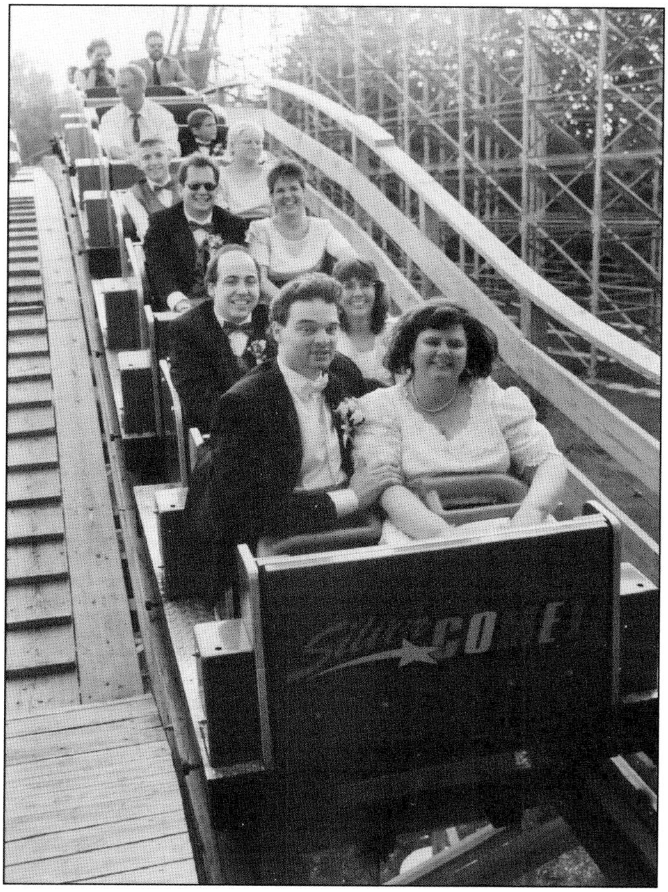

Roller coaster enthusiasts Tim and Rose Ann Hirsch rode the Silver Comet on their wedding day, September 9, 2000, along with their wedding party, family, and friends. Starting in the front seat from left to right are Tim Hirsch, Rose Ann Hirsch, Scott Zuris, Kathy Loveland, Steve Skidmore, Belinda Houck, Carl Ruchalski, Colleen Ruchalski, Ted Regluski, Joel Regluski, Mary Ann Pendrys, and Mark Loveland. (Author's collection.)

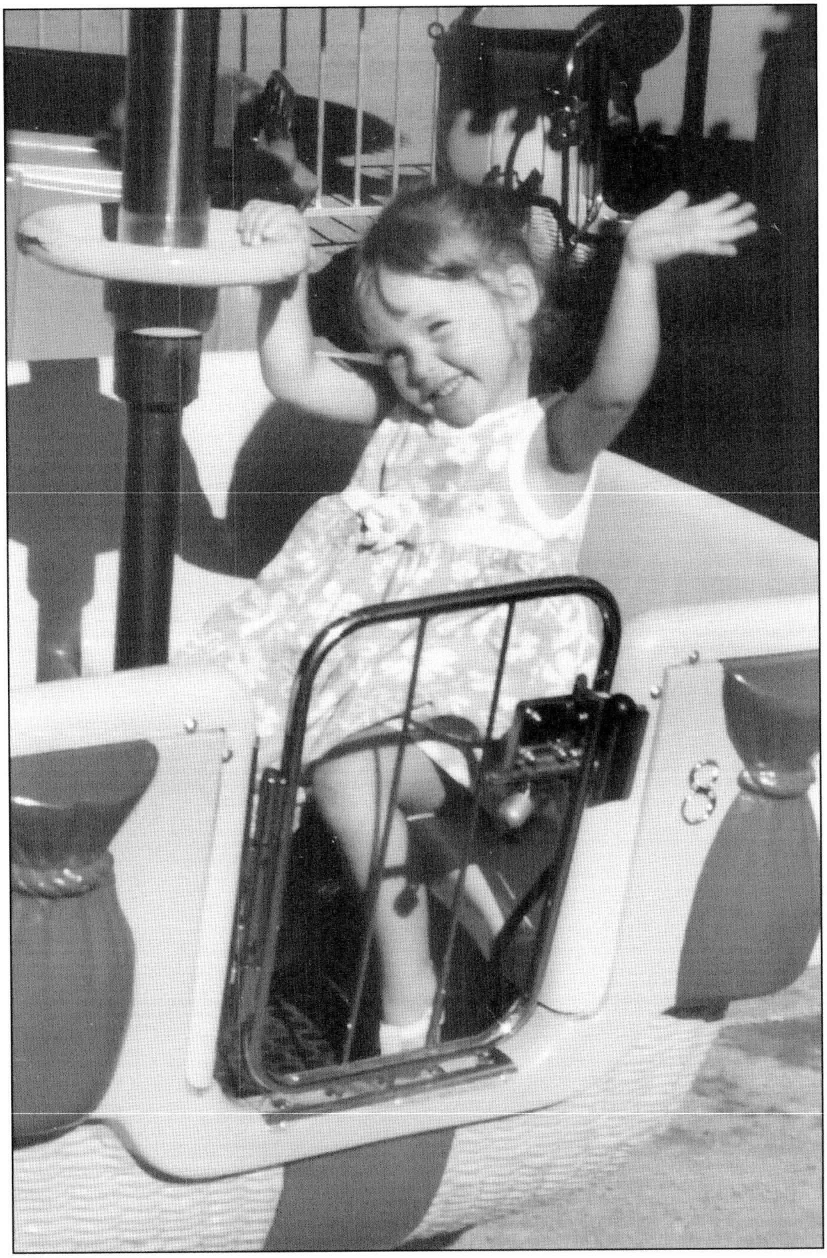

DiPietro continues to add new and exciting thrill rides like the spinning Crazy Mouse roller coaster and the breathtaking Flight swing ride as well as contemporary kiddie rides such as the Jack and the Beanstalk–themed drop tower. Tradition plays a big part in the park's lineup. At Fairytale Theater, stories are told in song and dance by the Fantasy Island Princess and friends. High-kicking stage shows bring visitors into the Golden Nugget Saloon where folks can belly up to the ice cream bar for sundaes. In Western Town, the Brandon brothers are still trying to outwit the marshal and his deputy. The original Gingerbread House has been converted into a new Birthday House. Families with young children are Martin's Fantasy Island's niche, but for the baby boomer generation, a visit to Martin's Fantasy Island is a step back in time to the park they remember and can share with their grandchildren. (Courtesy MFI.)

Seven

Fun in the Country

Buffalo businessman Paul Snyder purchased 164 acres of land with seven small lakes on Route 77 near Corfu as a getaway for his family. The founder of Freezer Queen Foods soon realized that his country property was the perfect getaway for other families as well. He developed a sandy beach on the large lake, hired lifeguards, built a refreshment stand, and around 1955, opened Darien Lake to the public as a picnic park with "excellent swimming." In 1964, he added 23 campsites, accommodating tents and trailers, and put up a small restaurant.

After a Cornell University study recommended developing the property into a large camping facility, Snyder began turning Darien Lake into a resort that would attract patrons from all over New York State. He purchased more land, expanding the resort's holdings to 1,000 acres, and added more attractions. A representative of Huss Trading Corporation of Switzerland was impressed with Snyder's vision for a theme park, and in 1980, the two parties signed a seven-year agreement in which Huss would provide Darien Lake with 17 major rides and a waterslide complex, and Snyder would pay Huss a percentage of the park's revenue. A theme park was born.

Over time, the park has undergone major changes that have brought it into the foreground as one of New York State's finest theme parks. Radical roller coasters on the edge of technology as well as an assortment of thrill rides appeal to a wide audience looking for a day of excitement in the country.

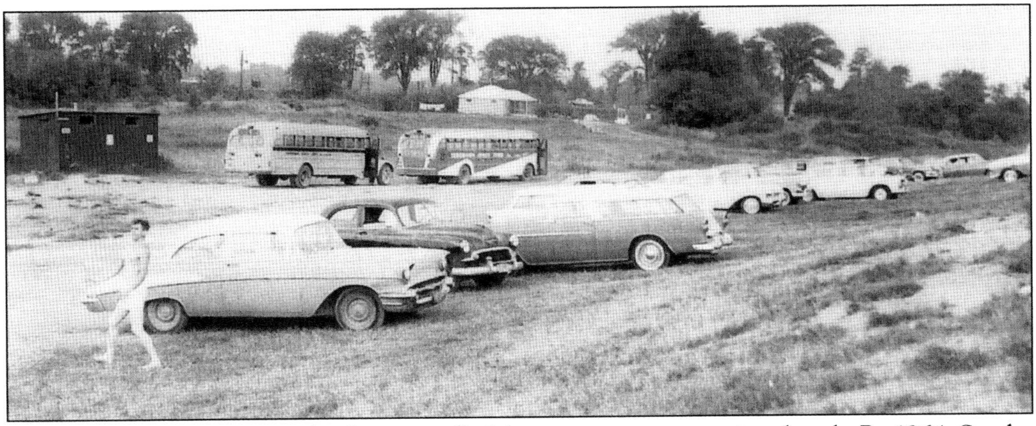

This image shows Darien Lake during its fledgling years as a recreational park. By 1964, Snyder had added campsites, a clubhouse, a general store, a baseball diamond, tennis courts, basketball courts, and children's playground equipment. During the 1970s, the NBA's Buffalo Braves practiced at Darien Lake. (Courtesy DLR.)

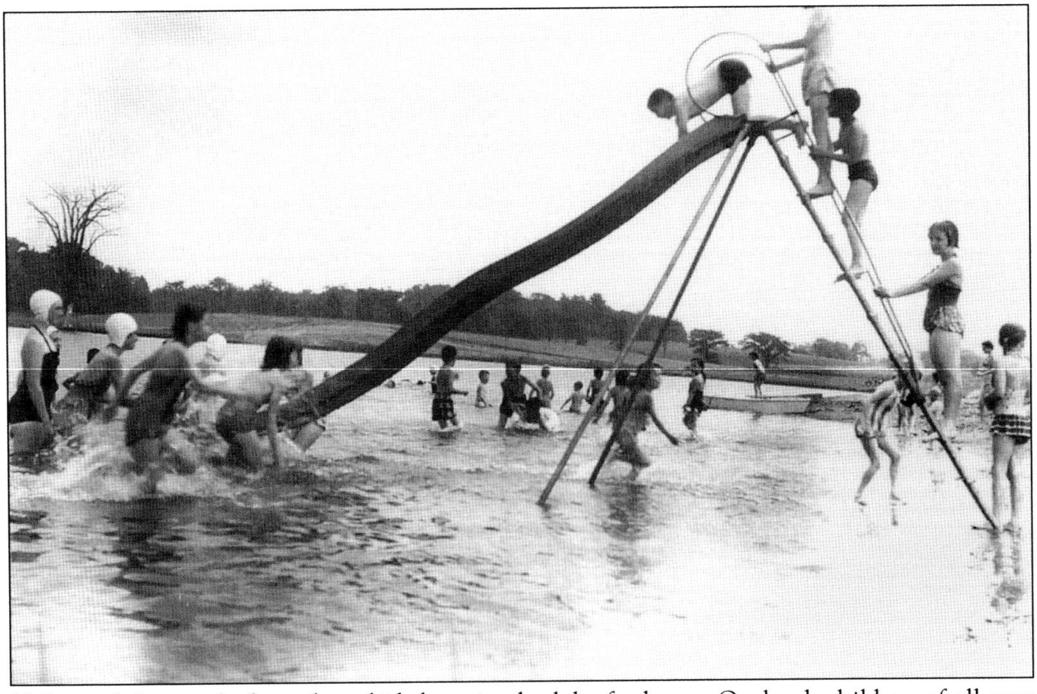

Slides and diving platforms kept kids busy in the lake for hours. On land, children of all ages could enjoy arcade games, air hockey, and billiards in the clubhouse. Cartoons and movies were shown in the clubhouse, which also had a snack stand and general store that provided campers with needed items. (Courtesy DLR.)

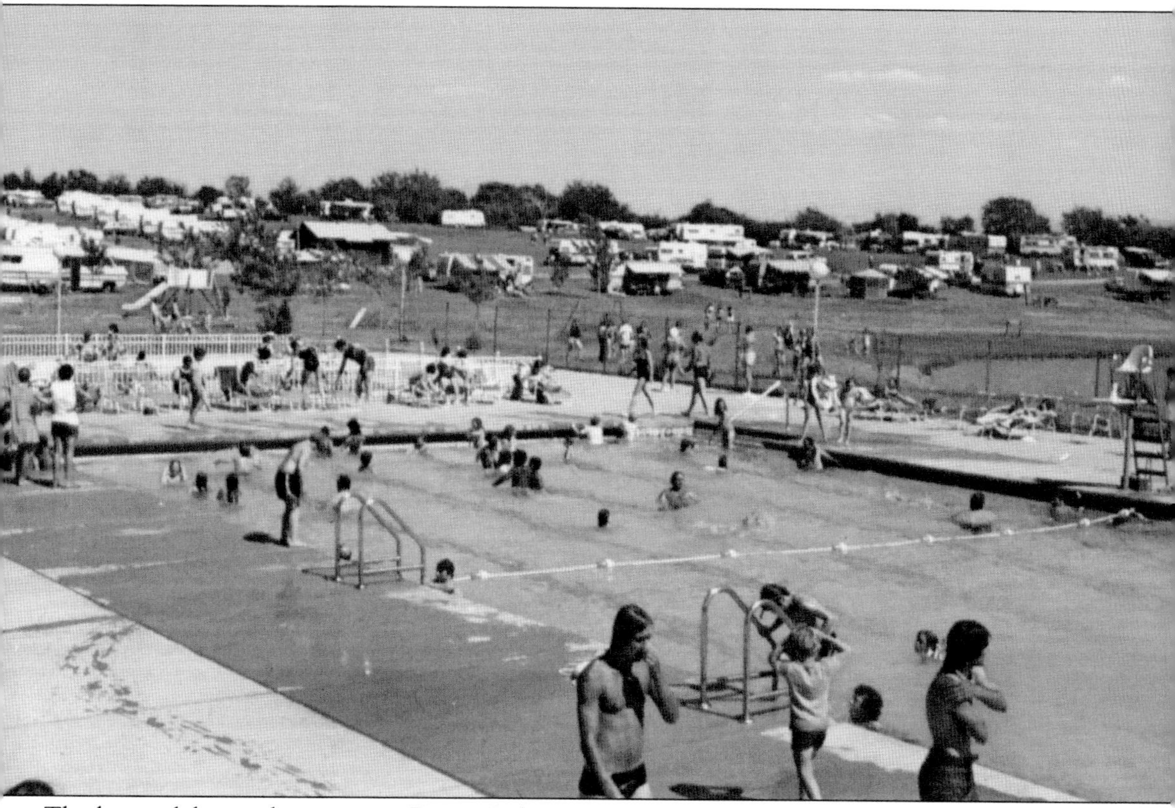

The largest lake on the property, Darien Lake, continued to be used for swimming. One of the smaller lakes, Trout Pond, was stocked with black bass, pike, and trout. Fishing contests were held annually, attracting fishermen from all over New York State, Pennsylvania, Ohio, and Canada. In 1975, Snyder brought recreational vehicles into the park, renting them out for a weekend or the entire season. Additional activities such as horseback riding, batting cages, a nature trail, miniature golf, petting zoo, paddleboats, and a skateboard park were added for the campers' enjoyment. Near the campground, Snyder built an Olympic-size swimming pool surrounded by a large concrete patio with lounge chairs for sunbathers. Hot tubs and a children's wading pool were set in a separate area. This photograph shows the campground directly behind the pool with the rental recreational vehicles on the left. (Author's collection.)

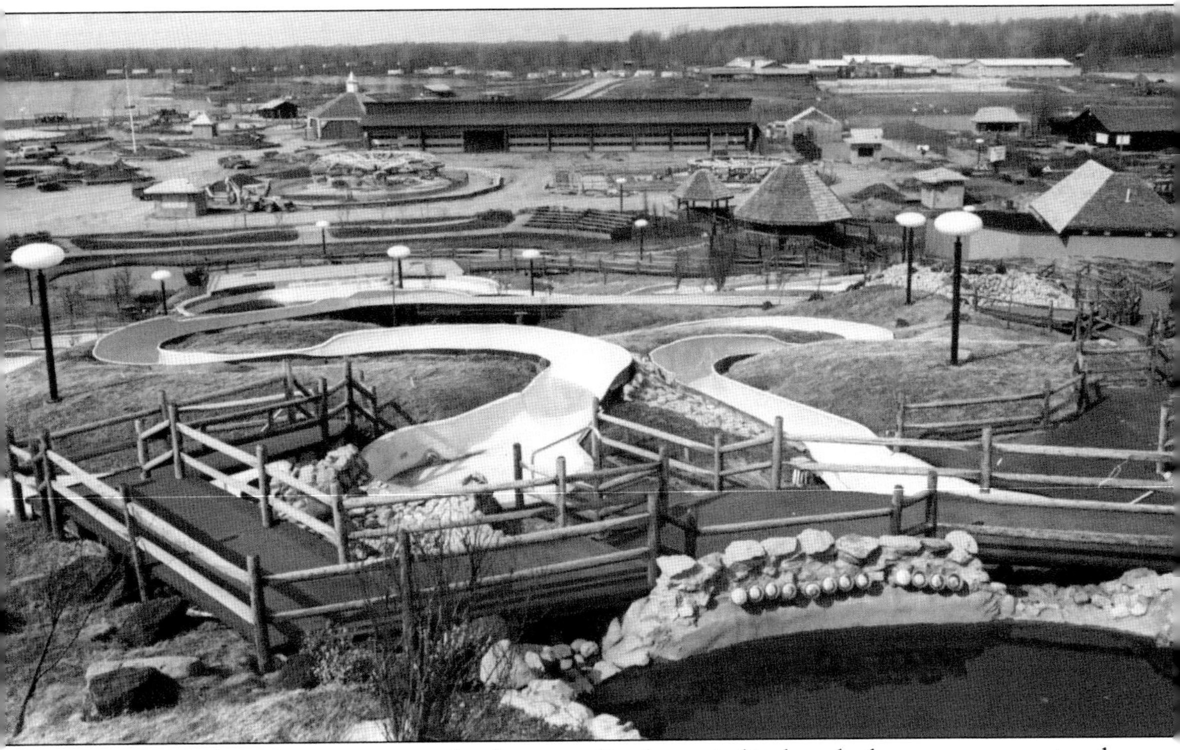

Always looking for new activities for the resort, Snyder capitalized on the latest craze sweeping the country—waterslides. In 1977, the man-made Rainbow Mountain debuted with four waterslides snaking down its side. Riders used rubber mats to slither down the concrete slides and up the banked turns. Keeping with the country theme, Rainbow Mountain had landscaping that featured shrubbery, wildflowers, decorative pools, and padded walkways with rustic fencing. Lighting was placed strategically around the mountain for nighttime sliding fun. A changing area with lockers and a snack stand rounded out the mountain's offerings. The waterslides were an immediate hit with campers and visitors alike. The success of Rainbow Mountain inspired Snyder to add more thrills to Darien Lake. The first of the mechanical rides arrived at the park in 1979, including a swing ride from Huss Trading Corporation. (Courtesy BSCACEC.)

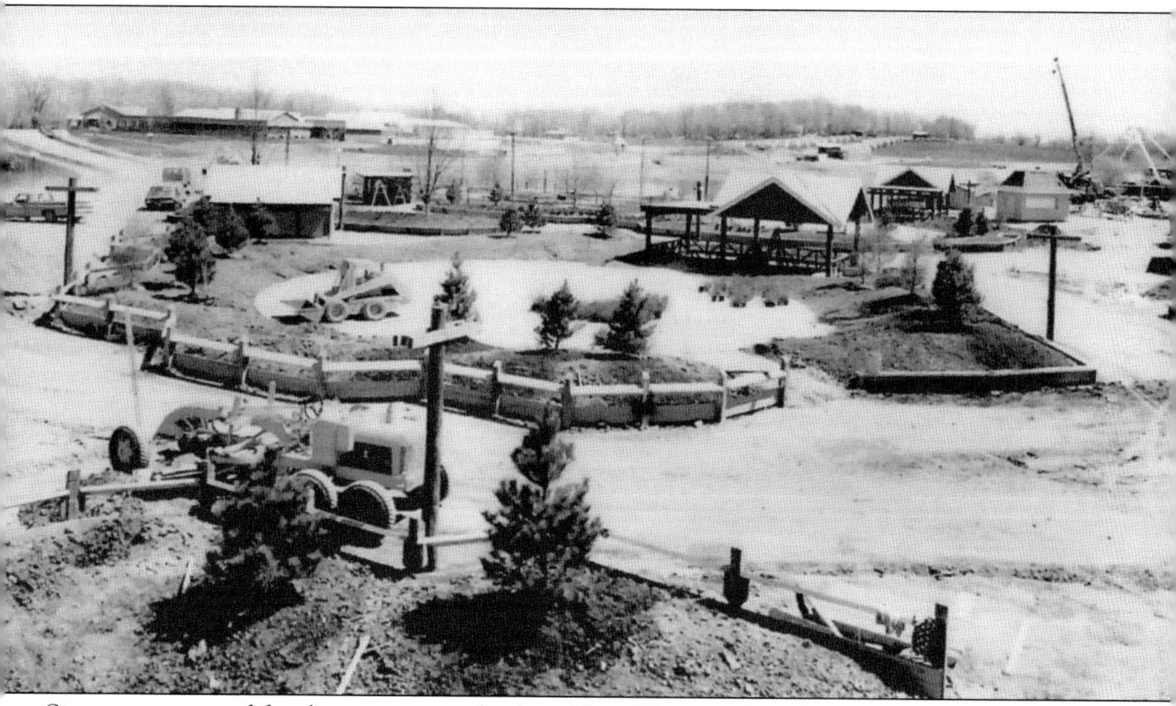

Sites were prepared for the prototype rides from Huss. These included the Pirate and the Corn Popper. Darien Lake was the perfect location for Huss to display its rides for amusement park, theme park, and carnival owners to observe them in full operation. Darien Lake Fun Country began the 1981 season with 11 new rides, including the antique auto ride, a riverboat ride on the lake, and the 11-foot high Lady Bug roller coaster for the kiddies. Admission was pay-one-price and included the rides, waterslides, and entertainment at the air-conditioned Jubilee Theater. An outdoor concert venue seating 8,500 people, the Lakeside Theater was developed on Darien Lake. For day visitors to the theme park section, 25 acres of land were paved for a parking lot, and a new front gate was erected. Everything in the park had a country theme, from the landscaping and ride names to the food stands and souvenir shops. (Courtesy DLR.)

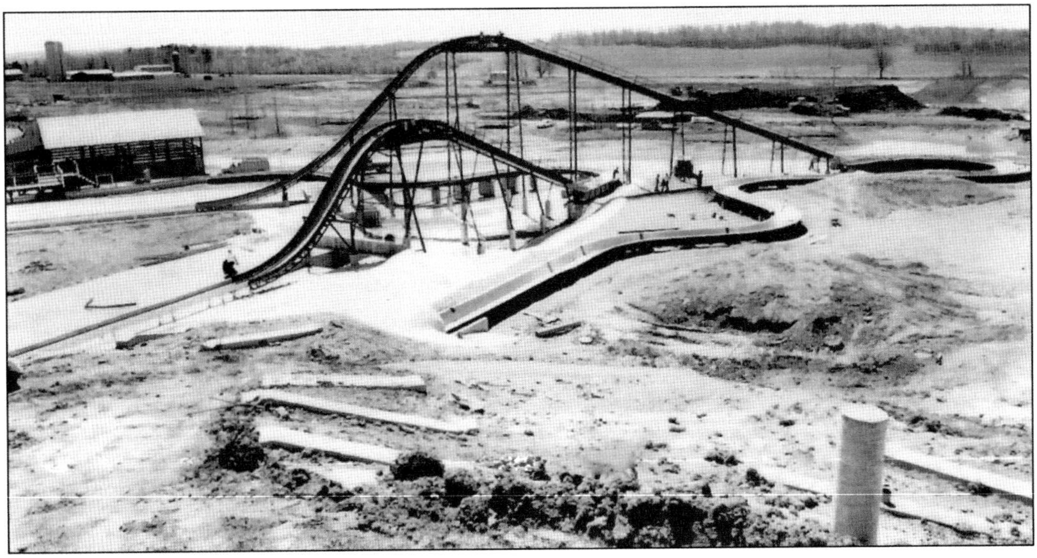

The flume was the largest ride built during the first phase of the theme park development. Passengers sat one in front of the other in log-shaped boats that wove through a tunnel in Rainbow Mountain. Two hills guaranteed that riders would get wet. The boats were carried up the hills on a conveyor belt and slid down the opposite side. The smaller of the two hills had less of a backsplash than the higher hill, which dumped water onto the riders. The trip up the taller hill afforded riders a bird's-eye view of the park and surrounding area. The barns and silo of a neighboring farm can be seen in the background on the left of the photograph above. (Above, courtesy DLR; below, courtesy of Dan Wilke.)

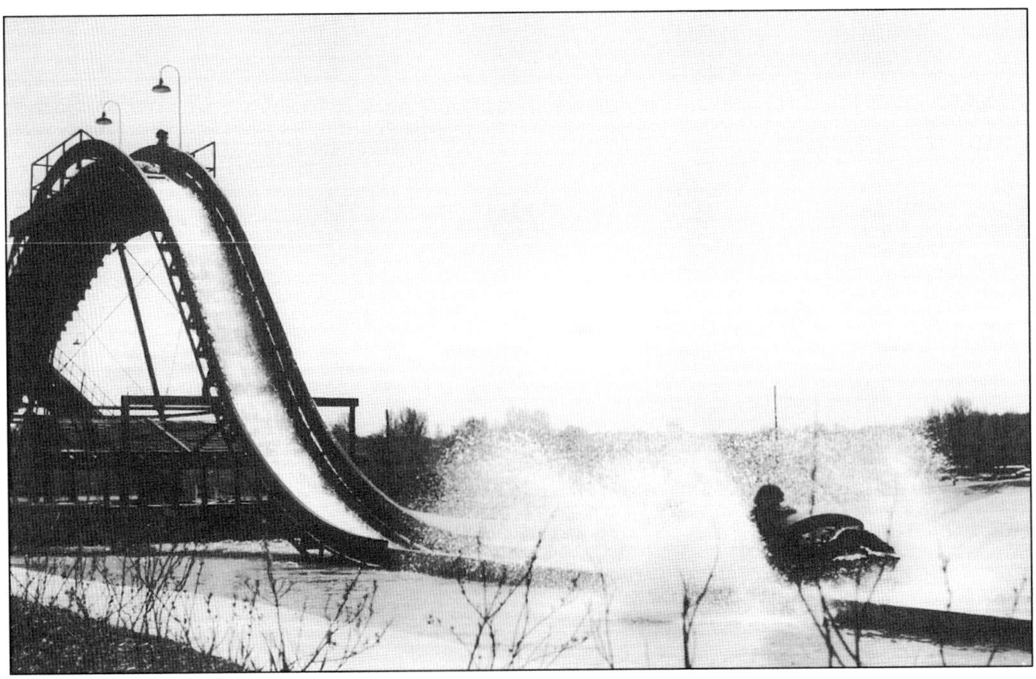

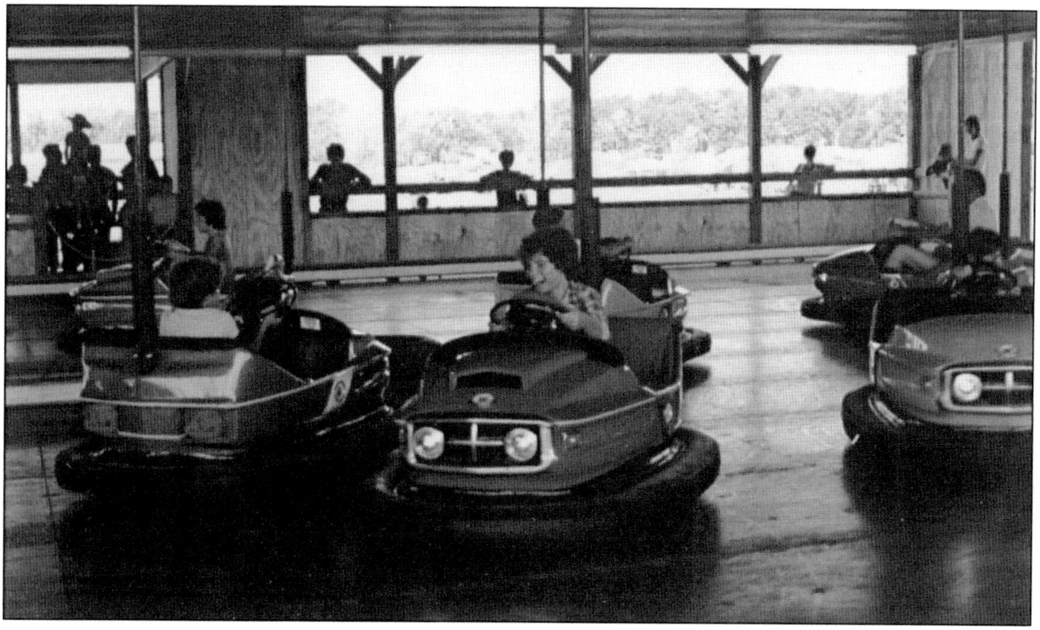

The bumper cars and carousel were among the first rides brought to Darien Lake. The carousel featured fiberglass horses that were reproductions of styles from several different carousel manufacturers such as Philadelphia Toboggan Company, Gustav Dentzel, and Herschell Spillman. The 1982 season is considered the first full year of operation for Darien Lake as a complete theme park, spread over 1,200 acres of countryside that included the campground. Over $10 million had been spent on the park. The addition of four waterslides and a raft ride to Rainbow Mountain created the largest water park complex in New York State. (Above, author's collection; below, courtesy of Dan Wilke.)

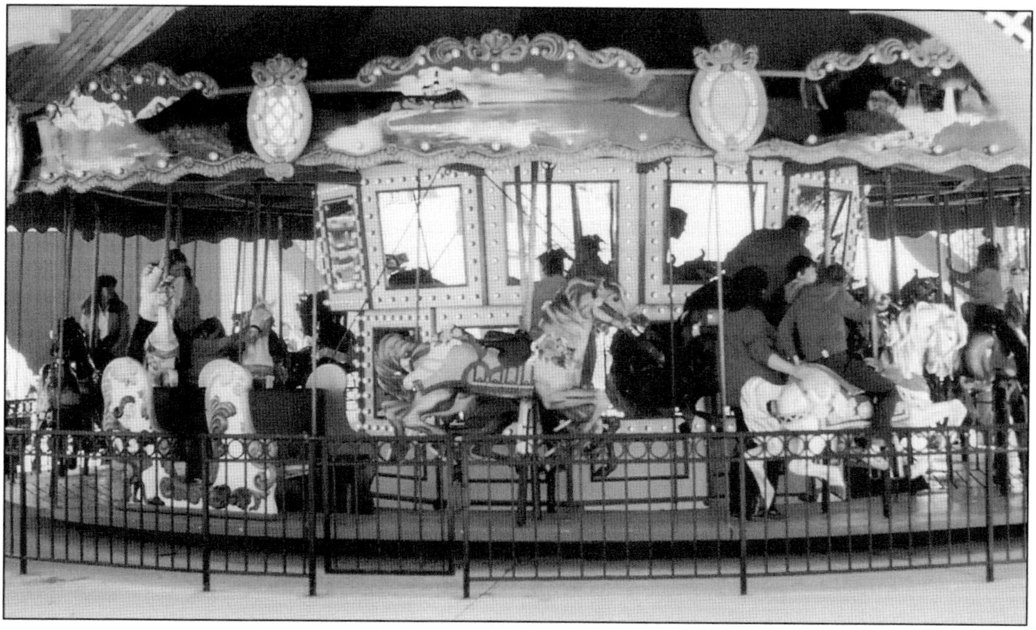

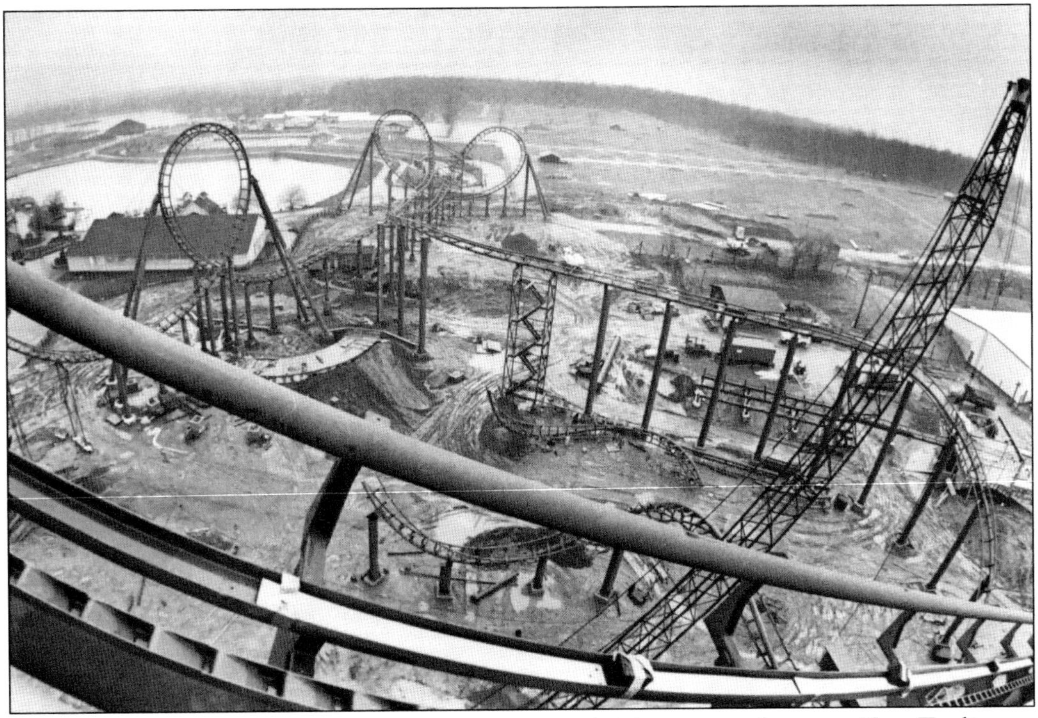

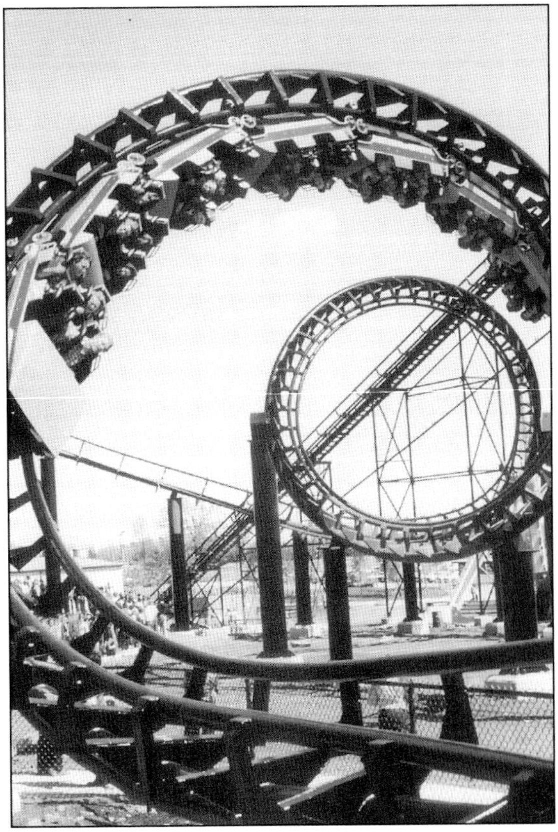

A joint venture between Huss Trading Corporation and Arrow Dynamics resulted in the Viper steel roller coaster. It was the largest roller coaster in the world when it opened in 1982 and was the first roller coaster to flip riders upside down five times. The Viper was Darien Lake Fun Country's signature ride, and it attracted the attention of roller coaster enthusiasts from all over the nation. (Courtesy BSCACEC.)

The Viper's first hill rose 120 feet into the air and dropped 75 feet before entering a vertical loop. That was followed by a boomerang inversion and a double corkscrew. The big finale was a spiral dip into an underground tunnel. Including all the elements, the Viper was 3,100 feet long. (Courtesy of Dan Wilke.)

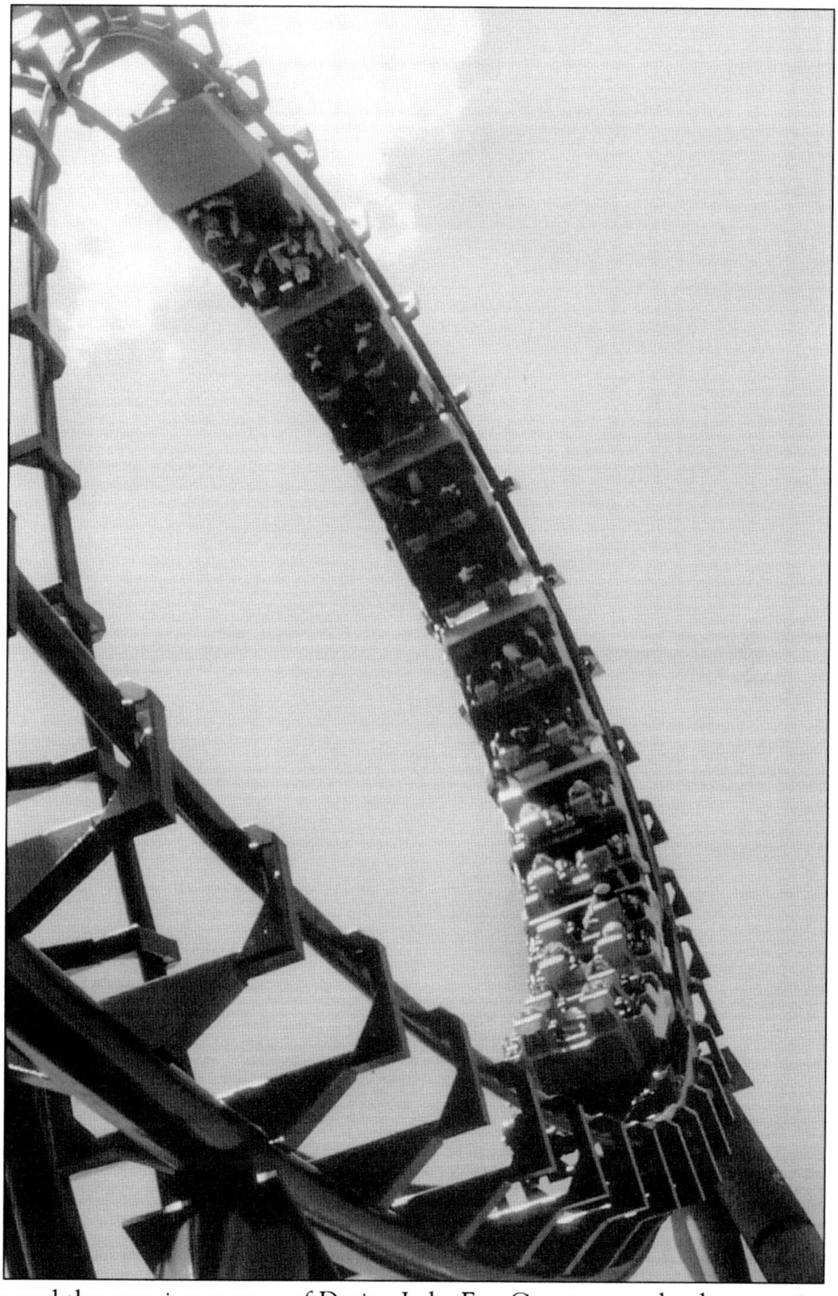

The Viper and the amazing success of Darien Lake Fun Country caught the attention of many in the amusement industry. A group of investors who made up Funtime, Inc., were looking for properties to purchase. The group owned Geauga Lake and Wyandot Lake Park, both in Ohio. Funtime had transformed Geauga Lake from a run-down amusement park to a major vacation destination in only 10 years. Snyder, who had spent more than $75 million to build Darien Lake Fun Country into the largest theme park in the state, agreed to sell 50 percent of the resort to Funtime in 1982. Fun Country was dropped from the park's name the following season. Under combined ownership, the rapid expansion of the past few seasons slowed. One major ride was added in 1983 that changed the park's vista: the Giant Wheel. (Courtesy of Dan Wilke.)

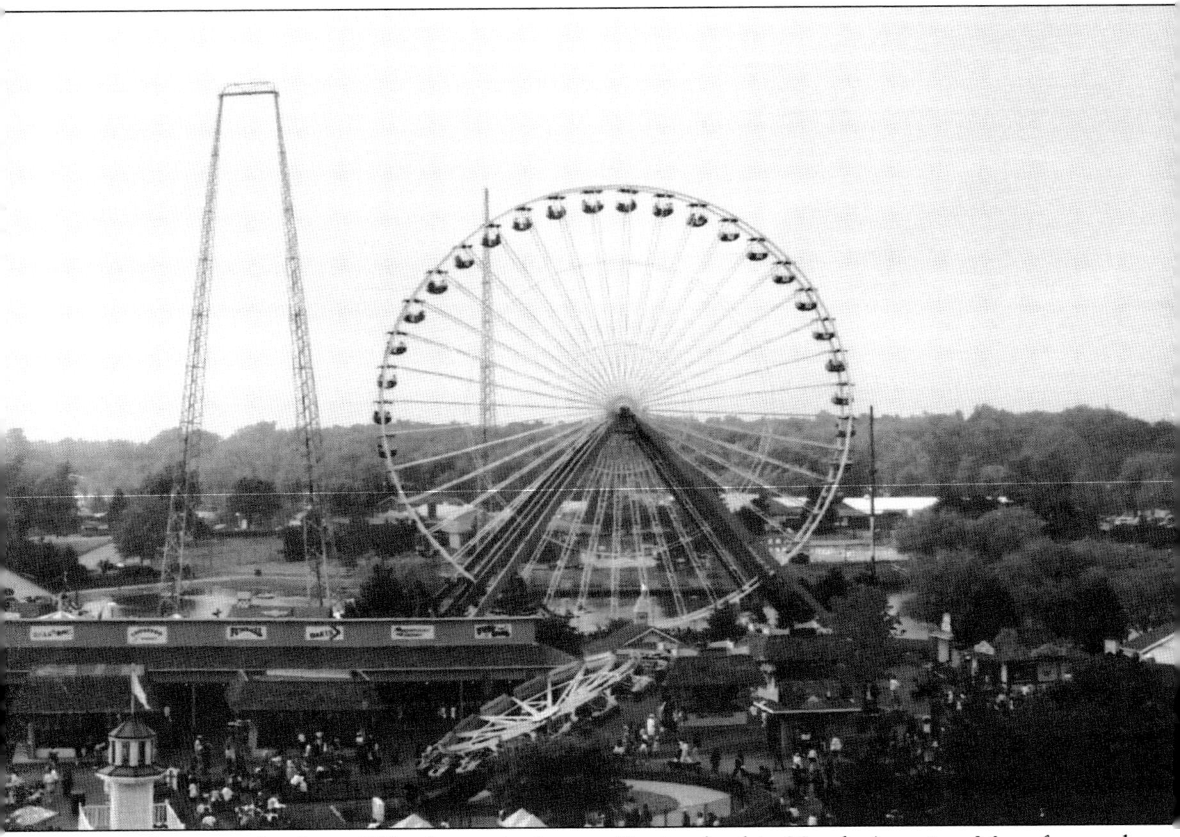

At the time, the Giant Wheel was the largest Ferris wheel in North America. Manufactured by Vekoma of the Netherlands for the 1982 World's Fair in Knoxville, Tennessee, it stood 165 feet tall and could handle 240 passengers per ride. With 15,000 computerized lights creating an amazing nightly show, the Giant Wheel became an icon for the park. Funtime obtained full ownership of Darien Lake in 1985. Cosmetic improvements were made to the park the following season. A five-year capital expansion plan began in 1987 with the addition of the Big Top Circus, a water-ski show, and the Grand Prix Go-Kart Speedway. The second year of the plan introduced Adventureland for kids and the expansion of the campgrounds with the addition of 68 new recreational vehicle sites and 228 new sites for camping trailers. Darien Lake became one of the largest campgrounds in the United States. (Courtesy DLR.)

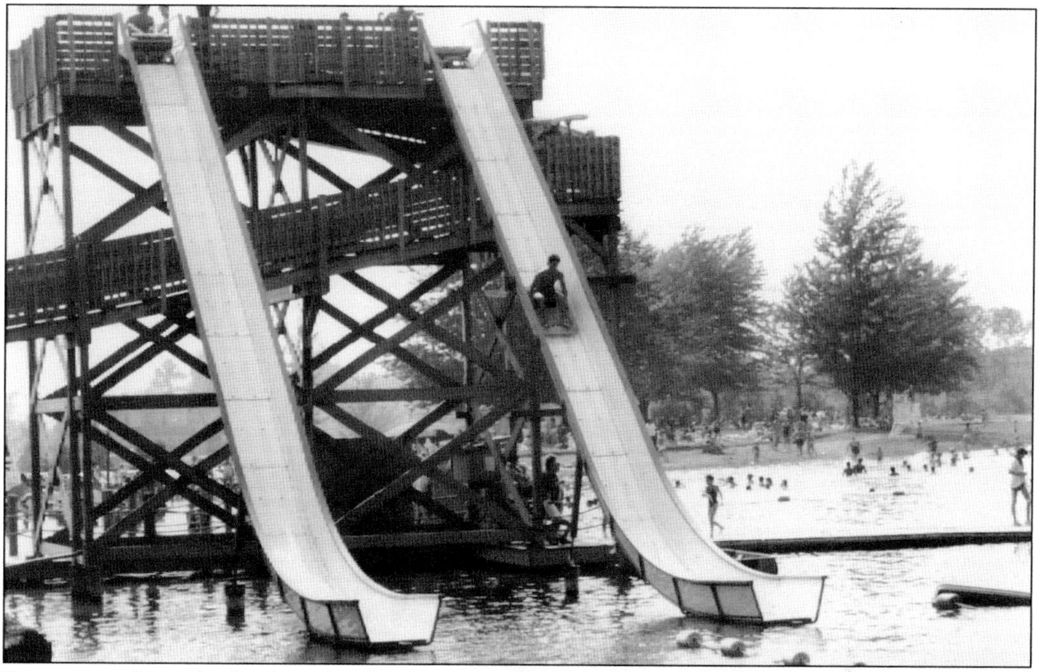

Expansion along the bathing beach also took place with the addition of Hydroforce, twin 35-foot high slides that sent riders aboard toboggans flying across the surface of the lake. Over the next several seasons, visitors to Darien Lake found new and exciting additions like the Grizzly Run, a white-water rapids ride. (Courtesy DLR.)

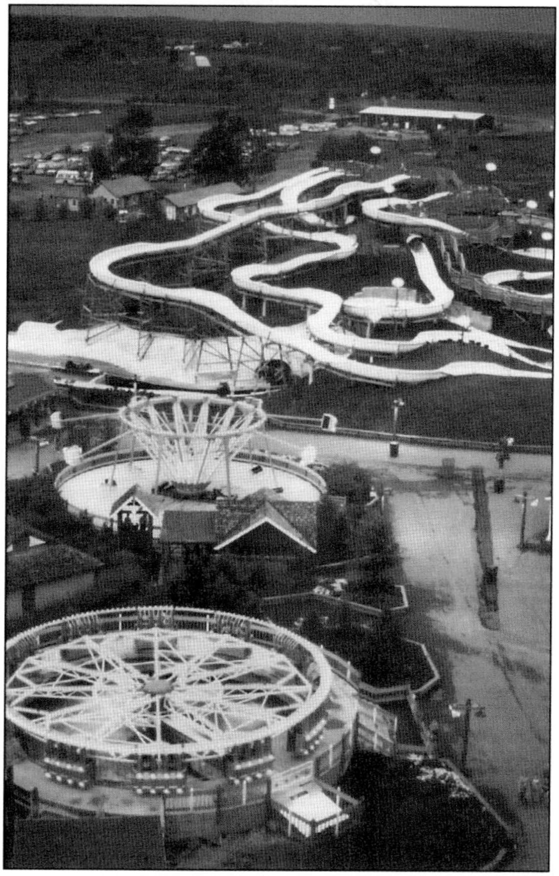

By this time, Rainbow Mountain had become outdated. Over one cold winter, it was transformed into Barracuda Bay, featuring 14 thrilling waterslides and an exciting water raft ride through dark tunnels. In 1994, four new twisting waterslides using inflatable tubes were introduced as 'Cuda Falls. (Courtesy Dan Wilke.)

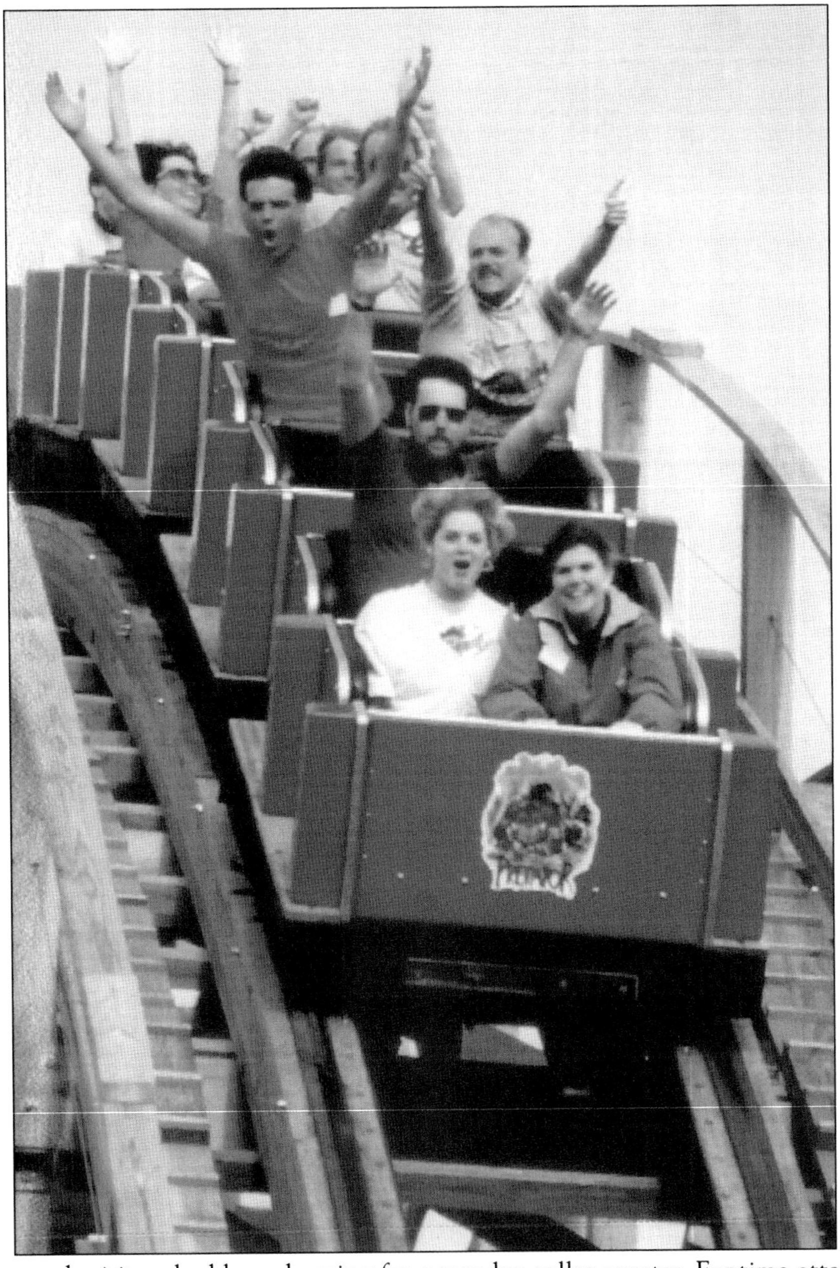

For years, park visitors had been begging for a wooden roller coaster. Funtime attended the auction of Crystal Beach Park in 1989 with intentions of purchasing the Comet, but lost out to Charley Wood in the bidding. This left Western New Yorkers without a wooden roller coaster. Deciding to build their own wooden roller coaster, Darien Lake owners turned to well-known roller coaster designers and builders Dinn and Summers. They wanted a midsized roller coaster that packed plenty of thrills into a compact area. The result was the Predator. Rising 90 feet into the air and with 3,400 feet of track, the Predator opened to rave reviews in 1990. Its rolling hills were reminiscent of the old wooden roller coasters of the 1920s, providing plenty of airtime in its fabulous drops and a quick downward turn that barreled riders into the final lap before returning to the station. (Courtesy DLR.)

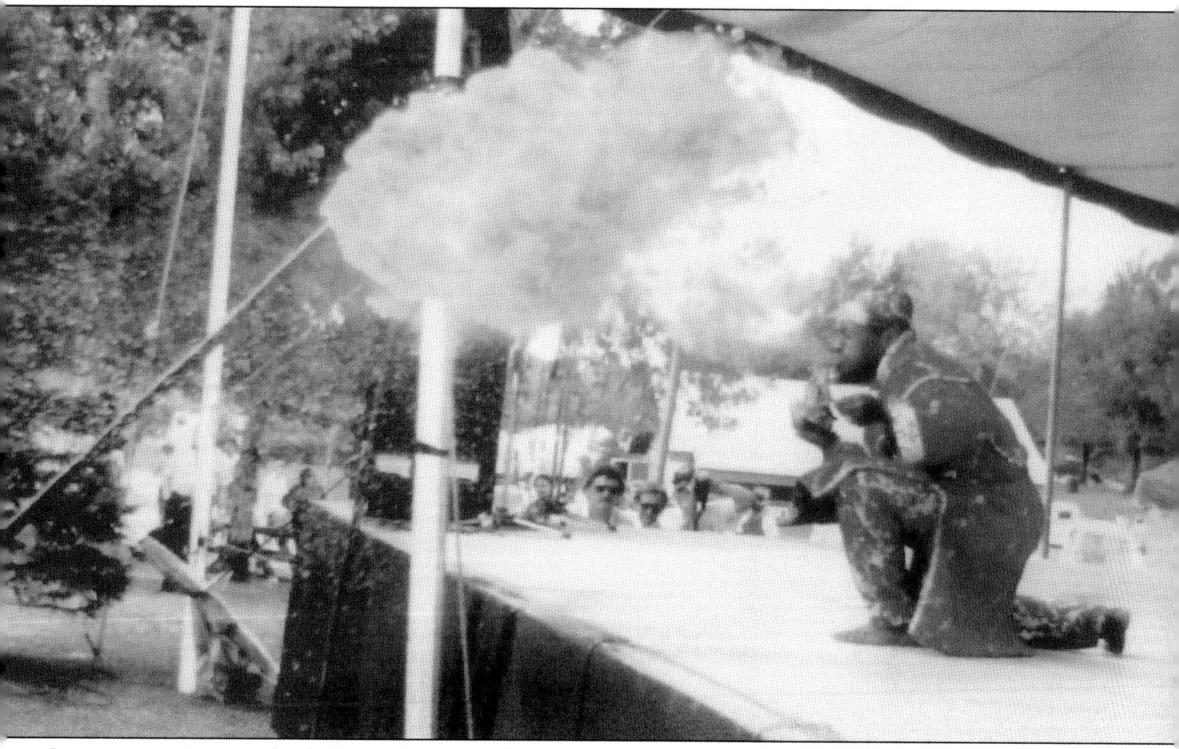

Live entertainment had always been used to attract visitors to Darien Lake. Often the small outdoor stages throughout the park were the site of daily shows and special engagements. In 1992, a new form of entertainment took place. The Laserlight Fantasy Show originally premiered on the park midway in front of Barracuda Bay. Everything came to a standstill when the light show was on; the midway was jam-packed with visitors watching the show. In order to ease the blocked midway, the show was moved to the Lakeside Amphitheater the following summer and renamed the Laserlight Reality Show. Accompanied by music, lasers projected moving images onto a massive screen, creating a story. To accommodate the ever-growing concert crowds, a new Performing Arts Center with a capacity for 20,000 people opened in an undeveloped area of the park in 1993. The center has hosted famous acts and bands such as REO, Santana, the Osmonds, Pink, and Buffalo's own Goo-Goo Dolls. (Courtesy DLR.)

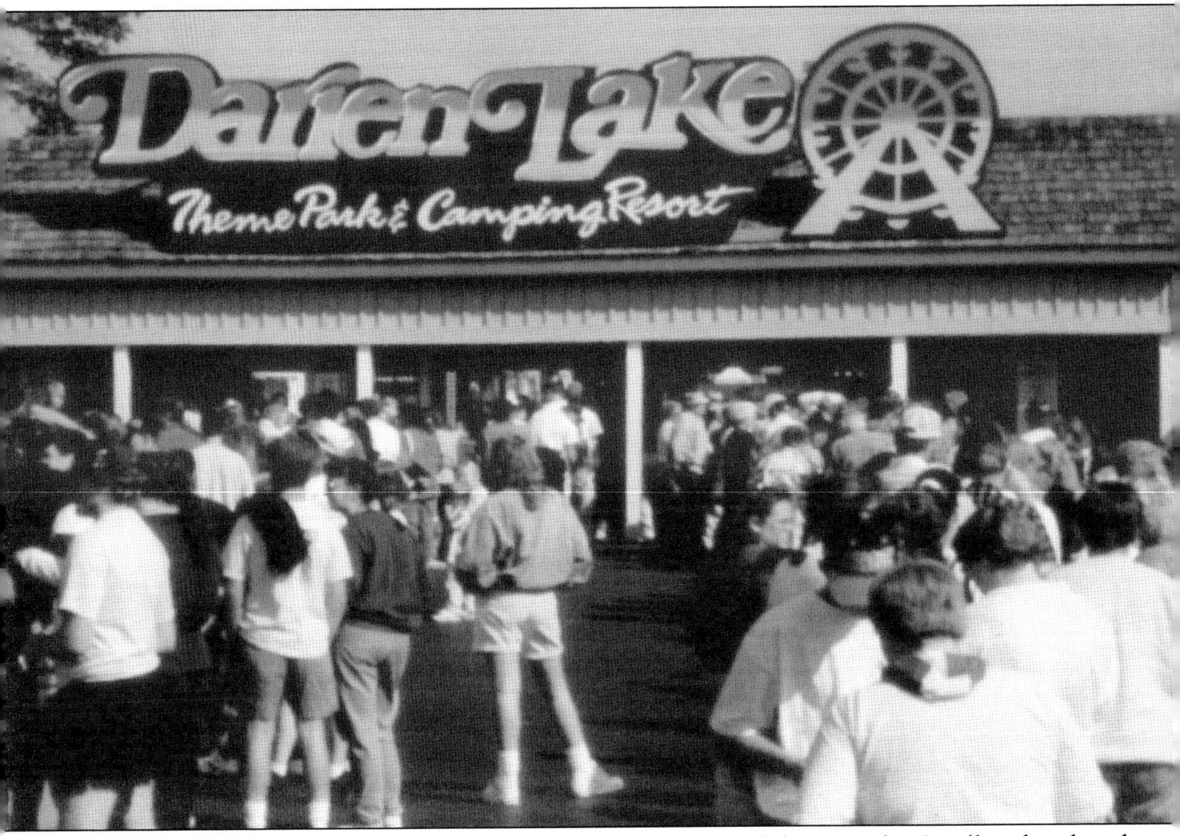

Across the country, things were changing for amusement and theme parks. Small and midsized parks that had not closed during the previous decade were bought up by investors looking to consolidate many parks under one name in order to achieve greater economic success. A group of investors from Oklahoma formed Premier Parks, Inc. Premier Parks had acquired the dilapidated Frontier City with intentions of a different development, but when the economy took a downturn, Premier Parks renovated Frontier City instead and saw an excellent return. Their next venture was the purchase of Wild World in Largo, Maryland, in 1992. Premier Parks began purchasing midsized parks throughout the United States, and in 1995, the company bought Darien Lake from Funtime. Premier Parks had discovered that investing heavily in new attractions in the recently acquired parks sparked patron interest, which resulted in increased revenue. (Courtesy DLR.)

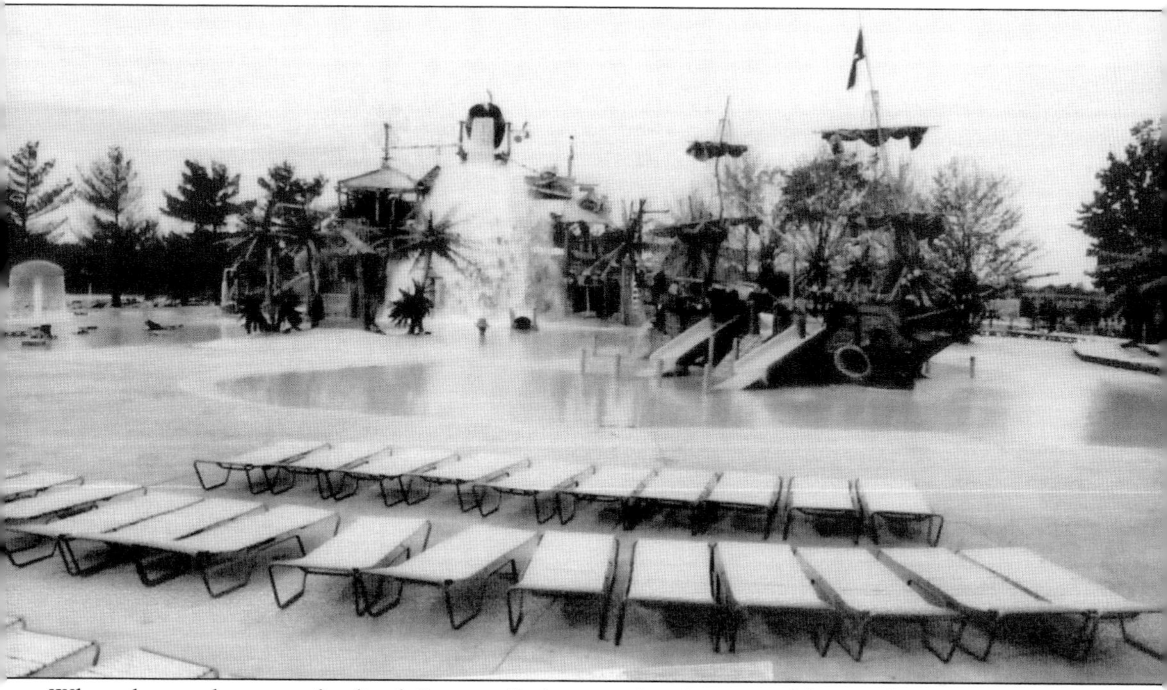

When the purchase was finalized, Premier Parks immediately pumped $8.6 million into Darien Lake. The 1996 season opened with upgrades to the Performing Arts Center and the campgrounds. A steel roller coaster was brought from Premier Park's Kentucky Kingdom, enclosed within a concrete building, and named Nightmare at Phantom's Cave. The kids were not forgotten, either: Treasure Island miniature golf was replaced with Popeye's Seaport, which opened with a play area and 10 kiddie rides, several of which were able to accommodate adults, allowing families to ride together. The largest addition was Hook's Lagoon, an interactive aquatic play park that opened on the former site of Adventureland. The new themed area was connected to Barracuda Bay by a bridge that spanned the main midway. Hook's Lagoon had 75 water-play features and three themed wading pools, one of which sported a replica pirate ship with kid-sized waterslides. (Courtesy DLR.)

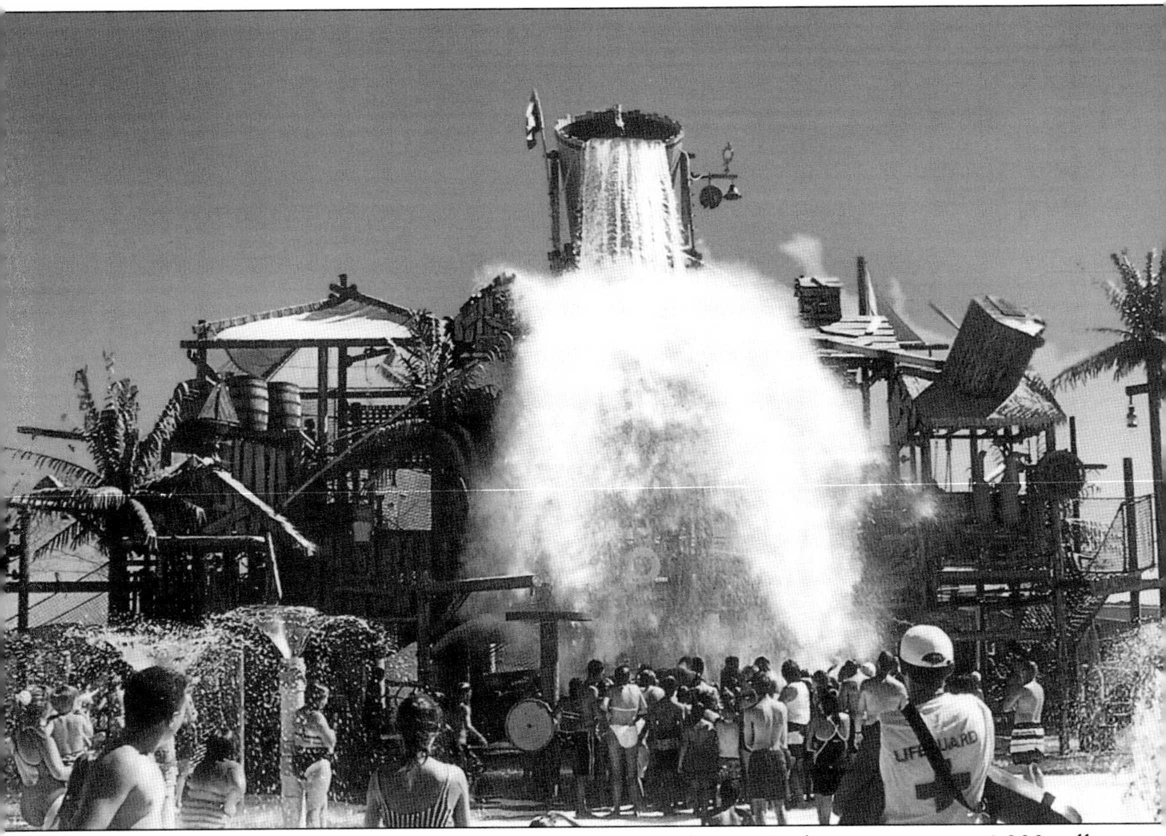

The main feature of Hook's Lagoon was the 40-foot tree house. At the very top was a 1,000-gallon water barrel that tipped over every five minutes, drenching anxiously waiting patrons below. New York's first inverted looping roller coaster was unveiled in 1997. The Mind Eraser was a standard model built by Vekoma. The cars were suspended from an overhead track, and riders' legs dangled as the train whipped through the course. Reaching a height of 105 feet with an 86-foot first drop and five inversions, the steel roller coaster was an exciting addition to the park. The nearby Lady Bug kiddie roller coaster was painted colors to match the Mind Eraser and renamed Brain Teaser. The water park was expanded again that year with the addition of Crocodile Isle. It featured a million-gallon wave pool and a sun deck. (Courtesy DLR.)

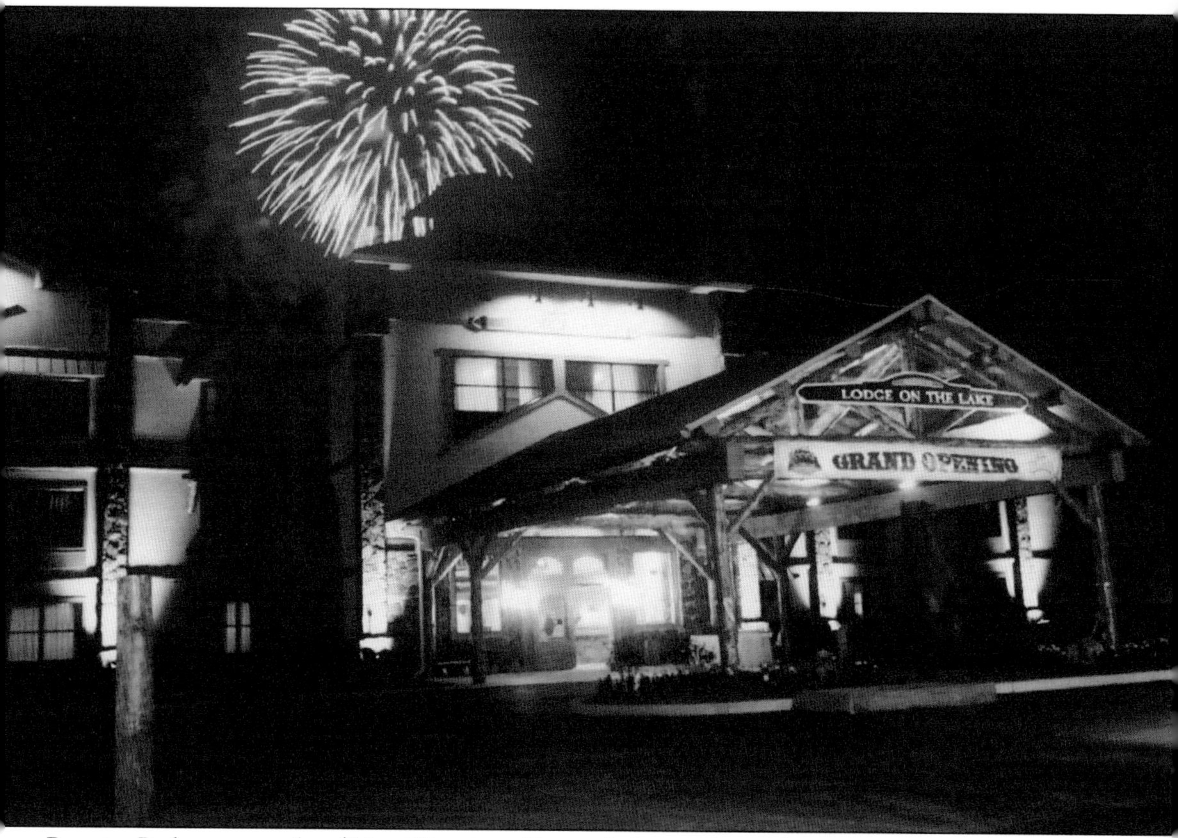

Premier Parks put another $12 million into Darien Lake in 1998. The park's first on-site hotel, the Lodge on the Lake, designed with a North Woods theme, opened on Memorial Day weekend. With 161 rooms, two suites, and an outdoor heated pool, it was the perfect addition to entice non-camping families to come to the resort for an extended stay. Keeping with the woodsy theme, Beaver Brothers Café opened later in the summer, offering three meals a day to visitors and campers alike. The steel Boomerang Coast to Coaster also opened that same year. Riders were hauled backwards up a 125-foot incline, then dropped. The train screamed through the station, flipped twice in a bat-wing inversion, then entered a single vertical loop. Out of the loop, the train flew up a second 125-foot incline, then dropped again, following the same route, backwards. (Courtesy DLR.)

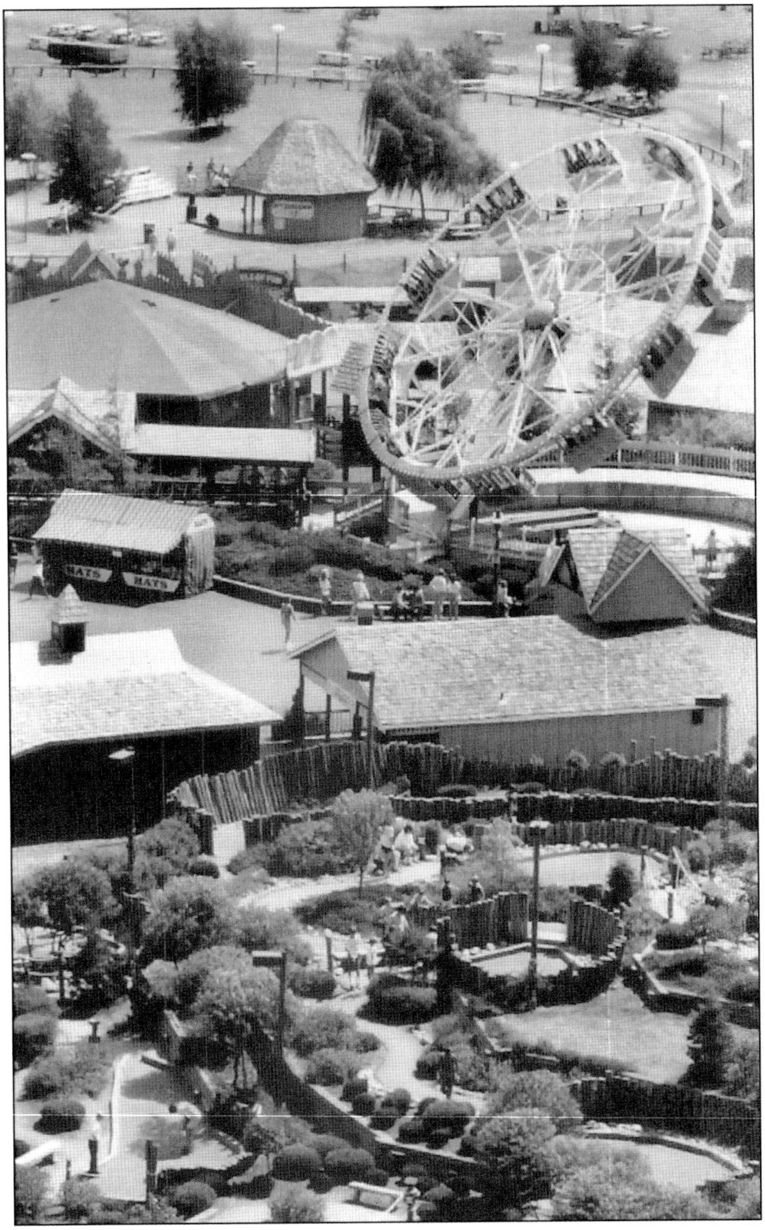

Premier Parks had changed Darien Lake into a destination theme park, but more changes were ahead. The company had continued to buy up amusement parks and turn them into sought-out theme parks, increasing their holdings enough to make them the third-largest amusement park chain in the country. Then in October 1998, Premier Parks shocked the amusement industry when it acquired the nation's second-largest amusement park chain, Six Flags Theme Parks. Darien Lake was one of five Premier Parks properties placed under the Six Flags brand. The park opened in 1999 with vast improvements, including a newly revamped central plaza and Looney Toons and Marvel Comics Justice League characters. The roller coaster from Nightmare at Phantom's Cave had been removed and sent across the state to Great Escape. The building was converted into a 1,200-seat theater featuring the Batman Thrill Spectacular Stunt Show, complete with fantastic stunt motorcycles and fiery explosions. (Courtesy DLR.)

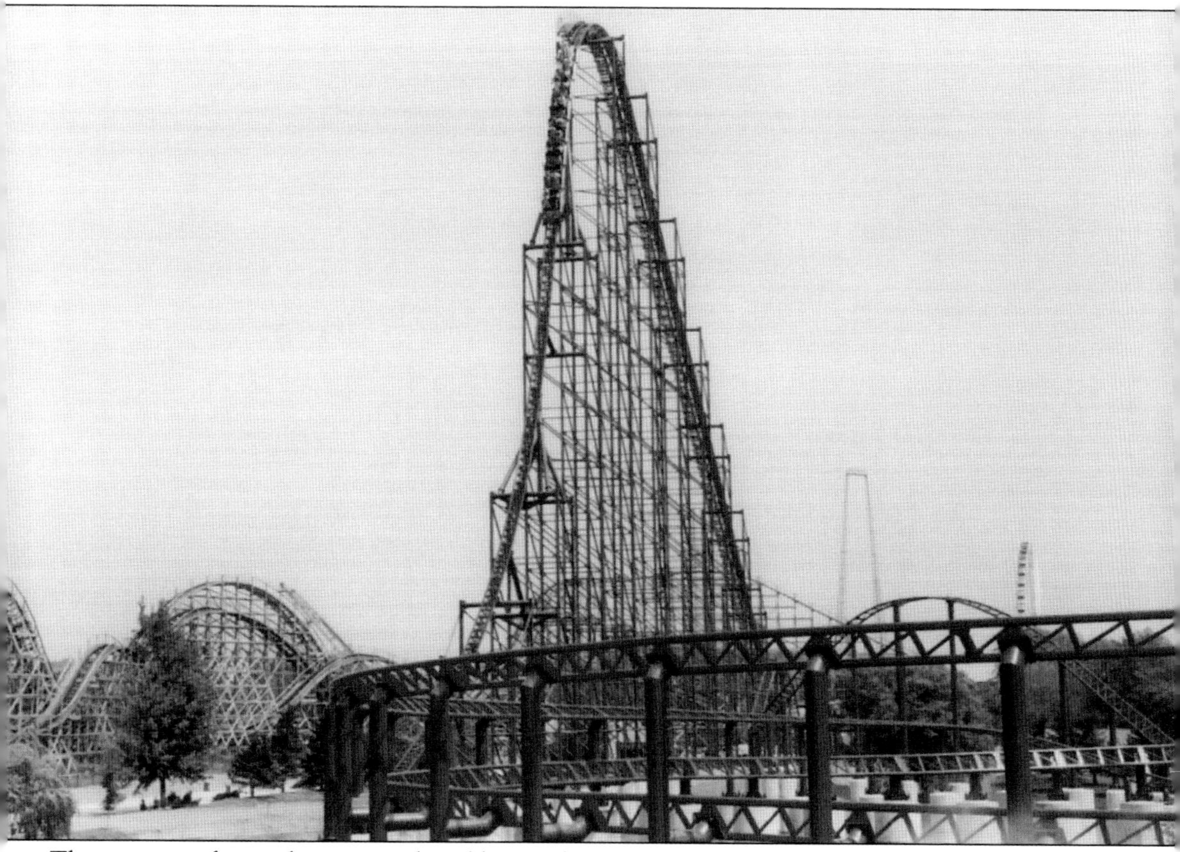

The most significant change was the addition of a steel roller coaster on the brink of technology, Superman Ride of Steel, which debuted in 1999. Built by Swiss amusement-ride manufacturer Intamin, the non-looping roller coaster dominated the park's skyline with a 208-foot-high first hill that could be seen from miles around. Situated near Route 77, its very presence initiated anticipated excitement for visitors entering the park. The first drop plunged 205 feet to the ground at a 75-degree angle over misters placed in the trout pond. Highly banked low turns, a steeply banked double helix, two large hills that produced a sensation of floating, and negative-G camelback hills on the return made Superman Ride of Steel a spectacular ride. The roller coaster was smooth and extremely fast, reaching a blazing speed of 72 miles per hour. (Courtesy DLR.)

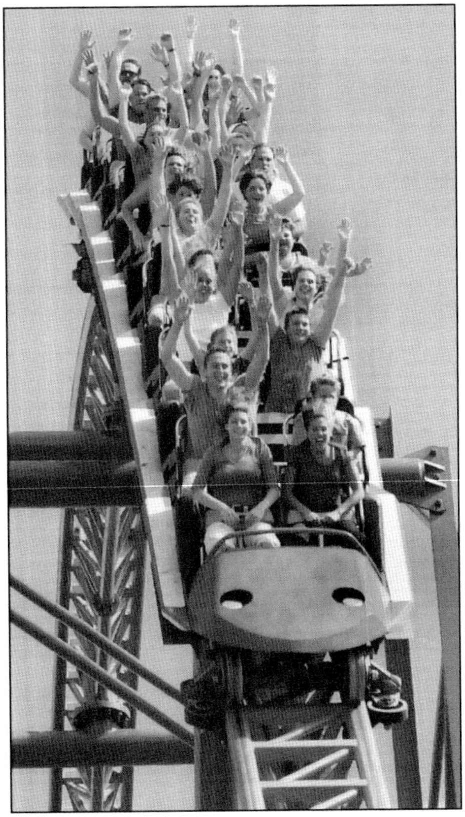

Stadium seating on the open-sided cars allowed riders in the back to see over the heads of the riders in front so that they were able to experience the same visual thrill. Superman Ride of Steel overshadowed every other roller coaster in the park, including the Predator, which appeared a great deal smaller in comparison. The word Superman was dropped from the ride's name in 2007. It is still the most extreme roller coaster in Western New York and the entire state, but its reputation has reached farther, drawing roller coasters enthusiasts from Ohio, Pennsylvania, New England, Canada, and even Europe. (Left, courtesy DLR; below, author's collection.)

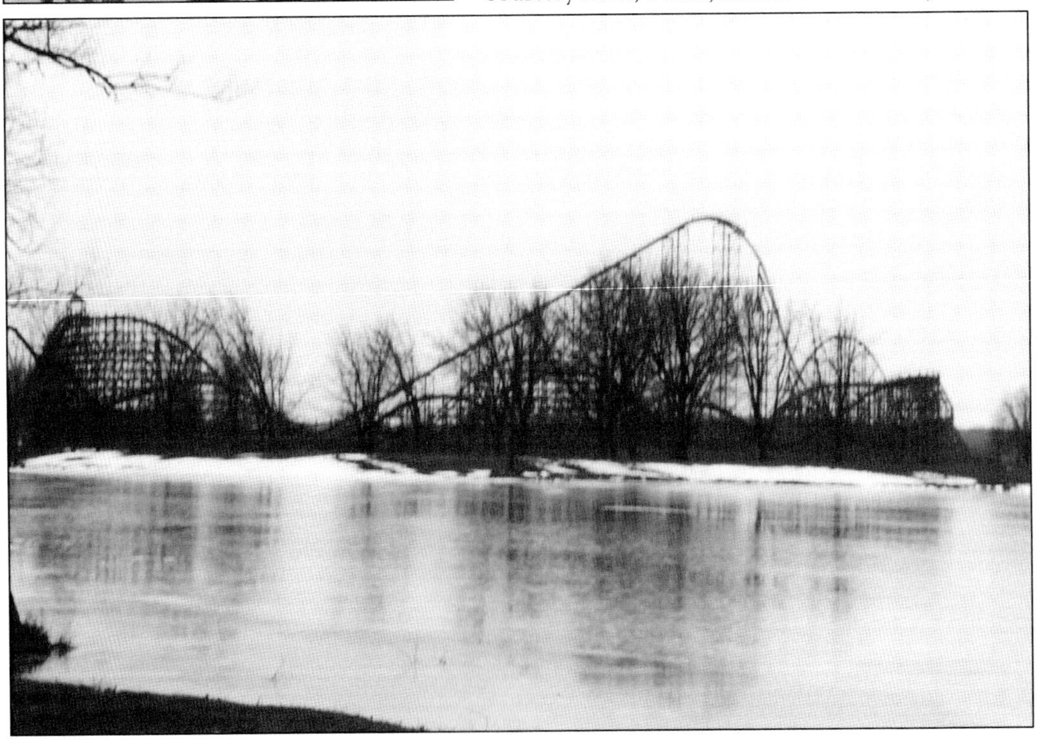

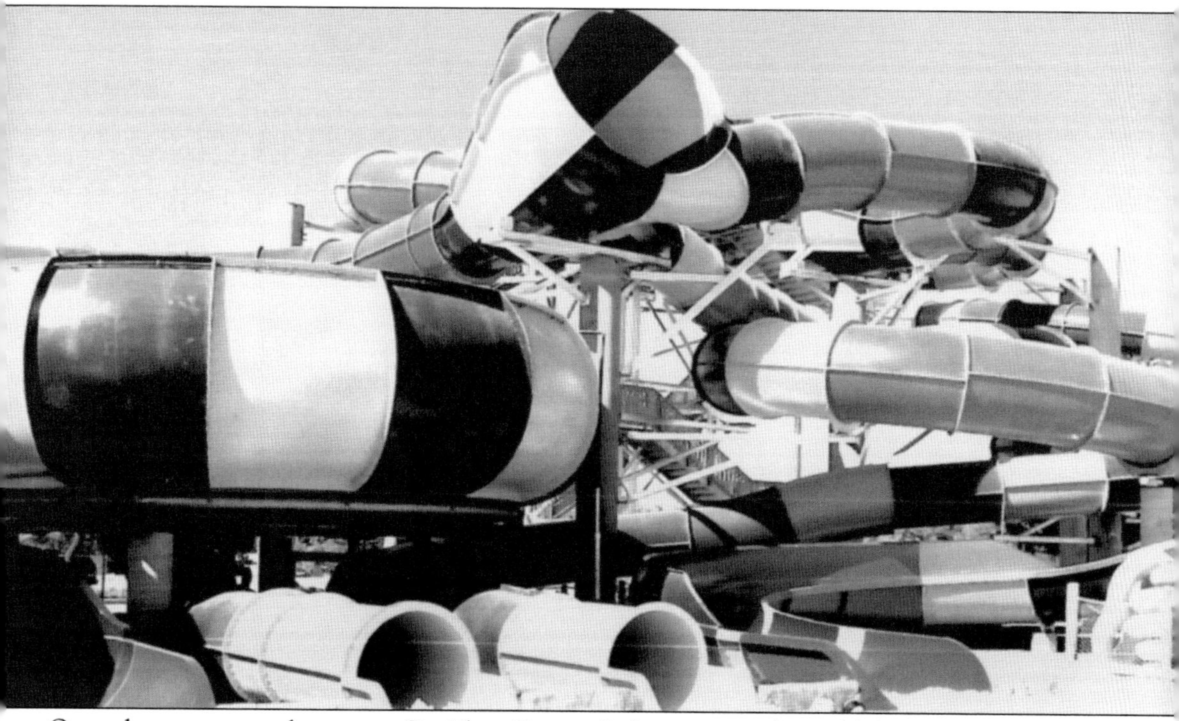

Over the next several seasons, Six Flags Darien Lake continued to add fantastic rides and attractions, but by 2006, Six Flags was experiencing financial troubles, and some of the parks in the chain were closed permanently. Company-wide, there were changes and cutbacks throughout the summer. In April 2007, Darien Lake and five other parks were packaged and sold to PARC Management. Upon completion of the sale, PARC Management entered into a 50-year contract with CNL Income Properties, under which CNL would purchase the properties from PARC and then lease them back for operation. This freed up enough funds to allow PARC to add new attractions on a yearly basis. (Courtesy DLR.)

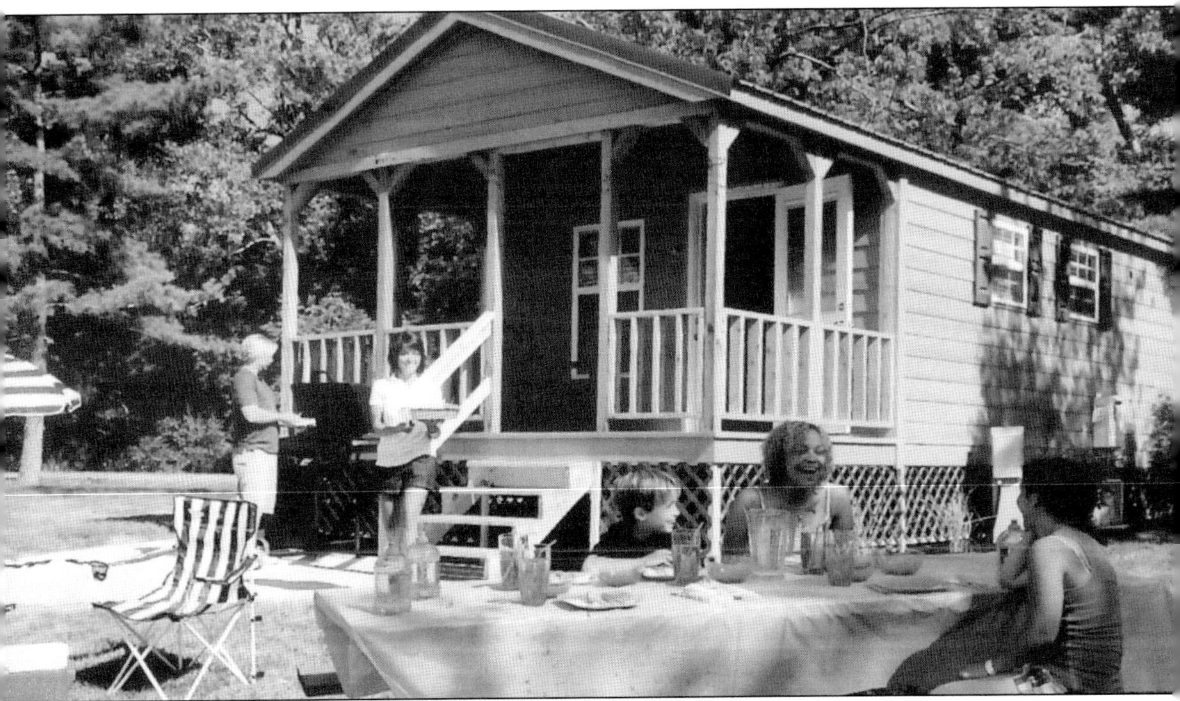

Darien Lake Resort opened for the 2007 season with fresh entertainment and a new Laserlight show. MotoCoaster arrived in 2008. Its riders straddle motorcycle-style cars and are launched from zero to 35 miles an hour in only three seconds. The themed cars then ricochet around figure eights and negotiate tight turns on more than 1,100 feet of track at 40 miles per hour. Children's television cartoon character, Bob the Builder, joined Darien Lake Resort for a live show in 2009. Another show debuting that year was *Survivor, Live*, where audience members participated in competitions against each other. When the unexpected recession befell the nation, Darien Lake Resort took steps to make it easier for families to enjoy a day at the park by lowering gate prices. Packages were offered that included overnight stays at the lodge, campground, or new lakeside cabins, plus admission to the theme park. (Courtesy DLR.)

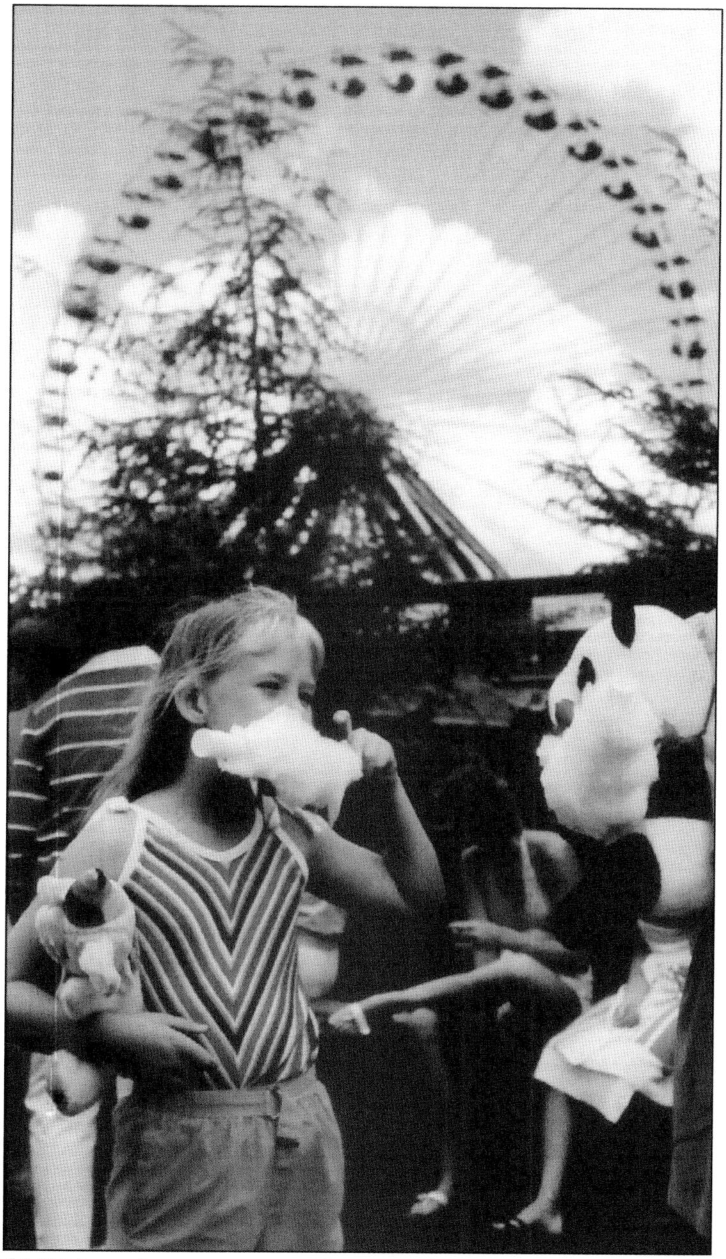

The summer of 2010 brought a new era to Darien Lake Resort with the opening of a themed water park, Splashtown. Park patrons now have a choice to enjoy either the theme park or the water park—or both—in one day. The new water park incorporates some old favorites like Hook's Lagoon, 'Cuda Falls, and Crocodile Isle with new attractions such as Swirl City, showcasing twisting, swirling water adventures; Flotation Station Lazy River; and Lazy Days Lagoon, which features a wave pool and "beachfront" deck space. What began as a picnic park in the country has blossomed and grown into a major theme park and resort. Changes in ownership have pushed Darien Lake to the cutting edge of amusement entertainment, and the future holds unlimited possibilities as Darien Lake Resort continues to appeal to people from Western New York and beyond. (Courtesy DLR.)